The Puritan Pulpit
The American Puritans

Ebenezer Pemberton
(1704-1777)

Compiled and Edited by
Dr. Don Kistler

Soli Deo Gloria Publications
. . . for instruction in righteousness . . .

Soli Deo Gloria Publications
A division of Ligonier Ministries, Inc.
P.O. Box 547500, Orlando, FL 32854
(407) 333-4244/ FAX 333-4233
www.ligonier.org

*

*

ISBN 1-56769-084-X

*

Library of Congress Cataloging-in-Publication Data

Contents

Contents

Ebenezer Pemberton

(1704-1777)

Ebenezer Pemberton was born in Boston in 1704 and graduated from Harvard College in 1721. His father, Ebenezer Pemberton, was also a distinguished clergyman.

The Presbyterian Church in New York City, having dismissed their pastor in 1726, invited Pemberton to preach for them. So acceptable was his preaching that the congregation, though greatly divided previously, united in giving him an affectionate and urgent call to become their pastor. He accepted, and returned to Boston to seek ordination, having only been licensed to preach to that point. His ordination sermon was preached by Benjamin Colman. He entered upon this pastoral charge in 1727 and remained for 26 years.

The congregation was relatively small, but in 1739, and for two years following, an extensive revival of religion took place in New York City, and the congregation grew rapidly.

In 1740, George Whitefield visited New York, and Ebenezer Pemberton was the only clergyman in the city who invited him to fill his pulpit. In succeeding visits, Whitefield often preached for Pemberton and drew multitudes of various denominations, some of whom ultimately joined as members.

In 1753, Pemberton accepted a call to the New Brick Church in Boston. He was installed in 1754 and remained there until his death on September 15, 1777. In 1770 he received the degree of Doctor of Divinity from the College of New Jersey, the first degree of that kind ever conferred by that college.

(Abridged from Sprague's *Annals of the American Pulpit*)

1

The Knowledge of Christ Recommended

A sermon preached at Yale College
April 19, 1741

"For I determined not to know anything among you save Jesus Christ, and Him crucified." 1 Corinthians 2:2

An unquenchable thirst after knowledge was originally implanted in the nature of man, and designed by our all-wise Creator, for the most excellent and valuable ends. This, though innocent and commendable in itself, proved to be an unhappy temptation to the first apostasy, and involved the race of mankind in universal ruin. A criminal ambition to be wise above the privilege of their natures allured our first parents to violate the law of their creation and eat of the fruit of the forbidden tree, by which they forfeited the divine favor and incurred the dreadful penalty of eternal death. Aspiring to become as gods, discerning between good and evil, they fell from their exalted station and rendered themselves viler than the beasts that perish.

But (blessed be God) there is a knowledge by which we may be delivered from the ruins of our apostate state and recover our forfeited felicity. This is not an acquaintance with the terrors of nature or the intrigues and policies of art, but a knowledge of Christ and Him crucified.

The great doctor of the Gentiles determined to make this the principal scope of his public preaching and private conversation. He counted all things but loss and dung for the excellency of the knowledge of Jesus Christ our Lord. This blessed subject filled the apostle's heart and triumphed in all his discourses; to know Christ Himself was his first concern; to bring others to a saving acquaintance with Him was his highest ambition and the great design of his ministry. This resolution was not a sudden flash of thought, occasioned by some present surprise; it was not taken up in a melancholy disposition of mind when his understanding was disordered with the fumes of enthusiasm, but was the effect of calm and mature deliberation.

Paul was brought up at the feet of Gamaliel and was instructed in the doctrines and traditions of the Jewish rabbis. He was acquainted with the celebrated authors of antiquity—their orators, philosophers, and poets—but when his eyes were opened by a divine illumination, he saw the vanity of these boasted attainments and became a humble disciple of the despised Jesus. From henceforth, therefore, avoiding the enticing words of man's wisdom and renouncing the empty flourishes of human eloquence, he resolved to preach the gospel with great plainness and simplicity and recommend divine truths in their native excellency and glory.

Though the doctrine of the cross was to the carnal Jews a stumbling block, and to the Grecian philosophers foolishness, yet Paul was not ashamed of this foolishness of preaching, but determined in Corinth itself, the seat of learning and politeness, to know nothing but Christ and Him crucified. In speaking to these words (by divine assistance) I shall:

First, explain the nature of this knowledge of which Paul had so high an esteem;

Second, recommend it to your diligent study and practice;

Third, apply my discourse to the students of this college, and in a special manner to those who are designed for the service of the gospel ministry.

1. First, I am to explain the nature of this knowledge. It certainly implies a doctrinal knowledge of Christ and the important truths revealed concerning Him in the gospel. This supposes that we are by nature in a guilty, polluted, and condemned state; we are enemies to God, the bounteous Author of our beings, transgressors of His laws which are holy, just, and good, and upon this account heirs of eternal damnation. It includes a knowledge of the wise and condescending methods of heaven to redeem the apostate progeny of Adam from these dark and disconsolate circumstances, and to restore His chosen people to a state of endless felicity and joy. To accomplish this wonderful design, the eternal Son of God, the Heir of His Father's love and glory, became the Son of Man and clothed Himself with the sinless infirmities of human nature. In our nature He perfectly obeyed the moral law, that everlasting rule of righteousness, fulfilled the entire will of God in our place and stead, and died as a sacrifice upon the cross for the sins of men. This same Jesus, who was arraigned at the bar of the Roman governor and executed upon a cross as a common malefactor, was the promised Messiah, the only Savior of the world. And accordingly, when He had finished the work of redemption, rose again by a divine power, ascended up into heaven in the presence of His disciples, and sits at the right hand of God forever and ever. All power in heaven and earth is committed to Him, and whoever believes in Him shall obtain the remission of sins through the virtue of His atoning blood, be sanctified through the powerful influences of His Spirit, justified at the tribunal of God through the imputation of His invaluable merits, and finally brought to the full possession of ineffable glory.

These are doctrines clearly revealed in the gospel, which every Christian must in some measure be acquainted with. But though a doctrinal knowledge is an essential part, yet it is by no means the whole of what the apostle intends. The most exalted degree of knowledge, unless it purifies the heart and influences the conduct, serves only to aggravate our guilt, and will, in the end, heighten our future condemnation.

The devils themselves are acquainted with many of the doctrines of the gospel, for they believe and tremble. And many who have had their understandings enlightened with divine truths have had their hearts filled with inveterate enmity against the power of godliness. Men who have explained the mysteries of faith with the greatest clearness, and defended them with convincing strength and evidence, are oftentimes found enemies to the cross of Christ, and obstinately refuse to have Him to reign over them.

Therefore this knowledge implies a practical and experimental knowledge of Christ, a knowledge that is not confined to the head but seated in the heart. It is a knowledge that is not produced by the powers of human reason or the common methods of education or instruction, but is the effect of a divine illumination, a spiritual discovery of Christ to the soul. When Christ is fully known, the blessed Spirit of divine grace takes away the veil from our understandings, causes the scales to fall from our eyes, and gives us such a view of the glory of God and Christ as has a transforming efficacy upon the whole man, changing us into the divine image.

Therefore Paul prays for the Ephesians that "the God of our Lord Jesus Christ, the Father of glory, may give unto you the spirit of wisdom and revelation in the knowledge of Him; the eyes of your understanding being enlightened, that you may know what is the hope of His calling, and what are the riches of the glory of His inheritance in the saints" (Ephesians 1:17–18). This knowledge is clearly distinguished from all other knowledge by the following effects:

First, it humbles the sinner before God and fills him with a deep sense of his own unworthiness. Human knowledge puffs up the mind, raises the natural vanity of man, and is apt to fill them with scorn and contempt of others. But the knowledge of Christ opens the sinner's eyes to see his native guilt and deformity, and covers his face with the deepest confusion in consideration of his innumerable offenses.

No man ever attains to a saving acquaintance with Christ until he is convinced that he is a guilty, condemned malefactor, destitute of every qualification to recommend him to God, and the deserved object of his everlasting displeasure.

And the clearer views any person obtains of the excellency and glory of a Savior, the more abasing apprehensions he entertains of his own deformity and vileness. When the veil is in any measure drawn aside and he beholds the blessed Jesus seated upon a throne of grace, clothed with the garments of salvation, with peace and pardon in His hands, he is immediately struck with awful admiration at his astonishing condescension, falls down at his feet with transport and surprise and cries out with holy Job, "I have heard of Thee by the hearing of the ear, but now mine eye seeth Thee; wherefore I abhor myself and repent in dust and ashes" (Job 42:5–6).

This knowledge not only humbles the soul before God, but, second, it engages the soul to trust in Christ entirely for pardon and salvation. To know Christ is to believe in Him as our Savior, whose invaluable blood has redeemed us from the curse of the fiery law and the dreadful displeasure of almighty God; through whose immaculate righteousness we have a title to the inheritance of the saints in light, and may stand with safety at the tribunal of offended justice.

Whence is it that the Lord Jesus is no more valued, and an interest in Him so seldom sought after, by the perishing sons of men? Because the God of this world has blinded their eyes so that they should not see His excellency and glory. But when the sinner's eyes are opened to see the fullness of His merits, the boundless compassions of His nature, and the wondrous riches of His love, he immediately cries out, "This is such a Savior as my necessities demand and the circumstances of my guilty polluted soul require. O Jesus! How delightful is Thy name! How glad are the tidings of peace and salvation! With joy I accept the condescending offers of Thy grace, and with humble gratitude I commit my precious soul into Thy almighty and saving hands."

Thus they who know His name will certainly put their trust in Him. While others are depending upon their own righteousness, and endeavoring to pacify the offended Majesty of Heaven by their duties and endeavors, these will renounce all confidence in everything but Christ, and build all their hopes of happiness upon this unalterable Rock of Ages. They will depend upon the value of His merits, the prevalency of His intercession, the riches of His grace, and the power of His Spirit to cleanse their guilty souls and sanctify their polluted natures, to guide them through the howling wilderness of this world, and finally bring them safe to the heavenly Canaan. "I know whom I have believed," said St. Paul, "and I am persuaded that He is able to keep that which I have committed to Him against that day" (2 Timothy 1:12).

Third, this humble trust in Christ as our Savior is forever attended with an everlasting hatred against sin, which is so justly displeasing unto Him. The malignant nature and destructive tendency of sin is visible upon the face of the whole creation. It has destroyed the beauty and stained the glory of this lower world. Sin has introduced all those distresses and disorders which its guilty inhabitants are groaning under, and which have rendered this earth a valley of tears and a stage of affliction and darkness.

But never was the evil of sin so fully discovered, never was its fatal tendency so astonishingly revealed, as by the death and suffering of our blessed Redeemer. For it was this that brought Him down from heaven to earth, from the pleasures of His Father's bosom to the state of a servant. Sin was the accursed cause of all the distressing sorrows of His life, and all the tormenting agonies of His death.

Now when this is clearly manifested to the soul and it feels the refreshing influence of the Redeemer's blood taking away its guilt and absolving the sinner from the sentence of the law, it will certainly open all the springs of godly sorrow and fill him with an everlasting hatred against those sins which were the cause of these sufferings. When such look upon Him whom they have pierced (Zechariah 12:10), they cannot but mourn, as one who mourns for his only son. They must break out in such language as this: "Did my dearest Lord die a sacrifice for those sins which I had committed, and shed His invaluable blood upon the cross so that I might not suffer the terrors of eternal death? Oh, that my head were waters, and my eyes fountains of tears, that I might weep for my ingratitude and rebellion against Him! Were my sins the thorns that pierced His sacred head and the cruel spear that wounded His blessed side? Was it for my sake that He was nailed to the cursed tree and executed as one of the vilest sinners? Let me then forever renounce those sins which were the guilty cause of His sufferings. Let me forever abhor those murderers of my best Friend and Benefactor."

Fourth, this knowledge kindles in the soul the highest affection to Christ. Ignorant and besotted sinners, whose eyes are dazzled with the pomp and glitter of the world, and whose hearts are captivated with the pleasures of sin and sense, can see no form or comeliness in Christ wherefore He should be admired. Hence they argue, "What is thy beloved more than another?"

But a soul enlightened by the Spirit of God is immediately struck with a view of His divine and amiable glories, and at once pronounces Him fairer than the children of men, the chiefest among ten thousands, altogether lovely. But when they consider all the amazing evidences of His love to them, they are swallowed up with wonder and surprise, and break forth into the most affectionate strains of gratitude and praise: "What manner of love is this wherewith the Son of God has loved us? Who can comprehend the height, the depth, the length and breadth of the love of Christ that passes knowledge? What obligations you are under, O my soul, to this lovely Savior! What shall I render to the Lord for all His benefits? Unto Him who has loved me, and washed me from my sins in His own blood, to Him be glory and dominion forever and ever, Amen."

Men under the dominion of sin and sense esteem the yoke of Christ an intolerable burden, and obedience to His commandments an unprofitable severity. But those who have tasted that He is gracious are convinced of the justice and equity of His government, esteem His service as their highest honor, and account none of His commandments to be grievous. They are willing cheerfully to forgo their dearest interest for His sake, and to take up their cross and follow Him in the face of ten thousand dangers. They unfeignedly join with the devout psalmist, "O Lord, truly I am Thy servant. I am Thy servant, Thou hast loosed my bands" (Psalm 116:16). They say, "I am Thine, O blessed Savior, by the most indissoluble obligations. I acknowledge Thy sacred authority. I bow my neck to Thy gracious yoke, and swear allegiance unto Thee forever. Let Thy kingdom be set up in my soul, reign absolute in my heart, and let every rebellious passion be subject to Thy just and righteous government. Let all the faculties of my soul be employed in Thy delightful service, and all the members of my body be improved as instruments of righteousness to Thy glory. Let it be my continual employment to glorify Thee upon earth, and my everlasting happiness to enjoy Thee in heaven." These are the genuine effects of a saving knowledge of Christ, and distinguish it from a barren and empty speculation.

2. I now proceed to recommend this knowledge of Christ and Him crucified to your diligent study and practice. This is the most sublime and excellent knowledge. Christ is the sum and substance of both the law and gospel. The design of both Moses and the prophets was to point Him out as the Savior of a guilty world. In Him all created and uncreated glories meet as in their proper center, and render Him most worthy of our attentive study and regards. What a scene of wonders is united in His Person! What a series of miracles attended His birth and life, His death, resurrection, and ascension! What could be more astonishing than that the universal Lord of heaven and earth should be confined in a virgin's womb, that He who governs the nations by His powerful influence and orders all the affairs of the upper and lower worlds according to His sovereign pleasure, should appear upon earth in the character of a carpenter's son, and submit to the condition and figure of a servant; that the Lord of life should die, and the immaculate Lamb of God be made a sacrifice for sin; that by dying He should conquer death and him who had the power of death, and by rising again make way for the eternal triumph and victories of His people. These are astonishing mysteries fit for the entertainment of the most enlightened understandings.

The wisdom of this world is employed upon inferior vanities, and useful only for this transitory life. But the knowledge of Christ contains the treasures of divine wisdom and grace, and unfolds the secret counsels of heaven for the recovery of a wretched and miserable world.

Here all the divine perfections shine forth in their united glories with a bright and charming luster. The designs of mercy are accomplished without any disparagement to the sacred claims of justice. Here the personal and mediatorial excellencies of the Lord Jesus are displayed, who was from all eternity the brightness of His Father's glory, and the express image of His person; but in the fullness of time He appeared in the likeness of sinful flesh, and was clothed with the infirmities of human nature. Here a way is opened for our deliverance from the guilt and power of sin, and a sure foundation is laid for the enjoyment of all the privileges of a justified, adopted, and sanctified state. Here the glories and felicities of the heavenly world are presented to our view, and the methods described in which we may be recovered from the miseries of our apostasy, and advanced to a happiness as large as our capacities and immortal as our souls. Surely these are subjects worthy of our most raised thoughts and suited to the entertainment of the sublimest spirits.

But why should I expatiate upon a subject that is boundless and inexhaustible, a subject more fit to employ the eloquence of an angel than the faltering tongue of a feeble mortal? Yea, the angels themselves look into these things with wonder and adoration. And they unite their songs with the happy company of the redeemed in heaven, ascribing "blessing, honor, and glory and power, unto Him that sitteth upon the throne and to the LAMB forever and ever."

This is the most useful and necessary knowledge. Men are apt highly to value themselves upon the account of their human knowledge, and to look down with contempt upon others whom they esteem ignorant and unlearned. But the wisest philosopher, the greatest scholar, if ignorant of Christ and the way of salvation appointed by Him, will be finally rejected by God, and with all his attainments lie down in everlasting sorrow.

The wisdom of this world can attain no higher than to gratify a present inclination, or secure some slight, temporal advantage. But the knowledge of Christ aims at a nobler end; it advances the glory of God, and promotes the universal happiness of man. The voice of nature proclaims our guilt, fills the mind with anxious fears, and soon convinces us that we are miserable and mortal sinners. But all the writings of the Gentile sages, all the directions of their celebrated moralists, are insufficient to recover fallen man from the ruins of his apostate state and restore him to his original integrity and happiness. This is the peculiar glory of the gospel, and can be attained only by an experimental knowledge of Christ, and a lively faith in Him.

Without this men may be instructed in the doctrines of grace, and discourse of them with propriety and elegance; but all their knowledge is but specious ignorance, and is esteemed by God no better than foolishness. Without this, though men are adorned with many amiable qualities, and lead sober, regular, and (to all appearances) religious lives, yet they remain under the condemning sentence of the law and perish at last in a state of unsanctified nature. For there is no other name given under heaven by which we can be saved but the name of Jesus, and no salvation by Him until He is inwardly revealed in us by His Spirit.

We may bear the character of Christians, and be diligent and devout in our attendance upon the duties of divine worship, but unless our persons are justified through the imputation of Christ's perfect righteousness, and our natures are quickened by a principle of new life derived from Him, we are no better than whited sepulchers, painted Pharisees, and disguised hypocrites. Justly then does the great Doctor of the Gentiles place so high a value upon this divine and excellent knowledge. With the highest reason he determines to know nothing but Jesus Christ and Him crucified—and his example is certainly worthy to be diligently imitated by us.

What infinite madness is it then for the guilty children of men to spend their time and strength in the pursuit of those things which will leave them naked, destitute, and miserable, and neglect the knowledge of Christ which will justify, sanctify, and save them. Why, O sinner, will you waste the lamp of life in these specious follies and amusements which belong only to the present world, and despise those things which concern your eternal welfare? Would you not stand amazed to behold a condemned malefactor, under a sentence of death and in continual danger of being dragged out to execution, spend his time in mirth and diversion, or at best in worldly cares and business, without any concern to prevent the execution of the law or prepare for his approaching death? But this is the daily madness of thoughtless and inconsiderate sinners. Every soul in this assembly that does not have an experimental knowledge of Christ is under the condemning sentence of the divine law, exposed to an infinitely more terrible execution than any human power can inflict.

There remains but a short and uncertain time to fly from the amazing danger and escape the vengeance of eternal fire. Is it not then worse than brutal stupidity to neglect the present season and trifle away those flying moments, upon which an eternity depends? Rouse yourselves up therefore, my dear brethren. Awake out of this fatal security. Cry earnestly to God that He would bestow upon you the spirit of wisdom and revelation so that you may know Him, whom to know is life eternal. Resolve to make this your chief study, your great and principle business. Other knowledge may recommend you to the applause of men, but this will restore you to the favor of God and enable you to stand with safety at the awful tribunal of Christ. You may be ignorant of many things and yet wise for salvation. But if you are destitute of this divine knowledge, you are sons of death and must dwell in the melancholy regions of eternal darkness. Other knowledge will be shortly unprofitable and vain. It will afford you but a feeble support against the assaults of the king of terrors. But an experimental knowledge of Christ will enlighten the dark valley of the shadow of death and enable you to meet your last enemy with joy and triumph. If you truly know Christ, though ignorant of everything else, you know enough to make you happy in time and throughout eternity. For such as are justified by faith have peace with God, and are heirs of immortal glory. Neither the reproaches of an accusing conscience, the demands of a broken law, nor the flaming sword of divine justice; neither former sins or later transgressions shall ever be able to separate them from their supreme and eternal felicity.

3. Nothing now remains but to apply this discourse to you, my dear young friends, the students of this house, and in a special manner to such of you as are candidates for the service of the sacred ministry.

Your united requests have brought me into this desk at this time, and for your service this discourse is peculiarly designed. Suffer me then, with a tender concern for your present usefulness and eternal welfare, earnestly to exhort you to the diligent practice of the duty recommended in my text; resolve with the great Doctor of the Gentiles to know nothing save Christ and Him crucified.

Blessed be God, there are many of you inquiring with the young man in the gospel, "What shall I do that I may enter into life eternal?" This, I trust, is a token for good, a happy sign that God has mercy in store for future generations.

In your present circumstances you will easily find the insufficiency of all human teaching to deliver you from that depth of misery in which you are involved, and to guide your feet in the way to peace and safety. If you have a lively sense of your guilt and misery you will soon perceive that neither the writings of Plato or Seneca, the celebrated philosophers of Rome and Athens, nor the most accurate delineations of the religion of nature by the admired teachers of morality in the present age, will afford you a solid foundation of peace and comfort. To a conscience truly awakened, these will be found miserable comforters, physicians of no value!

Alas, what will a knowledge of the secrets of nature, what will an acquaintance with the mysteries of art, or the most eloquent harangues upon the beauty and excellency of moral virtue avail me while I am perishing under the guilt of sin, and subject to the disgraceful servitude of Satan? What if I had a genius so sublime as to contain the whole circle of learning in my capacious mind; a capacity so extensive that I could count the number of the stars and call them all by their names; though I understood all manner of languages, and could discourse with the tongues of men and angels—yet if I do not know Christ and Him crucified, all these will profit me nothing. These splendid attainments, which are so highly valued by the learned and polite world, will but render me a richer prey to Satan and lead me with so much more pomp and ceremony to the land of darkness.

Let me then never any more waste my time in the search of that knowledge which will not supply the wants of my immortal soul, nor spend my strength in seeking after those things which will at last leave me blind and wretched, ignorant of my duty and happiness. Let me seek after that knowledge which will restore peace to my troubled mind, that will rectify the disorders of my corrupted nature, that will deliver me from the tyranny of Satan to whom I am enslaved, and from the terrors of death of which I am in continual danger, that will rescue me from that unutterable misery, which I have deserved, and restore me to the joys of paradise which I have forfeited.

This, O my brethren, is that knowledge which alone is worthy of the study of a rational and immortal creature. This is that knowledge which is recommended to you in my text. Other knowledge may brighten and adorn the understanding, but this alone will purify the heart. An acquaintance with the arts and sciences may advance your credit among men, but this alone renders you a child of God and gives you a title to the Kingdom of Heaven. The study of other things may entertain and amuse you while you are flourishing in health and prosperity, but this will comfort you when languishing on a bed of sickness, and revive and support you in the gloomy hour of approaching death.

But, oh, what darkness and horror will surprise the secure and inconsiderate sinner who has spent his time in the empty speculations of science falsely so called, and the idle amusements of the gay and fashionable world when he comes to stand upon the awful confines of the grave, and finds himself just stepping into the amazing gulf of eternity. With what sorrow and regret will he reflect upon those many hours he has wasted upon unprofitable vanities, while he has neglected the one thing needful, the knowledge of Christ and the way of salvation by Him? With what anguish and despair will such look up to the mansions of the blessed and behold many whom they once despised as ignorant and unlearned, triumphing in endless joy and felicity, when they with all their blasted attainments are thrust down into unutterable darkness and misery!

Allow me, my dear brethren, to go on and say that not only your own personal welfare, but the prosperity of the church of Christ is greatly concerned in your compliance with this exhortation.

You are the hopes of our churches; and the flourishing of religion in future times depends upon your having this saving knowledge of Christ. Many of you are designed for the service of the sanctuary, and if you lay the foundation of your preparations for the work of the ministry in an experimental acquaintance with Christ, you will doubtless prove to be extensive blessings in your day, and be the happy instruments of propagating pure and undefiled religion to late posterity. But if you enter upon this sacred charge under the influence of carnal motives, while you are strangers to that Christ whom you are to preach to others, you will in all probability be the plagues of the church, and the unhappy occasion of the damnation of multitudes.

Remember then that the eyes of God, angels, and men are upon you, to observe with what temper and disposition, with what views and intentions you engage in the service of the gospel. I think I see the happy spirits of your pious ancestors, who have fought the good fight of faith and finished their course with joy, looking down from the lofty battlements of heaven to observe your conduct and see whether you will prove faithful to the cause of Christ, for which they forsook the pleasures of their native land and encountered all the difficulties of a howling wilderness. I think I hear them calling to you aloud from their exalted seats in glory, and solemnly adjuring you by all that is sacred and serious to choose the God of your fathers for your God, to keep the sacred deposit of the gospel uncorrupted in this day of prevailing degeneracy, and transmit the knowledge of Christ without any erroneous mixtures to their children's children forever.

To propagate the kingdom of our great Redeemer, and not to promote the designs of a party, was the blessed cause in which our fathers were happily engaged, and for which they underwent numberless hardships and trials. And this should be forever dear to their posterity, who now stand in their place and stead and reap the fruits of all their expense and labor.

Let me therefore, with the authority of a minister of Christ and with the tender affection of a friend who is zealously concerned for your and the church's welfare, entreat and persuade you to make this divine knowledge the great design you have continually in view; and let all your other studies be managed in such a manner as may subserve this noble intention. The honor of your profession as Christians, your usefulness as ministers, and the necessities of the perishing souls of men, loudly demand this from you. See that you have a saving knowledge of Christ yourselves before you pretend to preach Him to others. For if the blind lead the blind, what can be expected but that they both fall into the pit of everlasting darkness and misery?

And when you enter upon the work of the ministry, let Christ and Him crucified be the favorite subject of your private meditations and public administrations, without which your sacred performances, however beautifully they are contrived, however artfully they are delivered, will be no better than the sounding brass and tinkling cymbals. Remember the character you are to bear is that of a minister of Christ, and the commission you receive is to preach His unsearchable riches, to proclaim the glories of the amiable Jesus—a commission that would dignify an angel and adorn the character of the brightest seraphim. Let His name therefore triumph in all your discourses, and let it be the height of your ambition to bring sinners to a saving acquaintance with Him.

This was the method made use of by the apostles in the first ages of the church, which was owned and honored of God with vast and surprising success. This was the practice of our venerable fathers in the early days of New England, and they were the happy instruments in the hands of God of filling His church with numerous converts and preparing multitudes for the kingdom of heaven. And if you imitate those blessed examples, and with sacred courage and zeal endeavor to promote the practical knowledge of Christ in the world, you will have the same almighty power to assist, and the same glorious rewards to encourage you. Yea, if you will unfeignedly give up your names to this glorious Redeemer, and heartily engage in His service, you will be standard-bearers in the camp of Christ, and under the influence and conduct of the great Captain of our Salvation, shall lead forth the armies of Israel to certain victory and triumph.

Though this may expose you to the reproaches of your friends and acquaintances, though you may be called to oppose the united endeavors of earth and hell, yet be faithful unto death, and then you shall receive a crown of life. Yet a little while and that Savior, in whose cause you are engaged and whose kingdom you promote, shall appear in the defense of His despised interest and fill the whole earth with the glory of His name. Yet a little while and He who shall come will come, and shall not tarry. Then shall the wise men and disputers of this world who, with all their learning, remain ignorant of the mysteries of salvation, be found wandering stars for whom is reserved blackness of darkness forever. While you who have determined to know nothing but Christ and Him crucified, and made it the business of life to make Him known unto others, shall shine with uncommon brightness in the firmament of glory. While they shall be clothed with everlasting shame and contempt, you will appear in distinguishing circumstances of dignity and honor, shall receive the applause of your Lord and Judge, and enter into your Maker's joy, Amen.

2

The Nature and Obligation of Receiving Christ by Faith

"But as many as received Him, to them gave He power to
become the sons of God, even to them that
believe on His name." John 1:12

Our blessed Lord informs us that God "sent not his
Son into the world to condemn the world, but that the
world through Him might be saved." If we consider the
descriptions of this salvation that are given us in the gospel, the invaluable price that was paid for its purchase,
and the inconceivable blessings contained in it, we must
necessarily conclude that it is the noblest object of a rational desire and the most important business that can
employ the thoughts of an immortal creature. If we look
down into hell beneath and view the forlorn company of
abandoned sinners who have trifled away the day of grace,
who have forfeited this inestimable blessing, and are irrecoverably fixed in the melancholy regions of horror and
despair, they bewail their insufferable loss with incessant
agonies and tears; they curse their distraction and folly in
neglecting so great salvation when offered to their choice
and acceptance. If we cast our eyes up to heaven and inquire of the happy spirits above who have finished their
course and are triumphing in immortal glory, they declare
the excellency of this salvation with cheerful and united
voices, and shout forth songs of praise to the honor of
their almighty Savior.

It is therefore a matter of unutterable consequence to

us who are yet in a state of trial and, through the divine favor, who stand as candidates for celestial blessedness, to improve the happy opportunity that we enjoy and to work out our salvation with fear and trembling. To this end we must secure an interest in Christ by faith, and receive Him as He is offered unto us in the gospel. For to as many as receive Him, to them He gives power to become the sons of God. In speaking to these words, I shall, by divine assistance, explain the nature of thus receiving Christ, press this duty upon you by some powerful and persuasive motives, and then conclude with some practical directions.

1. I am to explain the nature of receiving Christ. This is a duty, my brethren, of the first importance to be understood by every Christian. Upon your compliance with it depends your present acceptance with God and your future acquittal at His tremendous tribunal. A mistake here is infinitely dangerous, and has betrayed multitudes into eternal perdition. May the divine Spirit assist me to speak upon this momentous subject with convincing light and evidence, and may He enable my audience to hear with the utmost attention and diligence!

To receive Christ is a duty frequently insisted upon in the gospel, and is the same with believing on His name. It includes the following particulars:

• A firm assent of the understanding to the truth of what the gospel reveals concerning the Lord Jesus Christ, the Savior of the world. This is an essential part of faith, and lays the first foundation for all its future acts and exercises. He who comes to Christ must receive the divine testimony concerning Him, and believe Him to be the true Messiah promised to the ancient fathers, the great Prophet foretold under the Old Testament dispensation, and the Mighty Savior who was shadowed forth by the types and ceremonies of the Jewish church and expected by the people of God from age to age. He must acknowledge Him to be the divine Person appointed by the wisdom and sovereignty of heaven to be the only Mediator between God and man; who was of the seed of David after the flesh, but with respect to His divine nature was God over all blessed for evermore; who from the days of eternity dwelt in the bosom of the Father and in the fullness of time was manifested in the flesh, tabernacled among men, and was declared with power to be the Son of God and the Savior of men; who proclaimed the joyful tidings of salvation to the apostate progeny of Adam, evidenced the truth of His doctrine by many mighty works of power and grace, and exhibited a perfect pattern of the most excellent virtues in His innocent and exemplary life; who died as a propitiatory sacrifice for sin in circumstances of ignominy and disgrace, and arose again for the justification of His people with astonishing glory; who, in the presence of His disciples, ascended up into heaven by His own blood, entered into the holy place to make intercession for us, and is set down at the right hand of the Majesty on high; from whence He has sent the ever-blessed Spirit of grace to sanctify His church and prepare His disciples for the inheritance of the saints in light; who now sways the scepter of the universe in equity and righteousness, governs the creation according to His sovereign pleasure, and will shortly descend a second time into this lower world to finish the designs of His mediatorial kingdom, to pass a decisive sentence upon all mankind and reward every one according to their works.

These are in general the great doctrines of the gospel which whoever would be saved must undoubtedly believe. And though some of these important truths were not clearly revealed by our Lord Himself during the time of His personal ministry upon earth, and were even concealed from the knowledge of His favorite disciples until the descent of the Holy Ghost on the day of Pentecost, yet since they are plainly taught by the apostles, the first ministers of Christ's kingdom, who were under the infallible guidance of the divine Spirit, they are to be entertained as the doctrines of Jesus and received with a firm and unshaken assent. But though this is an essential part of that faith that is unto salvation, yet it is not all that is required in the true believer. Even the devils believe and tremble; and many men in all ages, who have acknowledged the doctrines of the gospel to be true, have nevertheless been strangers to their sanctifying power and influence. Though they have made a high profession of the name of Christ, yet they have been enemies to His cross and rebels to His crown and government.

• Therefore it further intends a sincere approbation of His blessed designs, and unfeigned acceptance of Him in all His sacred offices and characters. A saving and justifying faith is not confined to the head, but descends into the heart and bows the soul to a cheerful compliance with the invitations of grace. The true believer not only assents to the divine testimony concerning Christ, but acquiesces in that method of salvation which is appointed and revealed in the gospel, and in conformity to it receives Christ as His Lord and Savior. Conscious of His guilt, misery, and danger; convinced that there is no other name given under heaven by which he can be saved but by the name of Jesus, and encouraged by the free and universal offers of the gospel, he accepts Christ as an all-sufficient Redeemer and earnestly desires to be numbered among His obedient subjects, His redeemed people, and His purchased inheritance.

Christ is proposed to our acceptance in all His saving offices: as a Prophet, to instruct us in the will of heaven and guide our perishing souls in the way to happiness and glory; as a Priest, to make atonement for our guilt and reconcile us to our offended God and Sovereign; as a King, to subdue our rebellious natures and govern us according to His sacred laws. And everyone who truly believes in Christ receives Him as He is offered, without exception or reserve, as a Priest upon a throne, a Prince, and a Savior. He cordially consents to the whole of His merciful designs, cheerfully submits to His most gracious terms, and comes to Him to be pardoned and justified by His blood, to be sanctified and renewed by His Holy Spirit, and to be universally governed by His righteous precepts.

This distinguishes the faith of the true Christian from the presumptuous confidence of the painted Pharisee. The hypocrite desires an interest in Christ only to silence the clamors of an uneasy conscience and save him from the terrors of death and hell; but he rejects His authority and government, and refuses to part with his beloved lusts and corruptions. He is willing to be saved from the guilt and punishment of sin by the merits of Christ's death and passion, but has no desire to be delivered from its power and dominion by the influences of His grace and Spirit; and therefore his faith is but presumption, and his hope of being saved by Christ will prove to be but an empty delusion. For Christ will redeem none from hell but those whom He saves from their sins; whom He justifies by His grace, them also He sanctifies by His Spirit. But the true believer comes to Christ with an unfeigned resolution to submit to His yoke and an earnest desire that Christ would perform in him the whole good pleasure of His grace, and bring everything into subjection to His authority and dominion.

• This acceptance is attended with a humble dependence upon the power and grace of Christ to do all that in us and for us which He has promised to do for His people. This is an act of faith frequently insisted upon in Scripture, which forever excludes boasting and ascribes the entire glory of our salvation to God. "I know," said St. Paul, "whom I have believed, and I am persuaded that He is able to keep that which I have committed unto Him against that day" (2 Timothy 1:12). It supposes that we are deeply convinced of our utter inability to deliver ourselves from

the condemning sentence of the law and the defiling
power of sin, but are firmly persuaded of the ability and
readiness of Christ to save all who come to Him. We therefore commit our precious and immortal souls into His safe
and gracious hands, trust in Him as our only sanctuary
and refuge, and lay the stress of our eternal salvation upon
His powerful mediation and merits. We renounce all dependence upon our own works and rely on the sacrifice
and righteousness of our exalted Redeemer to cleanse our
guilty souls and justify us at the enlightened tribunal of a
holy God. We resign our polluted natures unto the power
and influence of His grace to mortify our sins and prepare
us for His heavenly kingdom, humbly confiding in the precious promises of His Word that He will guide our steps in
the paths of peace and holiness, and finally bring us to the
full possession of perfect and unalterable happiness. This
is to receive Christ by faith, and thus must we rely on Him
alone for salvation.

And now, upon the whole of what has been said under
this heading, we may plainly perceive that this grace of
faith is admirably calculated to humble the pride of rebellious sinners, to exalt the glory of divine grace, and to
promote the holiness and comfort of men. Boasting is entirely cut off, for by grace we are saved through faith, and
that not of ourselves; it is the gift of God. The true believer
may indeed triumph in the cross of Christ and rejoice in
the invaluable benefits purchased by His death and passion, but has nothing to boast of in himself but guilt, deformity, and danger. The way of salvation by faith obliges
the soul to renounce all dependence upon self, and to receive all from mere unmerited mercy. Man forfeited an
earthly paradise by trusting his own wisdom and power,
but is restored to the heavenly happiness by depending
upon the grace and righteousness of another. How illustriously does the glory of the divine attributes shine forth in
this wonderful dispensation! How vast the condescension

of heaven to the guilty progeny of apostate Adam! We have forfeited the favor of God by our willful transgressions, lost His amiable image which was our primitive glory, and are by nature sons of death and destruction. But, behold, a method contrived by the wisdom of God by which we may be admitted to the divine favor, be made partakers of the divine nature, and be enrolled among the family of heaven. The law of nature thunders out its curses against the sinner and proclaims indignation and wrath, tribulation and anguish, to every soul that does evil, without exception; but the soft and gentle invitations of the gospel offer peace and pardon, immortality and glory, to everyone who believes, whether Jew or Gentile.

Though this doctrine has been unreasonably reproached as flattering the vices of men and encouraging a licentious life, yet certainly nothing has a more powerful tendency to promote sincere and universal holiness. That faith by which we are saved purifies the heart, overcomes the world, and is a living principle of all good works. That Savior in whom we trust is commissioned by the Father to redeem from sin as well as from wrath, and will be the Author of eternal salvation only to those who obey Him. None can come to Him aright but those who are sensible of the corruption of their nature and groan under the burden of their sins. None are received and accepted by Him but such as are redeemed from their vain conversation, turned from all iniquity, and made a peculiar people, zealous for good works. Therefore, though boasting is excluded by the law of faith, yet holiness is secured and advanced. By this method the glory of God is wonderfully displayed, the pride of human nature is subdued, and guilty and rebellious sinners are saved.

2. Next I wish to press upon you this duty of receiving Christ by some powerful and prevailing motives. And here consider that you are by nature exposed to the wrath of God; and there is no other way of escape but this of re-

ceiving the Lord Jesus Christ by faith, and so securing an interest in His invaluable merits. You have become guilty before God by innumerable actual transgressions added to original sin, and have departed from the ways of His commandments times without number. Look back, O sinner, to the day of your nativity, and consider that you were shapen in sin, and in iniquity did your mother conceive you. From the earliest bloom of youth you have misimproved your time and talents, and wasted your strength and vigor in the disgraceful service of sin and Satan. From the first dawnings of reason you have rebelled against the sacred authority of God, your Maker and Sovereign, despised His condescending goodness, which is the fountain of your being and the bounteous spring of all your mercies. You have joined in conspiracy with Satan, the prince of the kingdom of darkness, to dethrone the eternal Majesty of Heaven, to wrest the scepter out of His hands and place the crown upon the head of an impious usurper; and is not this an insufferable contempt of the everblessed God, whose infinite power produced you into being at first, whose gracious providence has supported and preserved you ever since, and who can with infinite ease fearfully destroy you in a moment! And can you suppose He will pass by such insolent affronts, and suffer such daring transgressions to escape with impunity? Will He not vindicate the honor of His despised laws and revenge the quarrels of His abused authority? Has He not declared in His inalterable Word that He loves righteousness and hates iniquity, that the foolish shall not stand in His sight, and that He hates all the workers of iniquity?

Know then, O sinner, and tremble at the amazing thought that while you continue in your present condition, God is angry with you every day, and you stand exposed to all the curses written in the book of His law; that God is your Enemy, who governs the whole creation according to His uncontrollable pleasure, and can commis-

sion the most contemptible insects to be the ministers of
His awful vengeance. Oh, who can stand before Him once
He is angry? Who can abide the day of His indignation? Is
it not better to have the united power of angels, men, and
devils engaged against you than to be exposed to His almighty wrath, who is able to destroy both body and soul in
hell! Look into that dismal vault below and consider what
the apostate angels are groaning under in those regions of
torment and misery. Meditate upon the forlorn state of
those spirits in prison who are encircled with the terrors of
eternal darkness, and are sweltering in the lake that burns
with fire and brimstone. And let this inform you what a
fearful thing it is to fall into the hands of the living God,
and to feel the weight of His infinite displeasure. And to
this you are every moment exposed while you continue in
a state of guilt and impenitence.

Nor is there any other way to escape the distressing
scenes of wrath and misery than by hearkening to the invitations of the gospel and receiving Christ as your Savior
and Lord. He is the only Mediator between God and man;
outside of Christ, our God is a consuming fire. It is vain to
harbor any fond imaginations of being saved by the prerogative of mercy while you continue in your sins and at a
distance from Christ; for we are positively assured that the
wrath of God abides on he who does not believe on the
Son. God will never exalt the glory of His grace to the
point of diminishing the sacred claims of His justice. If
ever peace is made between an offended God and offending sinners, mercy and truth must meet together; righteousness and peace must kiss each other. If ever the
clouds of divine wrath are blown over and we see the face
of God in glory, it must be through the atoning sacrifice of
the Son of God applied to our souls and received by a living faith. The most exact obedience to the divine precepts
which any of the children of men could ever boast of, the
most costly sacrifices that were ever offered up to appease

the offended vengeance of heaven, will not vindicate the honor of the law and procure a favorable acceptance at the bar of unspotted purity and holiness. Could we fill the air with distressing groans, the seas with our sorrowful tears, and pierce the very heavens with our importunate cries for mercy, it would not make satisfaction to offended justice or purchase for us a title to the pardoning grace of God. If we build upon anything but Christ, our foundation will deceive us in the day of our extremity and danger, and we shall stand exposed to the desolating storms of divine fury. If ever, therefore, you would escape the wrath to come and lay hold of eternal life, which by your iniquities you have so justly forfeited, you must obtain redemption through the blood of Jesus and accept Him as offered to you in the gospel.

Which brings me to say, you are compassionately invited to receive Him with all His inestimable benefits and blessings. While multitudes of your fellow creatures inhabit the regions of darkness and are perishing for lack of knowledge, you, through the tender mercies of our God, have had the Dayspring from on high visiting you with His refreshing beams and clearly discovering the way of salvation by Christ. God, your Creator and Preserver, whose justice you have offended and whose wrath you have highly provoked, solemnly declares that He does not desire the death of the sinner, and with bowels of compassion beseeches you to regard the welfare of your perishing souls. The blessed Jesus, the only Mediator between God and man, shows you His sacred body that was nailed to the accursed tree, and His precious blood which was shed to satisfy the demands of justice, and adjures you, by all the distressing sorrows and afflictions of His life, by all the tormenting agonies of His death and passion, that you would not reject His offered grace and trample under foot the unsearchable riches of His kindness and love. He presents Himself before your eyes in His all-sufficiency and glory, with peace and pardon in His hands, to attract your affection and esteem, and to persuade you to submit to His conduct and protection. He commands you to come to Him so that you may have life, and all the blessings you stand in need of, for time and for eternity. He counsels you to buy from Him gold tried in the fire so that you may be rich, white raiment so that you may be clothed, and eyesalve so that you may see. He invites you to come and take of the waters of life freely, to buy wine and milk, without money, and without price.

And now, my brethren, shall all this astonishing kindness and condescension of heaven be in vain with respect to you, and serve only to aggravate your guilt and increase your eternal condemnation? Did the Son of God forsake the delightful bosom of His Father, clothe Himself with the infirmities of flesh and blood, stoop to the disgraceful state of a servant, and submit to the painful death of the cross in order to save the guilty children of men from their sins and deliver them from the wrath and curse of God, which were the just demerits of their crimes? And shall such a Savior be treated with scorn and contempt? Shall so great a salvation be rejected and despised? Shall you perish in your sins when so blessed a remedy is provided, and pine away in your iniquities when an almighty Physician may be obtained? Certainly this will be an instance of astonishing stupidity and madness! Such hug their chains and court destruction and misery. They make a covenant with Satan and are at an agreement with hell. The blood of the obstinate transgressor will therefore be upon his own head. God and His throne will be clear and guiltless forever.

But by rejecting Christ you astonishingly increase the number of your sins and expose yourselves to a severe and aggravated vengeance. You may now perhaps be insensible of your guilt, and imagine it but a slight and venial fault to turn a deaf ear to the calls of mercy and refuse the offers

of a Savior. But, alas, it is an evil of the first magnitude, a
most provoking affront to the God of your life and the Father of all your mercies! It is daring rebellion against your
rightful Lord and Lawgiver, who alone has power to save
or to destroy. Hereby you spurn the bowels of mercy, offer the vilest indignity to the Lord of glory, and are guilty
of bloody cruelty to your own souls. Was it not an instance
of wonderful condescension and grace in God the Father
to contrive the scheme of man's redemption in His eternal
counsel, to part with His Son out of His bosom in the fullness of time, to deliver Him up to suffering, affliction, and
death for guilty rebels who were unworthy of His favor,
and had deserved His everlasting displeasure? Was it not
an unparalleled expression of the kindness of God our
Savior, who is equal with the Father and the heir of His
love and glory, to appear in the humbling circumstances
of human nature, to clothe Himself in the livery of guilt
and shame, to die an infamous and accursed death so that
sinners might not suffer eternal destruction from the
presence of God and the glory of His power? Is it not marvelous goodness in the blessed Spirit of grace, that He is
willing to apply these inestimable benefits of the gospel to
the souls of men, to sanctify them by His heavenly influences, and to seal them to the day of redemption? And
shall all these miracles of mercy be slighted and neglected?
Is this your kindness to your best Friend and Benefactor,
who shed the sacred treasure of His blood for your ran-
soms? Is this your affection to your invaluable and immortal souls which, if you die in your sins, must perish without
remedy? What punishment can be equal to such a heinous
and aggravated offence! What doom is too severe for such
willful and resolved offenders! This sin is of such an uncommon malignity that it exceeds the abominations of
Sodom and Gomorrah, which brought down vengeance
upon those detested places and consumed them by showers of brimstone and fire. Yea, it in some respects exceeds

the sin of the very devils, for which those once happy and glorious spirits were banished from their first habitation and are reserved in chains of darkness forever. This not only unalterably binds upon you the sentence of the law, but exposes you to a more fearful and intolerable condemnation!

And finally, He who now addresses you in the gentle voice of an indulgent Savior will shortly appear in the surprising terrors of an incensed Judge, to pass an irrevocable sentence upon those who reject Him. He once appeared in this lower world in a humble and inglorious state, clouded with poverty and disgrace, a Man of Sorrows and acquainted with griefs. But He will shortly descend in all the grandeur of an incarnate God, clothed with light as with a garment, in sparkling majesty and glory. In the days of His flesh He passed through innumerable agonies and torments, and poured out His soul unto death to purchase salvation for a guilty world; but He soon arose from the dust of death and went up into heaven to appear in the presence of God as an Advocate for His people. The darkness and dishonors of His suffering state are forever blown over, and He is continually magnified and adored by the innumerable company of angels and the universal society of perfected spirits above. From these happy realms of light and joy, He sends the messengers of His grace to plead His cause with a rebellious world and persuade them to accept peace through the blood of His cross.

But He will shortly send for the executioners of His justice and command that His implacable enemies be brought forth and slain before Him. He is now seated upon a throne of grace and stretches forth His compassionate arms to embrace all those who will accept the offers of His love; but He will shortly erect a tribunal of justice and pass an irreversible sentence of misery upon those who reject His invaluable blessings. Look forward, O my brethren, to that great and tremendous day when this Savior whom you now despise shall appear in the majesty and authority of the Judge of heaven and earth, when you must stand at His impartial bar and give an account of what entertainment you have given to the invitations of His mercy. Behold, He comes in the clouds of heaven, riding upon the wings of the wind, attended by the dreadful artillery of His wrath. Lo! He descends from heaven with a shout, with the voice of the Archangel, and the trump of God. Behold, the dead are raised, the judgment is set, the books are opened, and all nations are summoned to appear before Him. How can you support these scenes of terror and distress! How can you bear this amazing sight, who now prefer your sins before your Savior, and refuse all His merciful and condescending offers! With what confidence can you expect to appear before Him, who cast contempt on His blood and crucify Him afresh by your daily iniquities! What would you give in that day for one of these offers that you now disregard, and for an interest in Christ, which you now so stupidly neglect.

Since then we look for this great and terrible day, with what earnestness should we seek for a title to His favor! With what speed and diligence should we receive Him on the terms on which He is offered to us in the gospel, so that we may welcome our descending Lord with shouts of joy and triumph, and may stand before Him with confidence when He shall appear the second time without sin for the salvation of His people.

3. And now, may I not hope that some of my hearers are convinced of their obligation to receive the Lord Jesus Christ by faith, and are desirous to believe in Him to the saving of their souls? To such, then, I would address myself in a few practical directions, and so conclude my present discourse.

First, see that you do not mistake a presumptuous confidence for the faith of God's elect. Many perch themselves upon the pinnacle of the temple and imagine that they have received Christ because they have been baptized in His name and made a public profession of His religion. They believe that Christ died for their offenses, and that through Him they shall obtain the pardon and remission of their sins; upon this alone they say they depend, and this they make their only support and confidence! But, alas, how many of these vain pretenders are uncircumcised in their hearts and vicious in their lives and conversations? The faith of such is but a deluding dream, and their most plausible profession is but hypocrisy and deceit. Take heed then that you do not deceive yourselves in this important affair. See that you receive a complete Savior in all His offices, as a King to reign in your souls as well as a Priest to atone for your sins; for He will save none by the merits of His cross but those who submit to the scepter of His government.

Second, give no ear to the delusions of Satan, who would insinuate that it is time enough hereafter to perform this important work. This is one of the most successful stratagies of Satan, the grand adversary of souls, and proves the irrecoverable ruin of multitudes under the gospel. The miseries of an unconverted state are so plainly set before them, the necessity of an interest in Christ is so frequently and solemnly inculcated upon them, that they can't think of dying in their present state and being herded with the forlorn company of unbelievers in the day of the final judgment. But they flatter themselves with hopes of some more convenient opportunity, when they shall be more freed from the encumbrances of the world and more happily disposed for the work of religion. By this temptation numbers have been prevailed upon to evade the thoughts of these things for the present, and have provoked God by their unreasonable delays to cut them down by the stroke of His justice, and appoint them their portion with hypocrites and unbelievers. Oh, then, consider your danger, and let this excite you to the utmost speed and diligence. Now is the accepted time; now is the day of salvation. What is your life but a vapor which may vanish in a moment? What are your days but a span which may suddenly come to an end?

Third, to conclude, cry mightily unto God to enable you to come to Christ by faith, and receive Him with your whole heart. Faith is the gift of God; no man can come to Christ except the Father draws him. Renounce therefore all confidence in yourselves; depend entirely upon almighty grace to produce within you the work of faith with power; and never cease your importunate supplications till all your difficulties are removed, till your prejudices are conquered, and you are enabled to open the everlasting doors of your souls to receive and entertain the King of Glory, to whom be all honor, blessing, and praise forever and ever, Amen.

3

The Method of Divine Grace in Conversion

"Thy people shall be willing in the day of Thy power."
Psalm 110:3

The depravity of mankind is in nothing more visible than in their profane contempt of redeeming love and their obstinate continuance in their evil ways, notwithstanding all the endearing methods of divine grace to reclaim and recover them. If we consider the melancholy state of guilt and misery in which mankind are involved by their apostasy from God, and the innumerable evils to which they are exposed by the righteous sentence of the divine law, reason would suggest that every one of this unhappy race would receive the glad tidings of a Savior with the highest transports of gratitude and joy, and submit to the conduct and government of Christ upon the first intimations of His willingness to entertain them in the arms of His mercy. But, alas, this is directly contrary to the general temper and practice of sinners. The compassionate Savior of the world uses the most indulgent means to engage them to consult their duty and happiness, and by the most pressing solicitations urges them to accept the condescending offers of His love. But such is the stupidity and ingratitude of rebellious sinners that they stop their ears against His persuasive charms, and, in contempt of offered grace, resolutely persist in the embraces of their enchanting lusts. Their understandings are so fatally blinded by the god of this world, their wills so madly bent upon the gratification of their sensual inclinations, and their affections so fondly engaged to the defiling pleasures of sin, that they will not come to Christ that they may have life. And this unhappy disposition would be universal in all the children of men, without exception, did not God, by a miracle of mercy, show compassion to a chosen number, and by His omnipotent arm subdue the perverseness of their wills and effectually incline them to accept of the saving mercies of the gospel. This is a truth clearly revealed in the words of my text, a truth which has the greatest tendency to humble the pride of man and exalt the name of our great Redeemer.

This psalm is an illustrious prophecy of Christ; it celebrates the glory of His exalted state, and shows us the method by which He gains for Himself the victory. He is appointed King in Zion by the unalterable decree of heaven, and sits at the right hand of God until all His enemies become His footstool. His implacable opposers shall be destroyed by the iron rod of His justice, and His people shall be made willing to submit to the scepter of His government by the irresistible power of His grace.

In discoursing upon these words I shall:

1. Inquire in what manner sinners are made willing to submit to the scepter of Christ, and comply with the calls of the gospel;

2. Show that this is a work of almighty grace, and performed in the day of God's power.

1. I am first to inquire in what manner sinners are made willing to submit to the scepter of Christ, and comply with the calls of the gospel. And here I would observe in general that the great Author of our beings applies Himself to the minds of men in a way agreeable to our rational nature, and by no means destroys the essential freedom of the will by force or violence. Men are drawn to their duty by the cords of a man and the bands of love, by powerful and effectual persuasion. Their understandings

are illuminated by a ray from the Fountain of lights to discern the undoubted certainty, the transcendent excellency and glory of spiritual and eternal things; this is accompanied with a secret and prevailing influence on the will, by which they become freely inclined to embrace Christ and the blessings of the gospel as being most worthy of their choice and affection, and to reject everything else as dross and dung in comparison to them.

The great mysteries of faith are not barely proposed to the understanding in the external revelations of the gospel, and the most powerful motives made use of to induce the sinner to believe and accept them; but by an internal dispensation of light and influence, the mind is divinely illuminated to entertain these sacred truths as indisputable realities, and the will and affections are engaged to cleave to them with the highest alacrity and pleasure. Carnal prejudices are removed, and the soul strongly and sweetly disposed to comply with the terms of the gospel. No violence is offered to the will, but its corruption is purged away, its perverse inclinations are effectually subdued, and the man is persuaded and enabled to act according to the dictates of the highest reason. But I proceed more particularly to describe the methods of divine grace in converting sinners, by which they are made willing to yield to the scepter and government of Christ.

• They are convinced of the deplorable misery of an unconverted estate, and the amazing danger in which they are every moment exposed. Sinners are so fond of their beloved pleasures, so inviolably attached to the gratification of their sensual appetites and worldly lusts, that nothing will usually awaken them out of their security till the glittering sword of divine vengeance is brandished before their eyes and they have an experimental taste of the bitterness of sin. Not even all the invaluable promise of grace, not all the alluring prospects of heaven, nor all the attractive charms of divine love will persuade the sinner to renounce the enchanting delights of sin and submit to the unalterable terms of mercy till the terrors of the Lord are set in array against him, and a sense of guilt and wrath is deeply impressed upon his conscience.

The first work of the Spirit is to convince men of their sins, whereby they have offended the eternal Majesty of heaven; to alarm their guilty fears by a discovery of their infinite danger; to show them that the wrath of an avenging God is revealed from heaven against them, and that the fiery abyss below opens its devouring jaws to receive them; that the sentence of the law is pronounced against them, and there is but a step between them and eternal death; that they are in subjection to the tyranny of sin and Satan, and have no strength or power to knock off their captive-chains.

When these things are set before the mind in a clear and convincing light and deeply impressed upon the heart; when they see that they hang over the bottomless pit of hell by the single thread of life, which may be snapped asunder by a thousand accidents, and do not know but that the next moment they may be dispatched into endless and intolerable misery; when they find that they are utterly unable to help themselves, and that it exceeds the power of the whole creation to deliver them from so deplorable a ruin—then their hearts will be filled with distressing fears and they will anxiously inquire, "What shall I do to be saved?" Then they will be prepared, with transports of affection and joy, to welcome the news of a Savior and say, "How beautiful upon the mountains are the feet of those who bring the glad tidings of peace and safety!"

• Christ Jesus is proposed unto them as an almighty and compassionate Savior. The most penetrating conviction of guilt, the most terrifying sense of danger, will not subdue the obstinacy of rebellious sinners and persuade them to bow to the scepter of mercy till the eyes of their understanding are enlightened to discern the greatness and glory of Christ, and they are clearly convinced of His ability to save to the uttermost all who come to God by Him. Now the gospel represents our blessed Lord as a complete and almighty Redeemer who, by the transcendent dignity of His person, the unspotted innocence of His life, and the depth of His humiliation and sufferings, has offered up an acceptable sacrifice to God, fully atoned the just displeasure of heaven, and paid a sufficient ransom for the redemption of all His people. The sacred streams of blood that He shed upon the cursed tree are of infinite value to wash away the guilt of the greatest sins. That perfect obedience, which He yielded to the divine law is a satisfactory price to purchase the eternal happiness of all those to whom it is imputed; and as He died for the offenses of His people in a state of meanness and poverty, so He rose again for their justification in surprising power and glory, and ever lives at the right hand of the Majesty on high to make continual intercession for them. His blood, which was shed by the hands of violence upon the cross, is pleaded with unfailing success in the courts above, effectually secures the believing sinner from the condemning sentence of the law, and procures him a title to the ineffable glories of heaven. And as His merits are infinite, so His grace is irresistible. All power in heaven and earth is committed to Him. He is exalted as a Prince and a Savior, to give repentance as well as remission of sins.

These are truths clearly revealed in the gospel, and denied by none save the hardened infidels of the age. But, alas, multitudes who are favored with the light of the gospel, and thereby are distinguished from ignorant and uninstructed heathens, satisfy themselves with a cold and general assent to these important discoveries and never feel their power and influence upon their hearts. These things are continually sounding in their ears; but "the natural man receiveth not the things of the Spirit of God;

for they are foolishness unto him, neither can he know them, because they are spiritually discerned." The Lord Jesus Christ continually passes before them in His mediatorial excellency and glory, clothed with the garments of salvation; but they have no eyes to see, no ears to hear, nor hearts to perceive His loveliness and beauty. Their eyes are so blinded by the god of this world that they behold no form or comeliness in Him for which He should be desired.

But when God is pleased to effectually draw men to Christ, and to make them willing in the day of His power, He causes the light of the glorious gospel to shine into their hearts with such convincing strength and evidence, and gives them such a sense of the glories and excellency of His nature and the power and riches of His grace, that their darkness is in a moment scattered, their blindness is at once removed, and they cry out with pleasure and surprise, "We believe and are sure that Thou art the Christ, the Son of the living God." He appears now in their eyes adorned with the most amiable and alluring charms, and they join in the language of the transported spouse, "He is the chiefest among ten thousands, and altogether lovely." They are fully convinced that His merits are invaluable, sufficient to atone for their most aggravated offenses; that His power is almighty, and can easily subdue their most obdurate corruptions. They see that there is none in heaven or earth but Christ who can screen them from the wrath of an offended God, which they have justly deserved, and restore them to the divine favor which they have willfully forfeited; so that now they are more anxiously concerned to secure an interest in His love than to obtain the most desirable earthly blessings, and dread His displeasure as more terrible than death itself in its most frightful appearance. They count all things but loss for the excellency of the knowledge of Christ, and with the most ardent and intense desire seek after the manifestations of

His favor in all the appointed ways of duty. Their ardent cries ascend up to heaven in the pathetic language of the psalmist, "As the hart panteth after the water brooks, so panteth my soul after Thee, O God. When shall I come and appear before Thee? When shall I behold thy power and glory? When shall I taste the wonders of Thy grace and love!" Thus they long and pant after Christ as in a dry and thirsty land where there is no comfort, no refreshment.

• And while they are in this languishing state, God is pleased graciously to set before them the free and universal invitations of the gospel, and to give the highest assurance that if they will come to Christ. He will accept and save them. It is not enough that Christ is able to save to the uttermost unless He is also willing to exert His almighty power on their behalf. Those who feel the intolerable burden of sin and see their astonishing guilt in its proper colors are apt to entertain the most melancholy apprehensions of their case, and to imagine that their sins are too great to admit of a pardon. This mightily discourages them in their attempts for salvation; so that they are sometimes ready to cast off all hope and sit down in black despair. Now to remove this difficulty, God is pleased to unfold the unsearchable treasures of His grace and show them that the invitations of the gospel are universal, without excepting the greatest and vilest of sinners; that neither the astonishing number nor the heinous aggravations of men's sins will exclude them from a share in the divine mercy, unless by their obstinacy and impenitence they exclude themselves. Whoever will may come to the waters of life freely; and all who attend to these compassionate offers, and who apply to Christ upon the encouragement of the gospel call, shall infallibly obtain eternal salvation. The merciful Savior of the world speaks to them Himself in His unalterable Word: "Come unto Me, all ye that labor and are heavy laden, and I will give you rest." He who is the faithful and true Witness has expressly declared, "He that cometh unto me, I will in no wise cast out." This revives their desponding spirits, gives life to their fainting souls, answers their strongest objections and shows that it is not only their important interest, but indisputable duty, to commit their souls into the hands of Christ and trust entirely in Him for life and salvation.

Were not the invitations of the gospel general, without requiring any preceding worthiness in man to qualify him for the divine acceptance, the self-condemning sinner must necessarily sink into the bottomless gulf of despair and remain without help and hope forever. But since the love of Christ is free, without regard to any amiable quality in the object upon whom it is fixed; since He descended from heaven upon this gracious intention, to save the greatest of sinners. Since the offers of mercy are universal, without excepting the highest offenders; though their sins are of a crimson color and scarlet dye; since He has certainly promised that He will reject none who, from a deep sense of their guilt and misery, humbly apply to Him and believe on Him for help and deliverance—this removes the discouragements that the soul labored under through a distressing sense of its great guilt and unworthiness, and when clearly manifested into the mind, lays a firm foundation for the exercise of faith.

• They are further encouraged by the example of others who have accepted these gracious invitations and have freely attained salvation. Manasseh, a detestable sorcerer and idolater, who offered up his children as a sacrifice to the devil and deluged the land of Israel with innocent blood, yet, when he humbled himself before the God of his fathers and unfeignedly turned from his wicked ways, was accepted and pardoned. That the greatest sinners have obtained pardon and salvation is a truth represented in the parable of the prodigal, who had deserted his father's house, wandered into a far country and wasted his inheritance in rioting and excess; yet upon his return to his offended father, lamenting his folly and confessing his utter unworthiness of any favor, he received a free pardon for his past ungrateful rebellion, was embraced with the highest affection and joy, and admitted to the honor and character of a son. Mary Magdalene, who had been possessed with seven devils, had them all cast out and had much forgiven her. Saul, who impiously blasphemed the name of Jesus of Nazareth, and with unrelenting fury persecuted the disciples of Christ, was stopped in the midst of his unhallowed rage by the miracle of mercy, and was at once transformed by the power of almighty grace from one of the chief sinners into one of the most eminent and excellent saints, from a bitter persecutor into a devout and zealous confessor.

How many among the Corinthians, who were once a blemish to human nature and wallowed in the blackest defilements of sin, yet were washed, were justified in the name of Jesus, sanctified by the Spirit of our God, and are now triumphing in immortal bliss, celebrating the glories of redeeming love! These, with many others, stand recorded in sacred Scripture for the encouragement of awakened sinners in all ages of the world, to relieve them under their distressing difficulties and discouragements and to excite them to come to Christ for life and salvation, whose grace is sufficient to subdue the most obdurate rebels, and whose mercy has extended to the greatest and vilest of sinners. "For this cause (said Paul) I obtained mercy, that in me first Jesus Christ might show forth all long-suffering, for a pattern unto them who hereafter should believe in Him to life everlasting." The treasures of His mercy are not wasted, though they have been dispensed to thousands of unworthy objects; nor is the power of His grace abated by all the astonishing victories He has obtained. He ever was and always continues to be an almighty and compassionate Savior, the same yesterday, to-

day and forever. This oftentimes supports the trembling
sinner, when bowed down with an intolerable load of
guilt, and fills him with a reviving hope that he may attain a
share in that mercy which has been so freely extended to
others. This shows him that the greatest unworthiness does
not stop the current of divine mercy to the returning
penitent; but the most heinous transgressors shall be accepted if they come to Christ by unfeigned faith and bow
to His gracious yoke.

• Finally, these invitations and encouragements are attended with a powerful influence upon the wills of sinners,
which effectually determines them to comply with the offers of a Savior and submit to His conduct and government. The carnal mind is enmity against God, and filled
with innumerable prejudices against the way of salvation
established by the wisdom and sovereignty of heaven; this
enmity must be removed, and the will and affections must
be sanctified and renewed, or the sinner will never come
to Christ and submit to His righteous demands. A new
heart must be given and a new spirit infused, to incline
them cheerfully to receive Christ as their Lord and Savior
and account none of His commandments to be grievous.
Christ Jesus must be formed in their souls by the influences
of the Spirit or they never will be persuaded to go to Him
by faith and accept Him upon His own terms.

And when they have thus received power from on
high, they immediately receive Christ in His sacred offices
and resign themselves to be ruled as well as saved by Him,
fully persuaded of the equity and reasonableness of His
laws and abundantly satisfied that His yoke is easy and His
burden light. They join themselves to the Lord in an everlasting covenant, never to be broken. They see that He is
the invaluable pearl, in comparison of whom the whole
creation is but an insignificant cipher; and therefore they
wisely determine to sell all that they may obtain an interest
in Him.

Though they entertain distressing apprehensions of their unworthiness of any favor, and are oftentimes filled with many misgiving fears lest Christ should utterly reject them, yet since they are freely invited, they resolve to venture themselves upon that gracious encouragement and to trust in His infinite mercy, whatever may be the event. They have wandered from mountain to hill in search of happiness and safety, and have found nothing but disappointment and confusion; but now they are brought to a full stand, convinced that there is no other name given under heaven by which they can be saved, and made to cry out with the disciples of old, "Lord, to whom should we go? Thou hast the words of eternal life." They know that He is able to keep that which is committed unto Him, and therefore, with the greatest cheerfulness and freedom, they renounce all those refuges of lies and hiding places of deceit to which they formerly trusted, and by a solemn and deliberate act they surrender themselves into His saving hands to be justified by His grace, to be sanctified by His Spirit, and governed by His laws. They depend entirely upon His conduct and assistance to carry them through the difficulties and temptations of a defiling world, and to bring them safe at last to the possession of an unperishing glory. Thus the soul, in the day of its conversion, is effectually made willing to comply with the calls of the gospel and to submit to the scepter of Christ.

2. I now proceed to show that this is a work of almighty grace and is performed in the day of God's power. Sinners will never come to Christ if left to follow their own inclinations and desires. The human nature was universally depraved by the first apostasy so that, while in an unregenerate state, we are insufficient for any good thing and are entirely destitute of spiritual strength. The understanding is covered with a veil of darkness so that it cannot discern spiritual things in their reality and importance; the mind is filled with fatal prejudices against that way of salvation that

is revealed and proposed in the gospel; the will is stubborn and refractory, impatient of the divine authority; and the whole man is so deeply corrupted and disordered that they voluntarily choose the degrading tyranny of their lusts before the glorious liberty of the children of God. The Scripture therefore speaks of carnal sinners as dead in trespasses and sins, and represents their conversion as impossible by any human power: "Can the Ethiopian change his skin, or the leopard his spots? Then may ye also, who are accustomed to do evil, learn to do well."

To come to Christ is to deny ourselves under every form and to renounce all our carnal confidences. To fly to the righteousness and atonement of our great Redeemer for justification and life requires a humble acknowledgement of our inability to help ourselves, and an entire dependence upon the victorious power of His grace to mortify our corruptions and subdue our rebellious inclinations, to sanctify and save our souls. This is so contrary to the pride of man, so disagreeable to the appetites of flesh and blood, that degenerate nature will forever cry out, "These are hard sayings, and who can hear them?"

Nor will the most powerful external means conquer the obstinacy of the sinner and effectually persuade him to submit to those mortifying demands. The Word preached, which is the usual instrument of conversion, is but a dead letter if not attended with the ministration of the Spirit. The most divine preacher, though endowed with all the charms of art and eloquence, if left to his own strength and skill, will prove but as the sounding brass and tinkling cymbal. The inspired prophet Isaiah, who was a perfect master of the art of persuasion, and triumphed over the passions of his hearers by the most moving methods of address, was dispatched to a rebellious house and forced to breathe out that melancholy complaint, "Who hath believed our report, and to whom hath the arm of

the Lord been revealed?" Yea, though the ministry of the
Word were confirmed by the evidence of miracles, yet it
would be ineffectual to reform and sanctify the sinner
without the concomitant influences of divine grace. This is
evident by the behavior of the Jews in the days of our
blessed Savior, who spake as one having authority, and so
as never man spake, with such surprising majesty and
power as awed and silenced His most inveterate adversaries; who confirmed His heavenly doctrine with such
numerous and undoubted miracles as constrained the
very devils to acknowledge His authority and proclaim
Him to be the Son of the living God. Yet He was obstinately rejected by the self-righteous Pharisees, and finally
condemned and executed by the princes of this world.

Nay, should an extraordinary messenger be dispatched
from the bright realms of eternal day, shining in immortal
youth and beauty, clothed with the dazzling robes of celestial glory and declaring the joys of heaven in the language
of ecstasy and triumph; or were the mouth of the bottomless pit opened and one of those miserable spirits de-
tached from the place of unutterable torments, to describe the terrors of God's wrath in the most frightful colors, and warn a guilty world of their amazing danger;
whatever transient effects might attend these surprising
scenes, they would not produce an abiding change, nor
engage the sinner to renounce his beloved idols and unfeignedly to devote himself to the service of Christ. If they
do not hear Moses and the Prophets, Christ and His apostles, neither will they be persuaded though one arose from
the dead. We may then certainly conclude that nothing
but the unconquerable arm of God can break the rocky
hearts of sinners and bow their stubborn necks to the divine government. If ever they are made willing to believe
the gospel and receive Christ, it must be in the day of
God's power. Therefore St. Paul tells us that by grace we
are saved through faith, and that not of ourselves; it is the

gift of God. Our Savior assures us that no man can come to Christ except the Father draws him.

I now proceed to the improvement of my subject.

Application

1. This teaches us the deep and dreadful depravation of human nature. Look round upon the Christian world; how securely do they sleep upon the brink of eternal misery? How obstinately do they rush upon the point of the most shocking dangers? They are involved in a state of the most deplorable darkness and ignorance; and yet willfully shut their eyes against the Sun of righteousness, who alone can scatter their darkness and illuminate their minds with the knowledge of salvation. They are condemned by the sentence of the divine law and in continual danger of being delivered over to the bitter pains of eternal death; and yet they perversely reject a pardon, which was clearly purchased by the precious blood of the Son of God and is freely offered to them in the gospel. They are under the tyrannical dominion of Satan, the god of this world, and in a disgraceful servitude to their domineering lusts and passions; and yet they refuse an almighty Redeemer who offers to knock off their captive chains and to deliver them from the bondage of corruption.

Though they are perishing under the fatal wounds of sin and have the symptoms of death and damnation visible upon them, yet they neglect the great Physician of Souls who beseeches them to accept health and salvation. They will not come to Christ that they might have life. They hearken to the voice of Satan, the grand adversary of souls, and stop their ears against the invitation of the blessed Jesus, the compassionate Friend and Savior of men. The flattering allurements of the world have a more prevailing influence upon them than all the divine rhetoric of heaven.

Their rejection of Christ is willful, and flows from their strong attachment to their lusts; and therefore this will be their condemnation: that Christ is a light that has come into the world, but they have chosen darkness rather than light. Their misery is the effect of their voluntary choice; they delight in their fetters; and so their future damnation will be just, inevitable, and intolerable. Oh, how deep is the corruption of mankind! How fatal and bewitching is the power of lusts, which makes men secure in the midst of the greatest dangers and rocks them to sleep in the bosom of their sin, which will eternally torment and devour them!

2. This shows us from whence the various and surprising success of the gospel arises. The gospel is the blessed means appointed by heaven to bring the sinner from his natural state of darkness, sin and wrath into a state of grace and salvation. But how various and different are its effects! To some it is a savor of life unto life, to others a savor of death unto death. Some are blinded and hardened by the god of this world, and remain stupid and inflexible under the most awakening methods of address, while others are enlightened, melted into penitential tears, and made willing in the day of God's power. One is stopped in the midst of his rebellious course, humbled at the footstool of divine grace, and effectually engaged to commit himself to Christ, to be governed by His laws, and to be saved by His merits. Another, like the hardy leviathan, mocks at fear and remains unmoved, while the whole artillery of divine curses are leveled against him, and resolves that he will not have this Man to reign over him.

Yea, we oftentimes see at the same church and under the same sermon that one is softened and another is hardened. One is pricked at the heart, filled with awful surprise, and forced to cry out in anxiety and distress, "Men and brethren, what shall I do to be saved?" Another, who perhaps sits in the same seat, disregards the messengers of heaven and will neither be persuaded by the terrible threatenings of the law nor the alluring promises of the gospel. Now to what must we attribute these various and astonishing effects? Certainly not to the different complexions and tempers of persons, nor to their various natural powers. For oftentimes men, endowed with the most amiable dispositions and adorned with the most beautiful and engaging qualities, remain strangers to Christ, while persons of the most stubborn natures, of the most boisterous and unruly passions, are softened by divine grace and brought under subjection to the power of the gospel. Men of the brightest parts and shining accomplishments in human literature continue ignorant of the mysteries of faith, and perish through the pride and haughtiness of their understanding, while the simple and unlearned are enlightened from above and made wise to their eternal salvation. This must be ascribed to the distinguishing grace of God, who distributes His favors according to His sacred and unaccountable pleasure; who by an extraordinary dispensation of mercy snatches one as a brand out of the burning, and in spotless sovereignty leaves others to the destructive effects of their voluntary choice. To this it is attributed by our blessed Lord Himself, who dwelt in the bosom of the Father and was intimately acquainted with the secrets of the divine counsel: "I thank Thee, O Father, Lord of heaven and earth, that Thou hast hid these things from the wise and prudent, and hast revealed them unto babes; even so, Father, for so it seemed good in Thy sight" (Luke 10:21).

3. This should awaken us all to the most solemn inquiry whether we are of the happy number of those who have been made willing in the day of God's power. Many deceive themselves in this important affair and perish at last with a lie in their right hand. They triumph in the Christian name and glory in their high profession, as if these would be a sufficient defense against the terrors of divine

wrath, and would procure them an unfailing title to the merits of Christ—though they have never felt the operations of His Spirit upon their hearts, have never been brought to renounce their refuges of lies and accept Christ as their Prince and Savior. But, alas, my brethren, these are flattering dreams and will miserably disappoint your expectations and leave you destitute, naked, and forlorn! None will be saved by Christ but those who are made willing to forsake their darling sins, to deny themselves, and unreservedly resign to the direction and government of the great Lord and Head of the church. This is what we are utterly indisposed unto by nature, and indeed filled with inveterate prejudices against.

If we would therefore build upon a sure foundation that will not fail us in the day of our decisive trial, when the secrets of all hearts must be disclosed, let us inquire whether we have had such a discovery of our misery by nature as has filled us with unutterable concern for the safety of our perishing souls; such convictions of our blindness, guilt, and pollution as has destroyed our carnal confidences and made us sensible that we are lost and undone in ourselves, and unworthy that God should assist and deliver us. Have the eyes of our understanding been enlightened to see such attractive excellencies and glories in the face of Christ as has alienated our hearts and affections from all the alluring vanities of sin and sense, and influenced us to cry out in the divine language of the psalmist, "Whom have I in heaven but Thee? And there is none on earth I desire besides Thee." Have these things been impressed upon our minds with such irresistible light and evidence as actually to engage us to renounce all other objects of our confidence, and to venture our eternal salvation upon the infinite value of His merits, and the riches and power of His grace? Have we been brought to submit to His righteousness and to go forth in His strength? Have we freely committed our all unto Him, to be governed by

His law, to be guided by His Spirit, and disposed of according to His sovereign will and pleasure? Unless you have in this manner been enabled to come to Christ, your profession is but hypocrisy, your faith presumption, and you will be herded with the workers of iniquity. But if you have indeed been made willing thus to resign yourselves to Christ, without exception and reserve, a day of the divine power has passed upon you. And I may say to you as our Lord to St. Peter, "Blessed art thou, Simon Bar-jona, for flesh and blood has not revealed this unto thee, but My Father who is in heaven."

4. Let those who have hitherto obstinately rejected the calls of the gospel be excited earnestly to cry to God to exert His almighty power on their behalf. Without this, the most powerful means will but harden you in your wicked ways and aggravate your future destruction and misery. Though planted by the rivers of water and called the vineyard of the Lord, you will remain an unfruitful desert. Though watered with the dews of the sanctuary, you will bring forth nothing but the grapes of Sodom and the clusters of Gomorrah. Men may pour out their affectionate prayers for your spiritual welfare, and may use the most persuasive arguments to reclaim you from the paths of the destroyer, but it is the divine power alone that must cause the haughtiness of man to stoop, remove the carnal prejudices of sinners, and bow their will to an unfeigned compliance with the methods of grace. For this, therefore, lift up your voice to heaven through the prevailing name and intercession of Christ, with indefatigable diligence and zeal, remembering it is for the life of your immortal souls. Let a deep apprehension of your past ingratitude and folly humble you before the dreadful tribunal of God. Let a sense of your guilt and danger animate you with inflamed desires to pray for sanctifying grace and pardoning mercy. Oh, wrestle with God by continual and vehement supplications, and never relax the vigor of your endeavors till with

holy Jacob you have obtained the blessing.

5. Let those who have been made willing in the day of the divine power ascribe all to God, and celebrate the praises of distinguishing grace. This is your indispensable duty, your interest and happiness. To enlarge your hearts in this blessed exercise and inflame your gratitude and joy, consider that you were by nature as far from Christ as the most hardened and scandalous sinners, and were as averse to the power and purity of the gospel as those who still go on in their unbelief and rebellion. How long did God wait to be gracious before you would be persuaded to comply with the heavenly call? How ungratefully did you abuse His adorable patience, resist the sacred influences of His Spirit, and willfully persist in the practice of your sins? How justly might He have rejected you in wrath, who so often refused the offers of His love, and have left you to perish in your impenitence and guilt? How many of your friends and acquaintances remain in the valley of dry bones, destitute of spiritual life and strength, while you have been made to hear the voice of the Son of God, to stand up on your feet and live? Omnipotent grace has conquered your rebellious wills, taken away your native aversion to holiness, and by sweet and powerful constraints persuaded you to place your affections upon Him who has loved you with an everlasting love, and given Himself for you.

How happy and advantageous a change have you experienced! You are brought out of worse than Egyptian darkness into the marvelous light of the gospel. You are translated from the bondage of sin and corruption into the glorious liberty of the sons of God. From a child of wrath and an heir of the kingdom of darkness and misery, you are adopted into the family of heaven and have a title to an inheritance that is incorruptible and undefiled. So that you may join in that triumphant song of St. Paul, "I am persuaded that neither death, nor life, nor angels, nor principalities, nor powers, nor things present, nor things to come, nor height, nor depth, nor any other creature shall be able to separate me from the love of God which is in Christ Jesus, to whom be glory, dominion, and praise forever and ever, Amen."

4

The Importance of an Unreproaching Heart

"My heart shall not reproach me so long as I live."
Job 27:6.

The character of Job is one of the most bright and distinguishing among the Old Testament saints, and stands upon sacred record as an illustrious pattern of the most difficult and useful virtues. He passed through the most severe trials and was assaulted on all sides by the most dangerous temptations, yet he happily preserved his integrity and obtained the testimony from God Himself that he was perfect and upright in all his ways, one who feared God and eschewed evil.

We find this excellent saint for a time advanced to the height of dignity and power, appearing as one of the greatest men of the east, enjoying an affluence of wealth and plenty, blessed with a flourishing posterity, and honored with the respect and reverence of his numerous acquaintances. But this bright sunshine of prosperity was suddenly shaded with the dark clouds of adversity, and we behold him at once stripped of all his agreeable enjoyments and sunk into the most melancholy state of poverty and distress. His estate was destroyed in a moment by the hands of oppression and violence; his children were cut off in the flourishing bloom of youth by a sudden and irresistible stroke; his body was overwhelmed with the most loathsome and painful diseases, and his mind was afflicted with the most dark and distressing terrors. His friends, who should have assuaged his grief and administered comfort to him under his afflictions, aggravated his misery and persecuted him with the most severe and uncharitable invectives.

Though they were persons of uncommon piety and wisdom, yet they entertained some mistaken apprehensions of God and were sadly unacquainted with the mysterious dispensations of divine providence; and so they falsely imagined that his uncommon sufferings were the consequence of his aggravated guilt. They therefore zealously accused him of secret hypocrisy and severely condemned him for not giving glory to God by an open confession of his sins. Under all these various and uncommon trials we find this holy patriarch maintaining an inviolable fidelity to God and setting an astonishing example of patience for the world. He bravely supported himself under the severe censures of his uncharitable friends, resolutely defended his character, and vehemently asserted the righteousness and integrity of his conduct. "God forbid that I should justify you; till I die, I will not remove my integrity from me. My righteousness I hold fast, and will not let it go; my heart shall not reproach me so long as I live." This was a noble resolution highly becoming the character of this excellent saint, and worthy of the imitation of every Christian! In speaking to these words (by divine assistance) I shall take the following method.

1. I shall inquire when a person may be said to be free from the reproaches of his own heart.

2. I shall consider the importance of being free from these reproaches.

3. I shall give some directions for obtaining this invaluable blessing.

1. I am to inquire when a person may be said to be free from the reproaches of his own heart. By the heart is here meant the conscience, which is that principle in the soul of man that shows us the duties we are to perform and the

errors we are to avoid in our moral behavior; it likewise reviews our conduct and either justifies or condemns our actions according to the will of God, the only rule of our duty. In order therefore to have consciences free from reproach, these three things are required:

• They must be rightly informed in the will of God, who is the only Lord and Sovereign of conscience. God is our supreme Lawgiver and Judge, whose authority is sacred, and whose laws we are unalterably obliged to receive and obey. Conscience is his vice-regent in the souls of men, and is to exercise its authority in subordination to Him and according to the discoveries He has made of His will. If the conscience then is darkened by ignorance, vitiated by error, or corrupted by prejudice, it will be but an unsafe and delusive guide, and oftentimes precipitate us into the most dangerous and destructive courses. Under the influence of a blind and mistaken conscience, the most execrable vices have been canonized and the most excellent virtues have been reviled and condemned; the blackest crimes have been committed, not only with impunity, but uncommon applause; the most bloody and inhuman cruelties have been varnished over with the glorious pretenses of zeal for the glory of God and a care to preserve the true religion. Thus the consciences of the Jews, being blinded by ignorance and prejudice, engaged them to persecute the Christians with unrelenting malice and severity, and to imagine that they did God good service. And St. Paul, before his illuminations, being fired with a mistaken zeal, destroyed the churches of Christ with implacable fury and thought verily that he ought to do many things against the name of Jesus of Nazareth.

If therefore we would have the testimony of an unreproaching heart, our minds must be enlightened with the knowledge of the divine will and be acquainted with the rules of duty prescribed in sacred Scripture. For all true religion begins with the understanding, from thence descends into the heart, and regulates the life and conversation. To this end we must lay aside unreasonable prejudices and cast off the prevailing influence of carnal interests and affections; for these have an unhappy bias upon the mind and darken and defile the conscience. We must study the Word of God with impartiality and diligence, and accompany all our inquiries into the divine will with ardent supplications to the Father of lights, that He would scatter the darkness of our understandings, preserve us from destructive errors, and effectually reveal unto us what is the good and acceptable will of the Lord.

• It is requisite that we make the law of God the only rule of our actions, and obey it without exception or reserve. No pretences of promoting the glory of God or advancing the happiness of men must influence us to start beyond the line of our duty and do anything which is forbidden in the Word of God. For a good intention will not excuse an unlawful action; and we are expressly commanded not to do evil that good may come of it. The example of others, though they shine as lights in the world and appear as uncommon patterns of integrity and virtue, must not be made the standard of our behavior, nor any blindly followed in all their actions. For the most enlightened of men know but in part, and are liable to innumerable errors; the most eminent saints are sanctified but in part and are attended with a body of sin and death. The law of God is our only unerring direction, the unalterable standard of our duty; to this must we strictly adhere at all times, and by this must our actions be regulated if we would keep a conscience void of offense. Our conversation must be as "becometh the gospel, which teacheth us to deny all ungodliness and worldly lusts, and to live soberly, righteously, and godly in this present world"; for it is not enough that we know our duty unless we impartially observe it. Our obedience must be universal, without any hypocritical reserves; for the indulgence of any darling sin is inconsistent with that sincerity which the gospel requires, and evidences that all our pretenses to religion are but hypocrisy and deceit. We must delight in the law of God after the inward man, and subject our hearts to His authority and government; for God searches the hearts and tries the reins of the children of men, and outward performances will never atone for inward impurities. In summary, if we would approve ourselves to conscience and avoid its stinging reproaches, it must be the constant care, governing inclination, and endeavor of our lives to make the glory of God the end, and the law of God the rule of our actions. And then our consciences will not make us ashamed when we thus have respect unto all God's commandments; but on the contrary will afford us perpetual ground of joy and satisfaction; for "great peace have they that love God's law, and nothing shall offend them."

• We must obtain a pardon for our errors and imperfections through the blood of Christ our Redeemer. While conscience is burdened with guilt, it is impossible that we should be free from its just reproaches. For the guilty sinner stands exposed to the condemning sentence of the law and is an heir of eternal death. And while any soul continues under this dreadful imputation, conscience must speak to him in the voice of terror and declare him a prisoner of revenging justice, in continual danger of being consumed by the fire of the divine indignation. Now we have all become guilty before God through our innumerable offenses against him. There is not a just man upon earth, "that doeth good and sinneth not." The holiest of men, through ignorance and infirmity, through the remaining corruption of their natures or the violent assaults of temptation, are frequently betrayed into sin. Hence, if ever our consciences acquit us, a pardon must be obtained through the merits of Christ; our guilty souls must be adorned with the immaculate robe of His righteousness and our polluted services must be sprinkled with the blood of the everlasting covenant, which cleanses from all sin. And then our past offenses, though they afford perpetual ground for humiliation and sorrow, cannot justly reproach and terrify us. For "being justified through the redemption that is in Christ, we have peace with God," and peace in our own minds, even the peace that passes all understanding.

2. This brings me to consider the vast importance of being free from these reproaches. And this will appear if we take a view of the inconceivable misery of those who are exposed to the reproaches of their own hearts. This is certainly the most dark and disconsolate state that can possibly be imagined on this side of the grave. The royal preacher tells us, "A man may sustain his infirmity, but a wounded spirit, who can bear?" An upbraiding conscience enkindles a fire in the breasts of men which continually preys upon the most tender and sensible parts, devours every easy thought, and oftentimes renders the sinner a terror to himself and to those who are about him. It presents to his view a black catalogue of his numberless offenses, displays their deformity in the most frightful colors, and terrifies and surprises him with the hideous prospect. It calls to remembrance the sins of his earliest youth which have long been buried in silence and oblivion; it especially charges upon the soul the transgressions of his riper years which have been committed against light and love, against the most sacred promises and engagements. It sets the terrors of the Lord in battle array against the sinner, and represents the blessed God not as a tender and compassionate Father, but as a severe and inexorable Judge, clothed with vengeance as with a garment, condemning them to suffer the inexpressible horrors and terrors of the second death. What ghastly spectacles of wrath, what amazing visions of fear possesses the souls of men when plunged into these dismal and disconsolate circumstances!

No wonder they continually meditate terror and cry out with trembling Cain, "My punishment is greater than I can bear." For who can contend with an offended God, or support the weight of His heavy indignation? Where can you fly, O sinner, from His avenging wrath? Or how can you endure the heat of His almighty displeasure breaking into your conscience and kindling the fire of hell in your bosom? You may possibly fly from the wrath of men and escape to the uttermost parts of the earth beyond the reach of their arm, but the wrath of God will accompany you to the most forlorn corner of the world, and your own guilty fears will haunt you like so many specters, wherever you go. In vain shall you call upon the mountains of the earth to cover you, and upon the insensible rocks to hide you, from this scene of terror and amazement. For you carry your tormentor in your bosom; and it is beyond the power of the whole creation to screen you from its sharp and terrible reproaches. This is the miserable condition of the self-condemning sinner, whose soul is filled with a sense of guilt and whose conscience is let loose to upbraid and torment him.

Perhaps the sinner may endeavor to chase away this melancholy gloom and divert these uneasy thoughts by gaiety and diversion, by the business and enjoyments of life. But, alas, these are miserable comforters, physicians of no value! A reproaching heart dries up these broken cisterns and embitters all the gratifications of sense. A man under such circumstances has lost his relish for music and mirth, for entertainment and company. He may for a moment drown the reflections of his own mind by the draughts of intemperance, and stifle the voice of conscience by riot and debauchery. But conscience will suddenly awake out of its lethargy; it will, like an unwelcome guest, intrude upon his gayest hours, and with distressing accents whisper the most unpleasing truths in his ear. His own guilty fears will dash his pleasant cups with an envenomed bitter, and like the handwriting against the wall will strike him into Belshazzar's fit of trembling in the height of his intemperate revels. And while these inward accusations embitter all worldly comfort and satisfaction, they also aggravate all our disappointments and sorrows. They alarm the sinner at the least appearance of danger and make him fear that every affliction is a messenger of justice, commissioned to drag him to execution; that every disease is a presage of death, sent to dispatch him to eternal misery; in summary, that all these anxieties and terrors which at present he endures are but the beginning of sorrows and the first fruits of unutterable horror and despair.

And how dismal must be the state of that man who is thus incessantly racked with inward anguish, and has nothing from without to support and relieve him? Who can express the misery of those who are daily consumed by this gnawing worm, and continually tormented in this devouring fire? How much is it our wisdom and duty to foresee the evil and avoid everything that will wound and enrage our conscience, and lay a foundation for these severe and dreadful reproaches?

This is especially true if we consider the happiness of those who are free from these reproaches. As an evil conscience is a domestic fury and a lively representation of eternal misery, so a good conscience is a continual feast and a blessed earnest of celestial happiness. While the breasts of the wicked are like the troubled sea, in a continual tempest and commotion, the souls of the righteous are the abode of peace and rest, and are oftentimes filled with joy unspeakable and full of glory. The testimony of an unreproaching heart is a perpetual spring of pleasures, truly noble, rational, and divine—pleasures which incomparably exceed all the sordid satisfactions of sense, and give an agreeable relish to all the other enjoyments of life. Yea, this lays a solid foundation of peace and comfort under all the evils and afflictions to which we are exposed in this vale of tears. It shows us that the bitter cup of adversity is ordered by the Hand of love. It assures us that the most severe dispensations of divine providence are designed for our real advantage.

And what can afford such joy and refreshment under the unreasonable persecutions and uncharitable censures of men as this faithful witness in our breasts of our own innocence and integrity? This blunts the edge of malice and takes out the sting of the most bitter reproaches; for how we may despise the hatred and anger of men when we are assured of the favor and friendship of heaven! How little need we value the frowns of the world, how safely may we defy its most severe threatenings, when we have the light of God's countenance shining upon our souls, the divine providence engaged for our protection and defense, and His unalterable promise that the momentary sufferings of this life shall work out for us a far more exceeding and eternal weight of glory! This supported the primitive Christians, that bright cloud of ancient confessors, that noble army of martyrs, under all the methods of torture and revenge which the rage of hell could suggest, the malice of men invent, or the tyranny of princes inflict. This inspired them with undaunted courage in the face of the most distressing dangers, and made them count it all joy when they fell into divers temptations. For their rejoicing was this, the testimony of their conscience, that in simplicity and godly sincerity they had their conversation in the world (2 Corinthians 1:12).

But above all, the inward witness of an unreproaching heart will wonderfully revive and refresh us in the dark and melancholy hour of death when, if ever, we want all the assistance and support that can be afforded us. Nothing then so dismays and terrifies the sinner as a reflection upon his ill-spent life, the clamorous accusations of an upbraiding conscience, and the apprehensions of that wrath which is ready to be revealed. And, on the contrary, nothing so strengthens and raises the spirits of a dying man as the consciousness of his own integrity, a comfortable assurance of the divine favor, and the joyful prospect of a crown of immortal glory. This will be a mighty consolation amidst the agonies of an approaching dissolution, will brighten the gloomy horrors of the grave, and fill us with light and joy when walking through the dark valley of the shadow of death. For such may be assured that death is not their enemy, but their friend; that the king of terrors, though it destroys their clay-like tabernacle and turns them into corruption and dust, yet is only the messenger of their heavenly Father, designed to convey them to the joys of His immediate presence.

In a word, this will enable them to look forward with holy joy and transport to the Day of the Lord, that solemn and illustrious day when the Son of Man shall descend in the greatness and majesty of an incarnate God to judge both the quick and the dead; for they know it will be the time of their complete and eternal salvation. And therefore, though the pillars of heaven tremble and the foundations of the earth totter and shake, though the elements melt with fervent heat and universal nature sinks into ruin and confusion; yet having their consciences cleansed from guilt through the atoning virtue of Christ's blood and freed from the dominion of sin through the almighty power of divine grace, they may hold up their heads with joy amidst the astonishing scene, and sing with triumph in the words of the devout psalmist in Psalm 46:1–2: "God is our refuge and strength, a very present help in trouble; therefore will I not fear, though the earth be removed, and though the mountains be carried into the midst of the sea."

Though the sun shall be turned into darkness and the moon into blood to prepare for this great and terrible day of the Lord, yet these happy souls may, with confidence and comfort, look for this blessed hope, this glorious appearing of the great God their Savior; for when He who is their life shall appear, then shall they also appear with Him in glory. This is and will be the happiness of the man who is free from the reproaches of his own heart, whose conscience is rightly informed in the will of God, whose sins are forgiven through the blood of Jesus, and whose conversation is as becomes the gospel of Christ. Surely then it is of infinite importance that we make sure of this invaluable blessing.

3. And this leads me to the other thing proposed, and with which I shall finish my present discourse, which is to give some rules and directions for obtaining and securing this unreproaching heart. I shall reduce what I think fitting to offer at present under the following headings:

• Earnestly apply to God by prayer for His Spirit, to sanctify and renew your conscience. It is by the Spirit of holiness that we mortify the deeds of the body and are enabled to cleanse ourselves from the defilements of sin. The common principles of reason and the strength of resolution, the advantage of education and the force of external motives, may restrain men from vicious disorders and engage them to a conversation that is externally regular; but it is sanctifying grace alone that must cure the inward affection to sin, root out the inveterate habits of vice, and produce a universal change in the soul. This we must seek after by constant and importunate prayer, by which we acknowledge our inability to do that which is good, our absolute necessity of divine assistance, and give God the glory of all our victories over sin and temptation. This prayer must be earnest and uninterrupted. The excellency of the blessing bespeaks our most fervent petitions for it; and our constant necessity demands our unceasing applications to the Fountain of Grace. For we stand in continual need of the supply of the Spirit of Christ, without which we shall be foiled by every temptation and soon make shipwreck of faith and a good conscience. Our ad-

dresses must be offered in the name of Jesus, our enthroned Advocate; for He is exalted to give repentance to
His people, and communicates His fullness according to
their necessities. Through Christ strengthening us we can
do all things. Though the flesh, the world, and the devil
are in an accursed conspiracy to deprive us of the blessing
of a good conscience, yet, being fortified by divine grace,
we may steadfastly resist the assaults of earth and hell,
maintain our integrity to the end, and secure the happiness of an unreproaching heart.

• Attend diligently to the voice of conscience and impartially obey its dictates. For want of this, the unthinking
children of men wander out of the ways of understanding
and plunge themselves into innumerable mischiefs. They
inconsiderately rush into sin, as the horse rushes into the
battle without fear or concern. But if they would they
hearken to the silent whispers of their own heart and reverence this faithful monitor in their breasts, it would
mightily restrain them from the commission of sin and
powerfully engage them to the performance of their duty.
And surely nothing more highly becomes us than to attend
to the admonitions of our conscience; for conscience is a
domestic judge, the representative of the supreme Majesty
of heaven and earth. It is better to offend the mightiest
monarch, and to have the fury of earth and hell engaged
against us, than to sin against the light of our own mind
and expose ourselves to its terrible reflections.

We have the greatest reason to stand in awe of its
authority, next to that of our final Judge. "For if our heart
condemn us, God is greater than our heart, and knoweth
all things; but if our heart condemn us not, then have we
confidence toward God" (1 John 3:20–21). Happy is the
man who attends to the voice of conscience and does not
allow himself in those things for which it may upbraid and
condemn him. There is no safer way to heaven than to follow the dictates of a conscience enlightened by the Spirit

of God, and directed by his unerring Word. And there is no surer way to hell than to stifle the voice of conscience and boldly to venture upon those things that are contrary to the remonstrances of our own hearts, and are condemned by the light of God in our souls. St. Paul therefore made it his continual exercise and care to keep "a conscience void of offense toward God and toward man" (Acts 24:16).

• Keep your consciences pure and upright by the daily exercise of faith and repentance. Notwithstanding all our circumspection and diligence, sin will continually attend us while we dwell in this defiling world and have a deceitful heart residing within us. The most holy man living will always have a melancholy occasion to complain with the psalmist in Psalm 19:12: "Who can understand his errors? Cleanse Thou me from secret faults." Now all sin, while unrepented of, offends and irritates the conscience and exposes us to its just reproaches. This then is a necessary method to preserve the peace and purity of our hearts, frequently to examine our lives, humbly to confess, and truly to forsake our sins. For if we judge ourselves in this world, we shall not be finally condemned in the world to come. Blessed are they who now unfeignedly mourn for their sins, for they shall be eternally comforted. Not that the most afflicting sorrow for sin, and the deepest humiliation for our offenses, can make any satisfaction to the justice of God, or procure us a title to His favor. No, but it prepares for the reception of divine grace and excites us to fly to the pardoning mercy of God. It makes us watchful against sin for the time to come, and earnest in our applications to the blood of Christ, that Fountain which is set open for Judah and Jerusalem to wash in from sin and from uncleanness. To this Fountain we must daily be repairing, in the exercise of faith toward our Lord Jesus Christ, as well as repentance towards God. The cleansing virtue of the blood of Christ, applied by faith, will purify the heart and purge the conscience; and, having our hearts sprinkled from an evil conscience, we draw near to God in full assurance and with a holy confidence.

• Set the Lord continually before you, and live under an abiding sense of His presence. Wherever we are, whatever we are engaged in, the great and terrible God is present with us. His all-seeing eye pierces into the secret corners of our souls, and He is intimately acquainted with our retired thoughts and most secret transactions. Let these reflections dwell perpetually on our minds. Upon all occasions, especially when tempted to sin, let us say within ourselves, "God, my eternal Judge, now critically beholds me, and at His enlightened tribunal I must account for my present behavior. If I now insult and defy His vice-regent in my soul, I offer the highest indignity to God Himself and expose myself to the arm of His almighty vengeance." Such thoughts as these will strengthen the authority of conscience, and give a prevailing efficacy to its admonitions. They will damp the force of temptations and make us steadfast and impartial in the discharge of our duty. Thus the illustrious Joseph maintained his chastity unspotted in the dangerous hour of trial and rejected the impure solicitations of his mistress with a holy disdain: "How can I do this great wickedness, and sin against God?" Thus the divine Moses preserved his integrity in the midst of the greatest temptations, and chose rather "to suffer affliction with the people of God than to enjoy the pleasures of sin for a season; for he endured, as beholding Him that is invisible" (Hebrews 11:25, 27).

• And finally, live under a realizing view of that eternal world into which you are hastening. This world is our state of trial, and we are swiftly passing off the stage; an immortality awaits us, either of ineffable joys or unutterable torments, and according to our present conduct, an irreversible doom will pass upon us. Let us then apply this thought with a becoming solemnity to our own souls, and say, "I am now a candidate for eternity, and therefore it becomes me to consider that every step I take in this world is an advance to eternal glory or an approach to endless and intolerable misery. If I now expose myself to the condemning sentence of my own mind, I shall feel its stings and upbraidings, its terrors and tortures forever. If my heart justly reproaches me of disregarding the service of God and neglecting my own salvation in this world, I must suffer the infinite displeasure of an offended Deity and groan under the agonies of a guilty mind in the world to come. But if I now submit to the authority of an enlightened conscience, and thereby am influenced to a just conformity to the divine will, it will always be my friend and most agreeable companion; it will afford me a divine support under the sorest trials and distresses, and like a good angel stand by me and comfort me in the last agonies of nature."

O blessed souls, who have this to revive and to refresh them when the sorrows of death compass them about, and the pangs of a dissolving body take hold of them, who can with a peaceful conscience look back upon the life which they have lived in the flesh as lived by the faith of the Son of God, and can make that humble appeal of good Hezekiah, "Remember, Lord, I beseech Thee, how I have walked before Thee in truth, and with a perfect heart." These can look forward with constancy and courage to a future world, and say with St. Paul in 2 Timothy 4:7–8, "I have fought a good fight; I have finished my course; I have kept the faith; henceforth there is laid up for me a crown of righteousness, which the Lord, the righteous Judge, shall give me at that day."

To Him, with the Father and the Holy Ghost, be glory now and forever, Amen.

5

The Duty of Committing Our Souls to Christ

Preached September 13, 1742

"And I am persuaded that He is able to keep that which I
have committed unto Him against that day."
2 Timothy 1:12

It was doubtless an important question that was proposed to the apostles by the trembling jailor, "Sirs! What
shall I do to be saved?" And it is a melancholy evidence of
the folly of mankind that they are perpetually cumbered
about many things while the one thing needful, the salvation of their souls, is sadly neglected.

None is so stupid as to imagine that he has a charter of
exemption from the common law of mortality, none so
foolish as to suppose that this world is designed for the
place of his immortal abode. We all know that it is appointed for man once to die, and daily experience shows
us that there is no discharge in that war. And yet how
common it is to behold unthinking mortals spending their
days in vanity and pleasure, without ever seriously inquiring where their next habitation will be.

But surely, since death is the end of all mankind and
puts a final period to our state of trial (since after death
succeeds the judgments), the immediate consequences of
it are either a state of perfect happiness or else endless
and intolerable misery. To prepare for these grand events
must be the common concern of the children of men, the

first and most important business of life. This the united voice of reason and revelation declare.

Various are the methods which have been taken by mankind in all ages to secure the favor of heaven and a state of future felicity. But, alas, the greatest part have waxed vain in their imagination, have groped after happiness in the dark, or, at most, encompassed themselves with sparks of their own kindling, which served only to light them down to perdition. The Scripture affords us the only sure and unerring direction, and unto this we are to take heed as to a light that shines in a dark place. By this we are assured that there is no other name given under heaven by which men can be saved but the name of Jesus, no other way of salvation by Christ but believing in Him or, to use the phrase of our text, committing our souls to him. This was the method taken by St. Paul, and with what divine pleasure he reviews the sacred transaction! With what holy triumph! With what unshaken assurance does he rejoice in his happiness and safety! "I know whom I have believed, and I am persuaded that He is able to keep that which I have committed unto Him against that day."

May divine grace incline us all to imitate the example of this happy apostle, to resign our souls to the charge and care of Him who alone is able to keep them in safety to the day of the Lord.

In discoursing on this passage I shall (by divine assistance), first, explain the duty of committing our souls to Christ, and then, second, evidence the safety of those who do so.

First, I am to explain the duty of committing our souls to Christ, and this necessarily supposes:

1. A deep conviction of our inability to take care of our own souls and provide for their eternal welfare. The whole scheme of man's redemption by Christ is built upon the ruins of the first apostasy; had there been no sin, there would have been no need of a Savior; had man been

qualified to save himself, God would not at such an infinite expense have provided a way for his recovery. Had any finite being been equal to the mighty work, God would never have parted with His Son out of His bosom to undertake it. All the treasuries of divine love which are unfolded in the gospel, all the riches of almighty grace displayed in the face of a Redeemer, proclaim man to be a creature inclined to the divine displeasure, exposed to numberless distresses and dangers, and utterly unable to provide for his own safety. That this is the share of mankind the Scriptures plainly declare, and we all easily confess.

But, alas, while men confess these things with their mouths, we too often find they make but a slender impression upon their heart. What a careless and indifferent air do we see upon the face of an assembly, while the misery of men by nature is described in its most awful colors! With how little affection and concern do they hear the glad tidings of salvation! Now whence does this insensibility come in the midst of so many dangers, this stupidity in an affair of such infinite consequence? Are sinners in league with death? Have they come to an agreement with hell? Are they fond of destruction and misery? This cannot be the case; for there is a principle of self-love in man that naturally inclines him to seek after his own happiness and fly from impending danger. But it is owing to that fatal security that reigns in the hearts of men, and the little sense they have of things of an eternal nature. They love their sins; they are unwilling to be disturbed in the peaceable possession of their lusts; and therefore they stifle every serious thought that at any time arises in their minds, and banish as unwelcome guests all convictions of their guilt and danger. They flatter themselves into peace by vain and delusive hopes; they lull themselves asleep by the bewitching charms of sensual pleasure. Hence they do not hear amazing thunders of divine wrath that utter their voices against them; they are not startled, though the flaming sword of divine justice is continually brandished before their eyes. And while they continue in this deep sleep of security, they are deaf to all the offers of a Savior, though He passes before them in all the glory of His person, and in all the wonders of His grace and love. The whole do not need a physician, but those who are sick. Men must feel in some measure the misery of their apostate state before they will be persuaded to apply to the Redeemer for deliverance.

Therefore, the first method of recovering grace is to open the eyes of sinners to see their guilt and danger, so that they may be prepared with joy to receive the glad tidings of a Savior. In order to accomplish this, the Spirit of the Most High brings to remembrance their innumerable transgressions of God's holy law, and charges them upon the conscience in all their crimson guilt and terrible aggravations. He speaks to them in the voice of terror so that they may be awakened to fly from the wrath to come: "What have you been doing, O sinner, ever since you have been in the world? You have been violating the authority of heaven, offending your Maker to His face—and by this you stand condemned by His righteous law and are every moment in danger of being dragged out to a terrible execution. Wrath from heaven is revealed against you; there is but a step between you and eternal death."

This fills the soul with a trembling concern for its safety and causes the sinner to cry out, "O miserable man that I am, who shall deliver me from the vengeance of heaven! Wherewith shall I come before God? How shall I avert His threatened displeasure; if I should plead my innocence or attempt to extenuate my crimes, my conscience would fly in my face and my own mouth would condemn me. Shall I try by floods of tears to abate the fierceness of divine wrath, or by continual supplications to move the Almighty to pity and compassion? Shall I attempt by a stricter obe-

dience to make amends for all my past offenses, and recommend myself to His favor for the time to come? Alas!
My deepest sorrows will make no atonement for my guilt,
nor my best performances attain that purity which the law
requires. Besides, I am dead in trespasses and sins, without
any power to yield any acceptable service to my injured
Sovereign. All the powers of my soul are enfeebled and my
universal nature is depraved; all I do flows from a corrupted heart and is infected with the poison of sin. Oh,
that God out of His infinite mercy would have compassion
on my misery and stretch out the arm of His mercy to help
and deliver me! I am oppressed, Lord, undertake for me."

Thus the blessed God convinces the soul of its danger
and breaks it off from all self-dependence, and this prepares the way for a gracious discovery of the way of salvation by Christ, which I come in the next place to consider.

2. Committing our souls to Christ implies a firm persuasion of His ability and willingness to save all those who put
their trust in Him. Without this, a soul under a humbling
sense of its guilt would be destitute of all relief and sink
into black and melancholy despair. Were there no door of
hope open in the gospel, the convinced sinner would set
down in a state of disconsolate sorrows and never attempt
to seek deliverance. But the great Physician, who wounds
only in order to effect a cure, mercifully steps in and supports the soul in its extremity by showing him that there is
a possibility of escape; that there is a Savior provided for
perishing and undone sinners who came from heaven to
earth upon this gracious design, who has completely answered the demands of divine justice by the spotless sacrifice of Himself, vindicated the honor of the divine law by a
perfect obedience to its righteous demands, and thereby
purchased eternal redemption for those who by faith receive Him.

This great Redeemer is discovered not only in the glory
of His power, but in all the wondrous riches of His grace,

who is as willing as able to save all those who come to God in and through Him, whose invitations are universal, to men of all orders and degrees, without reserve or exception, and has positively declared that those who come to Him He will in no wise cast out (John 6:37).

These truths are discovered to the soul not only in the external revelations of the Scripture, but by the internal illumination of the Spirit. They break in upon their mind in the day of God's power with an irresistible light and influence. The veil is removed from the understanding; the darkness that hung upon divine things is immediately scattered. That God who commanded light to shine out of darkness shines into the heart, giving the light of the knowledge of the glory of God in the face of Jesus Christ (2 Corinthians 4:6).

Now the sinner receives it as a faithful saying, and worthy of all acceptance, that Jesus Christ came into the world to save sinners (1 Timothy 1:15). Now he cannot but cry out, "Lord, I believe that Thou art able to save to the uttermost. Lord if Thou wilt, Thou canst make me clean from all my guilt and pollution. Happy are they who are encircled in the arms of Thy mercy; they need not fear the challenges of the law, the demands of justice, nor the terrors of hell. Thou art able to keep that which is committed unto Thee even unto the day of the Lord. And, blessed be Thy name, the compassions of Thy heart are equal to the power of Thy hands; important as the concerns of my soul are, I desire to betrust them to Thy care; guilty and condemned as I am, I cast myself at Thy blessed feet. To whom else could I go, for Thou hast the words of eternal life."

3. From hence follows hearty consent to be saved in a way of free grace by the merits and righteousness of Jesus Christ. The doctrine of salvation by free grace is so clearly revealed in the gospel, and so often inculcated from the pulpit, that most of our people think they really believe it and that none but blind and ignorant papists are in dan-

ger of trusting themselves and their own performances. They bless God that they have been better instructed than to build upon their own works. But if we inquire into the affair more narrowly, and ask what the ground is of their hope, and why they expect to be saved by Christ, many will be ready to answer, "I am not among the number of profane sinners. I am diligent in my business, just in my dealings, constant in my devotions, and attend upon religious worship in the appointed seasons. When at any time I fall into sin, I am sorry for it and resolve to amend and reform." Upon this account they imagine they stand high in the favor of heaven, and are in the direct road to salvation.

Thus, after all their high professions of expecting to be saved by free grace and by trusting the righteousness of Jesus Christ, the foundation of their dependence is built upon themselves, their own duties and performances—and this is the exact character of the Pharisee as described by our blessed Savior in Luke 18:9.

They don't think they can merit heaven by their good works, but they think their prayers, their tears, and their reformations, procure the favor of God and give them a title to the salvation purchased by Christ.

This is further evident by the conduct of awakened sinners who can no longer continue in the security of these self-righteous moralists, but are convinced that they are guilty sinners and are filled with an anxious concern for the salvation of their souls. Even these are seeking for some qualifications to recommend them to Christ. Exhort them to believe in Christ and trust in Him for salvation, and, alas, they are not sufficiently humbled; they do not have those dispositions which are required in those to whom the invitations of the gospel are directed. It would be presumption in them to trust in the righteousness of the Mediator till their hearts are more broken under a sense of their sins and they are better prepared for the divine acceptance. Thus they go about to establish a right-eousness of their own and, notwithstanding all their pre-tenses to the contrary, are flattering themselves with the fond conceit of bringing something with them to qualify them for the mercy of Christ. This is a convincing evidence that they are strangers to the doctrine of free grace; for if salvation is of grace, it is no more of works. The only quali-fication we have to recommend us to the acceptance of the Redeemer is that we are perishing and undone sinners, and that all we can bring with us is guilt, unworthiness, and misery.

But this is so different from all the notions we naturally entertain of the way of salvation, so contrary to the pride and arrogance of mankind, that this, above all things else, increases the difficulty of conversion and renders the way to life strait and easily mistaken. Nay, I dare assert as an unfailing truth that not one unhumbled sinner really be-lieves the doctrine of free grace as revealed in the gospel; not one soul is ever convinced of the safety of trusting en-tirely in the Redeemer for salvation till the veil is taken away from his understanding and his mind is super-naturally enlightened by the Spirit of the Most High God. Therefore, when St. Peter made that noble confession of his faith and declared our Lord Jesus to be the Christ, the Son of the Living God, our Savior immediately replied, "Blessed art thou, Simon Bar-Jona, for flesh and blood hath not revealed it unto thee, but My Father which is in heaven."

This divine illumination is the principle of every true believer; by this they are persuaded and enabled to com-mit themselves to the power and grace of Christ; by this they are taught to renounce all other dependences as ref-uges of lies; by this they are instructed to buy wine and milk without money and without price. They are made willing not only to forsake their darling sins, which were once as dear to them as a right hand and a right eye, but to renounce self, the most beloved of all their idols. They can no longer trust in their own strength, which they know is but weakness, nor in their own righteousness, which they are convinced is but filthy rags, but join in the triumphant language of the prophet Isaiah from 45:24, "In the Lord Jehovah have I righteousness and strength." They commit themselves to the grace of Christ—not upon the encouragement that they are in any measure prepared to receive Him, or in the least degree qualified for His acceptance, but because they are indigent and perishing creatures, and Christ is an almighty and compassionate Savior, and as such is offered to the vilest sinners.

And then their language is, "Blessed Jesus, I am an ignorant and benighted sinner. I come to Thee who art the Sun of Righteousness, to scatter the darkness of my mind and enlighten me by Thy Word and Spirit. I am a rebellious and condemned malefactor, but I fly to Thy atonement and righteousness to deliver me from my guilt, and justify me at the tribunal of a holy God. I am a frail and feeble creature, surrounded with numerous and powerful adversaries; but I lay hold on Thy almighty and victorious grace to bear me up in the midst of all opposition, and finally conduct me to eternal happiness and glory. Detesting myself in every view, my only refuge is in Thy boundless and unmerited mercy, and my highest ambition is to be a monument of Thy free grace through the unalterable ages of eternity."

4. But I must further add that this implies that we commit our souls to Christ to be saved in a way of holiness. This is an essential part of that faith which is of the operation of the Spirit, and which in a great measure distinguishes the true believer from the painted formalist, the hypocritical professor.

While we are preaching the doctrine of free grace, many of our hearers seem captivated with the charming sound, and are ready to say aloud, "This doctrine is music

in my ears; this is the preaching that I admire; beautiful
are the feet of those messengers who bring those glad tidings of peace. I know I have no good works to depend
upon; my only hope is in the unmerited mercy of God."

But what do they mean when they declare that they
expect to be saved by free grace? It is to be feared that
multitudes intend nothing more than that since salvation is
freely offered in the gospel, and is not to be purchased by
our best performances, they need not be solicitous to renounce their sins and walk in the narrow way of holiness.
They imagine they may live as they please, and yet expect
to go to heaven when they die. But, alas, this is a vain
dream, and empty delusion! This is to extract poison out
of the richest cordial, to turn the grace of God into wantonness. Such men may talk of free grace in the strains of
angelic eloquence, and appear in the defense of the truth
with the zeal of flaming seraphs. They are scandals to the
Christian name and character, enemies to the grace of
God, and are to be numbered among the subjects of the
prince of darkness. Is the holy Jesus a minister of sin? Did
He come into the world to give His followers a license to
commit iniquity with greediness, and escape with impunity? Did He suffer, bleed, and die for the sins of His
people so that they might freely indulge and boldly commit them? Is the doctrine of justification by faith designed
to destroy the necessity of a holy obedience to the divine
law? No, verily! 1 John 3:8: "For this purpose was the Son
of God manifested in the flesh, that He might destroy the
works of the devil." The grace of God which brings salvation teaches us to deny all ungodliness and iniquity, and to
live soberly, righteously, and godly in this present evil
world. Our Lord died an immaculate sacrifice for sin, not
to give leave to His followers to continue as the servants of
corruption, but to redeem them from all iniquity and purify unto Himself a peculiar people zealous for good
works. He justifies us freely without the deeds of the law so

that, being delivered out of the hands of our enemies, we might serve Him without fear, in holiness and righteousness before Him all the days of our life (Luke 1:74–75).

Know then, O vain man, that faith which we preach, and by which we commit our souls into the hands of Christ, is not a dead, inactive principle, but a living spring of new obedience! That salvation which is so freely offered in the gospel is a salvation from the power as well as guilt, from the pollution as well as punishment of sin. That heaven which Christ has purchased with His sacred blood is not only a place of light and joy, but a state of purity and holiness. And everyone who is saved by the merits of His cross is brought to bow to the scepter of His government.

When therefore we commit our souls to Christ, we apply to Him as clothed with the united characters of a Prince and a Savior (Acts 5:31). We come to Him for both repentance and remission of sins.

"O compassionate Jesus!" says the believer, "I stand in need of the whole of that salvation which Thou hast purchased by Thy death and freely bestowed upon Thy people. Thou art welcome to my soul in all Thy sacred offices, in all the kind and condescending characters which Thou hast assumed for the benefit of Thy church. I joyfully receive Thee as a complete Savior, to perform within me the whole good pleasure of Thy grace. I resign myself unto Thee, who are my rightful Lord and Sovereign, to be sanctified by Thy Spirit, governed by Thy laws, guided by Thy providence, and kept by the victorious power of Thy grace, unto the day of the Lord."

5. Finally, this committing of the soul to Christ is not barely a single act, to be done once in our lives, but is the frequent practice of every Christian. The first act of faith unites the soul to Christ, and neither death nor hell shall ever be able to make a separation. But it is the duty and privilege of believers daily to renew the solemn transaction, and by a fresh surrender to resign themselves to the

care of their compassionate Savior. Therefore the holy apostle tells us, "The life which I live here in the world, I live by the faith of the Son of God, who loved me and gave Himself for me" (Galatians 2:20).

The Christian sees a continual need of Christ's atoning blood to wash away his guilt, of the renewing influences of the Spirit to subdue his rebellious lusts, of fresh supplies of grace to carry him through the duties of his pilgrimage state, and enable him to finish his course with joy. The people of God therefore continually apply to Christ as their living Head, from whom they derive all their strength, without whom their souls would immediately wither and die. Under all their darkness and difficulties, they take themselves to Him as their unfailing Refuge and Defense, without whom they would fall an easy prey to the policy and power of their spiritual adversaries.

The believer says, "To whom, Lord, shall I go but unto Thee, who art the Author and must be the Finisher of my faith? Be Thou my guide, for without Thy counsel I am every moment exposed to wander into the paths of guilt and folly. Be Thou my Shield, for without Thy defense I shall fall into ten thousand dangers. Let neither the insinuating charms of vice, nor the violent assaults of temptations, corrupt my fidelity to my Lord and Master. Cover my head in the day of battle; stand by me in all my contests with sin and Satan; enable me to fight the good fight of faith, till the last enemy shall be destroyed.

"Thus let me come out of the wilderness of this world leaning upon my almighty Redeemer; and when I come to the concluding scene of life, may I with security and joy lay down my head in the dust, and in the lively exercise of faith, commend my spirit into the hands of my blessed Savior. In that important hour, when the world vanishes from my view and vast eternity opens before me, let the everlasting arms of Thy mercy support my dissolving nature and Thy vital presence brighten my passage through the dark valley of the shadow of death. Let my last remains of health be spent in the praises of redeeming grace, and my faltering tongue join in the triumphant language of St. Paul, 'I know whom I have believed, and that He is able to keep that which is committed unto Him.' "

This is the language of the true believer. In this manner he commits himself to the care and protection of Christ. Happy are they whose interests are deposited in His safe and gracious hands. He will certainly keep them to the day of the Lord.

And this brings me to the second part of my discourse, the evidences. I refer you to my text, where this important truth is positively asserted. Or if any thing further were necessary, it might suffice to direct you to a few of those innumerable places of Scripture where the same thing is clearly revealed. But I think the power and grace of the Redeemer is so delightful a subject that I cannot satisfy myself to pass it over in so cursory a manner. This is the foundation of all our hopes, the vital spring of all our joys, the only source of comfort in life and in death. Fain would I speak upon this heading in such a manner (if the Spirit of divine grace shall succeed the attempt) as not only to convince the understanding, but impress the hearts of my audience so that the sinner, trembling under the apprehensions of his guilt, may be encouraged to cast his soul into the arms of this Almighty Savior; and that the weak believer who is ready to sink under discouragements may be strong in faith, giving glory to God. But the limits of my discourse oblige me only to insist on a few things. It may suffice to say:

1. The Lord Jesus Christ is endowed with all those qualifications which are necessary for the preservation and happiness of those who commit themselves to Him. The constitution of His person abundantly qualifies Him for this important work; for He is the great EMMANUEL,

God with us (Matthew 1:23). Were He only a creature, though of the most exalted order and character, we might justly tremble to commit our immortal souls into His hands and rest the vast weight of our eternal welfare on any finite power and goodness. But the Savior whom we adore is the only begotten of the Father, the express image of His person (Hebrews 1:3), and partaker of the infinite perfections of His nature. He is expressly called in Romans 9:5 the mighty God, and "God over all, blessed forever-more." Yea, He is that God who made the world at first by the authority of a command, and continually upholds all things by the word of His power (John 1:3). This renders Him the proper object of our trust and confidence, and gives us the highest assurance that we may safely depend upon His wisdom and power, His fidelity and grace.

But God absolutely considered is a tremendous name. The exalted glories of the divine nature are apt to strike our minds with a trembling awe under a conscious sense of our guilt and pollution. Therefore our blessed Re-deemer kindly accommodated Himself to the frailty of mankind, and concealed the luster of His divinity under a veil of humanity. It was fitting that the Mediator between God and man should partake of the nature of both; otherwise, He would have been incapable of satisfying the demands of offended justice and vindicating the honor of God's violated law.

To this end He who was eternally in the form of God appeared in the fullness of time in the fashion of a man. He who lay in the bosom of the Father condescended to tabernacle in flesh and dwell with man upon earth. But though clothed with the infirmities of flesh and blood, He was free from every defiling blemish; though He lived in the midst of a polluted world, He was holy, harmless, un-defiled, and separate from sinners (Hebrews 7:26). In our nature, He perfectly obeyed the law; with infinite exact-ness He underwent the dreadful penalty that our sins deserved. He submitted to the humbling circumstances of poverty and distress. He was blasphemed by the Jewish rulers, insulted by the misguided populace, forsaken by His faint-hearted disciples, and in a manner deserted by His heavenly Father in the hour of His extremity and danger. In time, having passed through the labors and sorrows of a mortal life, He suffered the agonies of a shameful and accursed death that He might make atonement for sin and bring in everlasting righteousness. How abundantly qualified does He then appear to assume the character of a Savior? How able to go through the mighty work He has undertaken? How safely may we rely upon His power who is the great God as well as the Savior of men? How cheerfully may we venture our most important interests in His hands who has given us such amazing evidences of His love?

He who descended from the glories of heaven, submitted to the miseries of this inferior earth, and humbled Himself unto the dust of death for His people certainly will not lose the sacred purchase of His blood, but will pursue the conquests of His grace and surmount all the difficulties that stand in the way of their souls' salvation.

Had He indeed always remained in a state of suffering and weakness, had He been reserved an everlasting captive in the dark prison of the grave, we might justly have suspected His power to deliver others, since He himself remained subject to the empire of death. But though He was dead, yet He is above, and behold He lives forevermore. He broke asunder the bars of death, burst open the doors of His marble sepulcher, and rose triumphant Conqueror, as the Head of the redeemed. He looks forth like the sun after a dark eclipse, and shone with a more surprising luster than before. Having finished the design of embassy upon earth, and settled the affairs of His kingdom here below, He returned to His heavenly Father. He ascended up to glory in a visible manner, in the presence of

His admiring disciples, and a cloud received Him out of their sight (Acts 1:9).

Would you then know how great and glorious a Savior He is? Then view Him not only under the darkness and dishonor of His humiliation, but in the splendor and majesty of His exalted state. View Him by faith, making the clouds His chariots, riding upon the wings of the wind, ascending triumphant through the regions of the air. Behold the heaven of heavens, the imperial palace of the living God, lifting up its eternal gates, and opening wide its everlasting doors, that this King of Glory might enter in. Behold angels and archangels, and all the illustrious inhabitants of heaven, dressed in their richest robes of glory, going forth to congratulate their victorious Lord and celebrate the mighty conquests of His grace and love. Behold Him exalted to the head of the celestial hierarchy, seated at the right hand of God, invested with all power in heaven and earth. Finally, view Him amidst all the dazzling glories of heaven, amidst the incessant acclamations of saints and angels, ever mindful of the concerns of His church, employing all His interest in the courts of heaven on behalf of His people upon earth, and ordering all the wheels of providence and grace for their comfort and advantage. This is the Savior whom we adore, in whom we believe, and from whom we expect complete and eternal redemption.

Conscience may call back the remembrance of our former sins or later transgressions, and terrify us with the apprehensions of approaching vengeance; but the blood of Jesus has a stronger cry for mercy. In that blood we behold the claims of justice answered by an adequate satisfaction, the honors of the divine law illustriously displayed, and a door of hope opened for the chief of sinners. Though we find our strength too weak to shake off the disgraceful servitude of sin, and our most vigorous efforts too feeble to stem the torrent of degenerate nature, yet our Redeemer is mighty to save even those who are dead in trespasses and sins. The law of the Spirit of life in Christ Jesus can in a moment make us free from the law of sin and death. Let Satan appear in all the forms of terror and use all his accursed arts of policy and power; our Lord sits at the head of the invisible world, holds the devils in chains, and can enable the weakest of His people to baffle the designs of the prince of darkness. Though death and the grave stand in the way and interpose between complete felicity, even these are conquered enemies; the appointed time will shortly come when all who are in their graves shall hear the voice of the Son of God, when the sleeping dust of His people shall be recollected, and the bodies of their corruption shall be fashioned like His own most glorious body (Philippians 3:21). Then shall the designs of His grace be completed, and His saving power appear in its highest glory.

2. But the Lord Jesus Christ is not only thus wonderfully qualified to procure salvation for His people, but He has graciously promised that He will employ His power on behalf of all those who commit themselves to His protection and care. You know, my brethren, He is the faithful and true witness, too wise to be deceived and too good to deceive any of His creatures. He is not a mere man that He should lie, nor like the variable sons of men that He should repent. How gracious are His invitations to the sinner, oppressed with a sense of guilt, and ready to faint under the weight of his own discouraging fears. Matthew 11:28: "Come to Me, all ye that are weary and heavy laden." How kind and condescending is His promise: "And I will give you rest." How universal are the offers of life to all who are sensible of their need of a Savior, and are willing to accept delivering grace: "Whosoever will, let him come and drink of the waters of life freely" (Isaiah 55:1; Revelation 22:17).

Neither the number nor aggravation of men's sins stop

the current of divine mercy, nor obstruct the efficacy of the blood of Jesus. All who accept the offers of His love, and who trust in Him entirely for salvation, may be assured of a cordial welcome. Hence He gives to His apostles the most extensive commission: "Preach the gospel to every creature" (Mark 16:15). In pursuance of these divine instructions, the apostles pronounce it as a certain truth that by Him, all who believe are justified from all things from which they could not be justified by the Law of Moses. They proclaim it as a faithful saying that Christ came into the world to save the chief of sinners.

But this comfortable truth is not only clearly contained in God's Word, but is plainly declared in His works. Why does He display the riches of His goodness and long-suffering to those who insolently transgress His laws and despise the tenders of His grace? Why does He give sinners a space to repent, and use the most suitable means to persuade them to embrace the happy opportunity? Why does He carry on a treaty of peace with a guilty world and dispatch His ambassadors to beseech sinners to be reconciled to Him? And when men resist the methods of His grace and will not come to Him that they may have life, why does He mourn over their obstinacy and commiserate their ruin? Surely the great Savior of the world does not compliment the sinner, nor delude wretched mortals with the offer of salvation, which He is not willing to bestow upon them when they are made willing to accept it. No! We have the strongest testimony of His love in dying for sinners. It is His Spirit that inspires them with ardent desires after the blessings of the gospel. It is a divine power that has made them willing to accept a Savior; they therefore who flee to this blessed hope that is set before them, and by a humble faith commit their souls to the charge and care of Christ, may be assured that He will keep them to the day of the Lord.

3. And this will be further confirmed if we consider

that multitudes in all ages have trusted His faithful Word, and have been made monuments of His surprising grace. I confess that the greatest part of mankind refuse the gentle yoke of Christ, and choose the degrading slavery of Satan and their lusts.

But let us review the history of former ages, and we shall find an innumerable multitude in every period of the church who have been delivered from the power of darkness, and translated into the kingdom of our dear Redeemer. Let us recollect the dispensations of heaven in the present day, and what illustrious triumphs of divine grace have we seen and heard! Our blessed Savior has been, as it were, riding in circuit through the land, clothed with the garments of salvation, going on from conquering to conquering. Persons of all orders and degrees, of all ages and characters, have been washed, sanctified, and justified in the name of the Lord Jesus, and by the Spirit of our God. Tender youths in the morning of life have felt the power of redeeming grace, and learned with their infant tongues to lisp forth the praises of their Almighty Deliverer. Aged sinners, who have long withstood the inviting language of divine love and were upon the very borders of hell, have been called at the eleventh hour and made wondrous examples of sovereign mercy. The poor of this world have received this salvation as the free gift of God, without money and without price, and have become rich in faith and heirs of the kingdom of heaven. The rich in earthly possessions have been enabled to renounce this world as their portion, and lie as humble petitioners at the footstool of Christ, having obtained through Him a title to the inheritance of the saints in light. Self-righteous Pharisees have been stripped of all their presumptuous confidences, and have been taught to esteem all their boasted attainments as loss and damage for the knowledge of Christ Jesus.

And that none might be discouraged under a sense of their guilt and unworthiness, persons of the most infamous characters, who were once a disgrace to human nature, have been persuaded to cast off the unfruitful works of darkness, to give up themselves to Christ, and have found the atoning virtue of His blood, cleansing them from their aggravated guilt, and the almighty power of His Spirit transforming them into the image of divine purity.

Each of these is convincing evidence of the grace and power of Christ, and affords abundant encouragement to the greatest sinners to surrender themselves into His saving hands. After all the victories He has gained, and the numbers He has redeemed, the infinite treasure of His merits is not exhausted, nor is His power in the least diminished. His ear is not heavy that He cannot hear, nor His arm shortened that He cannot save. Still He is mighty to save, and will persevere in the work He has begun till the whole number of His elect are accomplished, the very last of his enemies subdued, and the universal company of redeemed sinners are fixed in a state of perfect purity and bliss.

Application

1. How great is the danger of those who refuse this all-sufficient and gracious Savior? My brethren! How often have you been importunately called upon to commit your souls into the hands of Christ? How often from this desk have the ministers of Jesus proclaimed the terrors of divine wrath, and shown you the danger of persisting in your impenitence and unbelief? How often have these walls resounded with the alluring voice of mercy, inviting you to accept the blessings of the gospel? But what effect have these things had? What reception have you given to these repeated messages from heaven? Have you received these invitations with sacred joy? Does the Spirit of God bear witness with your spirits that you have been made wiling in

the day of the divine power? Can you say that under a deep sense of your guilt and vileness you have been humbled at the feet of a sovereign God, and been obliged to confess that He would be just in consigning you over to eternal flames? Have you had such a view of the enmity and rebellion of your natures as has caused you everlastingly to despair of all help and deliverance in yourselves? Have you seen such a fullness in Christ the Mediator as has rendered Him incomparably precious in your esteem, the most worthy object of your supreme trust and confidence? Have you been enabled to fly to His righteousness and atonement as abundantly sufficient to procure the forgiveness of your sins, and restore you to the favor of an offended God? Have you been enabled to resign yourselves to His power and grace, to renew your polluted natures and transform you into the divine image? In this way have you found rest for your weary souls, peace for your disquieted minds, and such a comfortable hope of the divine acceptance as has engaged you with a joyful consent to devote yourselves to His service forever? If the gospel has had this effect upon you, you are not the persons whom I would terrify with a sense of your danger, but would rather congratulate your safety.

This, I trust, is the case of some of you. But with respect to a great part of this numerous assembly, have not the ministers of Christ reason to take up that melancholy complaint, "Who hath believed our report, and to whom hath the arm of the Lord been revealed" (Isaiah 53:1)? God has, as it were, appeared in terrible majesty, and spoken to you in thunder and lightning; but have you not with the Leviathan mocked at fear? Jesus Christ has passed before you clothed in the richest robes of gospel grace, and addressed you in the soft and gentle strains of love; but have you not with the deaf adder stopped your ears against His endearing voice? Have not many of your acquaintances been roused from their fatal sleep and heard

the voice of the Son of God, and received a new and a divine life, while you are still involved in the chains of death,
are slumbering upon the borders of hell, insensible of
your guilt and danger? Some of you perhaps have been
now and then startled a little out of your security, and
filled with some concern for your immortal happiness; but
with Felix you have adjourned this affair to a more convenient season, or at best satisfied yourselves with some
partial amendment, and from thence concluded that the
bitterness of death was passed. Are not many of you conscious that these are your circumstances? Must not your
consciences declare, if you will allow them to speak freely,
that after all the means of grace you have enjoyed, all the
religious impressions you have been under, that you have
not to this day been stripped of the pride of your nature,
nor brought to commit yourselves to Christ in the manner
that has been described?

To such I would address myself with the tenderest pity.
Make a pause, I beseech you, and consider your danger.
Satan, I know, will endeavor to rock you asleep with a presumptuous hope, and a corrupt heart will strongly incline
you to give heed to his accursed insinuations. But open
your Bibles and see what the Word of God declares concerning you. He who is the Lord of the invisible world,
who came as the messenger of His Father's grace, has expressly said, "If ye believe not that I am He, ye shall die in
your sins" (John 8:24). This He commanded His apostles
to preach to all nations: "He that believeth not shall be
damned" (Mark 16:16). Yea, He assures such that they are
condemned already, and that the wrath of God even now
abides upon them (John 3:36).

Do not these awful sounds strike your mind with horror and surprise? Does not your nature shudder at the
thought of falling into the hands of the living God? Alas!
Sinners, what will you do when He rises up in all the terrors of wrath? Will you be able to resist His power, who

has all the legions of heaven at His command, and can set the whole creation in battle array against you? Where will you flee when the sword of His justice is lifted up to destroy you, and clouds of insulting devils stand ready to seize you, when the heavens from above shall shower down whole tempests of wrath upon your defenseless heads, and hell from beneath stands open to receive you into its flaming bosom? Can your hearts endure and your hands be strong when this amazing scene shall be presented before you; when all these things, and infinitely more terrible ones, shall befall you? Gird up your loins like men, O sinners, and answer me. Is this the portion you choose? Are these the rewards you desire?

Doubtless you will say, "God forbid! Infinite mercy will prevent it." No, my brethren, do not deceive yourselves with vain and presumptuous imaginations; if you despise the offers of a Savior and die in your impenitence and unbelief, the God of truth has determined the case; the decree is fixed; the irreversible sentence is passed; you cannot escape. Even now you stand upon the brink of ruin; there is not a step between you and death; and the next move is into the lake that burns with fire and brimstone. And will it not then be a dreadful aggravation of your misery, that it is owing to your own folly and the effect of your own vicious choice? What can be more terrible than to sink into hell between the arms of divine mercy that were stretched out for your rescue and deliverance? With what rage and despair will you then reflect upon your present madness! How importunately will you then cry out for that mercy which you now refuse!

Awaken then, O sinner, and admit the conviction of your danger while a way of escape is provided. Have pity upon your perishing souls, before the decree is issued out, and your eternal state is finally decided. Sleep on a little longer, and you will lift up your eyes in unutterable torments. Trifle away a few more of the invaluable seasons of grace, and the day of your visitation will be ended and the gate of mercy irrecoverably barred against you.

2. But my text gives the greatest encouragement to the awakened and convicted sinner. This elevated voice, this language of terror, is not designed, my brethren, to unnecessarily alarm your fears or torment you before your time. Were there no hope in Israel concerning you, no prospect of your deliverance from this amazing misery, I would gladly suffer you to sleep on and take your rest for the few remaining days that are before you, and never offer to disturb you till your eyes were opened in the eternal world. But through the infinite riches of forbearing grace, it has not come to this; your condition, though sad, is not desperate; though prisoners of divine justice, yet you are prisoners of hope, and a door of deliverance is opened before you.

I know if you are truly awakened to a sense of your danger, Satan will aggravate your guilt to the utmost and represent your sins as unpardonable, your circumstances as forlorn and hopeless. But do not believe him; he is the father of lies, and a deceiver from the beginning. The eternal Son of God stands this day in the midst of this numerous assembly and cries with a loud voice, "If any man thirsts, let him come to Me and drink." He sends His ministers to make a full and universal offer of Himself and all His benefits to every soul that is willing to accept Him. Let none of you reject this invitation from a false and pretended principle of humility; that which is freely given may certainly be thankfully received. He calls you to apply to Him, not because you have done any good works to deserve His favor, or have any virtuous endowment to qualify you for His acceptance, but because you are wretched, miserable, poor, blind, and naked (Revelation 3:17). He offers you His righteousness to adorn your naked souls, His Spirit to sanctify your polluted natures, His grace everlastingly to enrich you.

Hearken then, you stout-hearted who are far from righteousness, and stand upon the dreadful precipice of eternal fire. Behold, now is the accepted time; now is the day of salvation (2 Corinthians 6:2)! If you receive the message of divine grace and commit yourselves to Christ, notwithstanding all your former rebellions, and present unworthiness, this day, this hour shall salvation come to your souls, and you shall go down to your houses justified. What surprising grace! What an adorable mystery of love this is!

Were this salvation proposed to you upon the most hard and rigorous terms, were you to wade through seas of blood and pass through a course of the severest penance upon earth in order to obtain it, even upon these conditions it would be a most advantageous offer, worthy to be received with the highest thankfulness and gratitude. How much more, then, when we are only commanded to wash and be clean, to believe in Christ and be saved?

Were these proposals made to the prisoners of divine vengeance who are shut up under wrath and weltering in eternal fire, would not their hearts leap for joy at the blessed news? Would they not with their flaming tongues immediately begin a song of praise, till the realms of darkness resounded with cheerful hallelujahs? But their day is over; the Son of Righteousness never arises upon those melancholy regions; nothing remains to them but a long night of horror and despair, while you, O sinner, enjoy the light of the gospel; while you have the joyful tidings of salvation sounding in your ears. Why then will you not attend to the calls of incarnate love, and accept so great salvation, so freely offered unto you?

Look up by faith to the happy seats above, and behold the spotless inhabitants of heaven; in what beauty do they appear? With what glory do they shine? With what unutterable transport do they encircle the throne of God and triumph in the perpetual effusions of His love? Do you not long, my brethren, to ascend these mansions of eternal bliss and join the choir of pure and perfected saints? Why then should you not be united to this glorified society? You have the same omnipotent grace to assist you, the same compassionate Savior to depend upon, and through His merits may be assured of a gracious reception.

Do not say that you are sinners, and therefore unworthy of so great a mercy; for Christ did not come to call the righteous, but sinners to repentance. Though your sins have been committed against the clearest light and the most endearing love, yet He is able to save unto the uttermost. Come then, O sinners, of every order and degree, of every age and character; commit yourselves to the gracious hands of Christ. Behold, He is willing to receive you all, guilty, miserable, and condemned as you are. He is willing to clothe you with His righteousness and make you heirs of His everlasting glory. To you, my brethren, even to all who hear me this day, this word of salvation is sent. Take heed, therefore, that you do not receive this grace of God in vain. Do not trifle away the day of divine patience. Perhaps, as for some of you, this may be the last invitation you will receive, the last opportunity of securing your future happiness. To be sure, the day of grace has its appointed limits, and none of you know how soon it may end.

But this you know, that yet a little while and the trump shall sound, the dead shall arise, and you must all appear before the tribunal of Christ. Yet a little while and that Jesus whom sinners despise shall appear in all the glories of an incarnate God, in the pomp and character of the universal Judge, and shall call for those who are His enemies, who would not that He should reign over them, that they may be brought forth and slain before Him.

But since you are not yet in these deplorable circumstances, since the blessed Jesus has not yet assumed the character of an inexorable Judge, let me again repeat the exhortation and beseech you in the name of Christ, by all the sufferings of His life and all the bitter agonies of His bloody passion, to be reconciled to God and to fly to the hope that is set before you. Let me adjure you by all the ineffable joys of heaven that He has purchased by His death, by all the inutterable torments of hell, which will be the portion of those who despise His grace, to have compassion on your immortal souls and to commit them to the care of Him who is mighty to save.

Hark, He calls to you from His cross, where He died as a sacrifice for the sins of men. He speaks to you from heaven, where He now dwells in inaccessible glory: "Look unto Me, all ye ends of the earth, and be saved." He rises, as it were, from His throne to stretch out the scepter of His mercy to you. He opens those arms that were once nailed to the accursed tree to receive and embrace you. Why, then, will you not give yourselves up to so kind, so gentle, so condescending a Savior? Why will you not put your trust in that grace which has been the refuge of the saints in all ages, and never yet deceived any who put their confidence in it? Are you willing to be made clean from all your sinful pollutions? Are you willing to be saved from your guilt and danger? Are you willing to receive this as the free gift of God through the merits of Christ?

I think I hear some of you saying, "There is nothing I so earnestly desire! I pant after this as the dear pants after the water brooks!"

Arise, then, whoever you are. The Master is calling you. Cast yourself into His gracious arms. Or if this is too bold a thought, cast yourselves at His feet; trust in Him for all salvation. Fear not, for as you seek Jesus, a bruised reed He will not break, and the smoking flax will not be quenched (Matthew 12:20).

3. How great, then, is the safety and happiness of the true believer. When the Christian considers the weakness and corruption of his nature—the number, strength, and policy of his adversaries—he is apt sometimes to almost

sink down in discouragement, and to break forth in the melancholy language of the psalmist: "I shall one day perish by the hands of my enemies" (1 Samuel 27:1). But these are the dark suggestions of unbelief, which are highly dishonorable to Christ and prejudicial to ourselves. Why are you cast down, O you of little faith! Why is your heart disquieted within you? You are under the care of Christ, whose power is almighty and whose love is unchangeable. You have Jesus for your Captain and Leader, the invaluable promises of divine grace for your support, and the faithfulness of God engaged for your protection and defense. And therefore you may be persuaded that neither life, nor death, nor principalities, nor powers, nor things present, nor things to come, shall ever seperate us from the love of God, which is in Christ Jesus our Lord (Romans 8:38–39).

In the midst of threatening danger, when called to the most difficult duties and trials, you may say, "I know that my Redeemer lives, and therefore will I not fear what men and devils can do against me." Your deliverance is begun by Christ, and you may have the highest confidence that He will never forsake the work of His own hands.

Lift your heads then with joy, O Christian, for the day of your complete redemption draws nigh! The time of darkness and temptation, of difficulty and anger, is but short. In a little while all ignorance shall be removed from your minds, all sorrow banished from your breasts, and you shall view the beloved Jesus without this interposing veil of sense, without the reflecting glass of ordinances in all His original excellency, beauty, and glory. After a few more struggles between the flesh and the Spirit, a few contests with a subtle devil and this ensnaring world, and your warfare will be accomplished, your victory will be complete, and you shall enter triumphant into the city of the New Jerusalem. Death, the universal terror of human nature, the last enemy of the saints, shall release you from this vain world, the abode of guilt and sorrow, and translate you from these territories of darkness to the endless felicities of paradise. There your minds shall no more be filled with distressing fears, nor your comforts darkened with disquieting doubts; sin shall no longer defile, nor Satan distress you, but you shall dwell in the presence of God, where is fullness of joy, and at His right hand, where are pleasures forevermore (Psalm 16:11).

In the meantime, let us rejoice in hope of this blessed and desirable day, even now while at a distance from our Father's house, and in the land of our pilgrimage. Let us attempt the songs of Zion and anticipate the work of heaven; let our souls magnify the Lord and our spirits rejoice in God our Savior, who has delivered us from the dominion of sin and the tyranny of Satan by a high hand and an outstretched arm; who will yet deliver us from every evil work, and bring us to see the end of our faith, the complete salvation of our souls. Let us join in a cheerful consort with the universal church upon earth and the general assembly of perfected spirits above; saying with a loud voice, as in Revelation 5:13, "Blessing, honor, glory, and power be unto Him that sitteth upon the throne and to the Lamb for ever and ever. Amen."

6

The Duty of Imitating the Example of Christ

"Let this mind be in you, which was also in Christ Jesus."
Philippians 2:5

Example is one of the most excellent and engaging methods of instruction, and has a peculiar efficacy to reform the disorders of mankind and dispose us to the practice of sincere and universal holiness. When we sit down and consider the deep and diffusive corruption of our nature, and the power and policy of our spiritual adversaries, we are apt to sink into a melancholy despair and imagine that the duties of religion are an impracticable severity, and the yoke of Christ an intolerable burden. But when we look abroad and see the bright and amiable examples of others who were men of like passions with ourselves, and clothed with the infirmities of human nature, who yet have bravely conquered the difficulties of religion, escaped the dangerous pollutions of the world, and practiced the most sublime instances of virtue in the midst of innumerable temptations—this is a noble evidence that Christ is not a hard and unreasonable Master, nor is obedience to His laws a task altogether impossible to be performed. This may abundantly convince us that the most frightening dangers may be surmounted and the most difficult parts of our duty may be complied with by the strength of a vigorous resolution and the almighty aids of divine grace. And what reflection can have a greater tendency than this to awaken us out of our slothful frames, to animate our Christian courage, and inspire us with a generous ambition to be followers of them who through faith and patience inherit the promises?

For this end the examples of eminent saints stand recorded in sacred Scripture and are recommended to our exact and faithful imitation. And in this respect the Christian religion clearly has the advantage above any institution that ever appeared upon earth. The celebrated matters of morality among the heathen delivered many excellent precepts to their followers, and recommended virtue to the world in pompous harangues, but they were extremely deficient in their practice and oftentimes scandalously loose in their manners—and therefore no wonder their discourses made so little impression upon their hearers and were ineffectual to reform a degenerate age.

It is the peculiar glory of the doctrine of Jesus that it not only contains the most admirable precepts of piety and goodness, but is encompassed with a bright cloud of witnesses who have trod in the ruggedest paths of virtue and cast a glory upon their profession by their divine and heavenly conversations. But above all it furnishes us with a just and unerring pattern of the most complete and absolute perfection in the life of our blessed Savior, unto which we are continually to direct our eyes and to copy after it with the utmost fidelity and diligence. This is earnestly recommended unto us in my text: "Let this mind be in you, which was also in Christ Jesus."

The example of Christ indeed is here propounded upon a particular occasion, and more immediately respects those Christian graces which the apostle in the preceding verses had been inculcating on the Philippians; but it is equally binding upon us with regard to every other grace and virtue, and is often proposed in Scripture as a powerful engagement to universal purity and holiness. In this extensive view I shall consider the words now read, and in discoursing upon them I shall (by divine assistance) proceed in the following method: First, I shall inquire in what respects the example of Christ is proposed to our imitation; second, what obligations we are under to imitate Him.

1. I am to inquire in what respects the example of Christ is proposed to our imitation. To endeavor an unlimited imitation of Him in all the works which He performed while He tabernacled in the flesh and conversed with man upon earth would be a presumptuous as well as an impossible attempt. Many actions of His life were plainly miraculous, and performed by Him in the discharge of His mediatorial office. Thus He healed the sick by a touch of His hand and cast out devils by an authoritative command. He fasted forty days and forty nights immediately after His baptism, and fed the multitude with a few inconsiderable loaves and fishes. As the great Prophet of His church, He revealed the secrets of the divine counsel and sent forth His apostles to be the extraordinary ministers of His kingdom. As our great High Priest, He died a sacrifice for the sins of the world, and rose again from the dead for the confirmation of His doctrine and the eternal justification of His people. In these things He is infinitely above our imitation, and to pretend to copy Him in them would be the height of madness and blasphemy. But we are to imitate Him in those actions which He performed as man, and in those duties which are suitable to our state and condition in the world. In these instances, the more closely we follow His example, the more exactly we walk even as He also walked in the world, the more perfectly we are conformed to the divine will, and the more acceptable is our obedience to our heavenly Father.

But it is necessary to mention a few particulars in which we are in a special manner called to imitate the bright and unerring example of Christ.

His amazing condescension and humility is an excellent pattern for our imitation. Of this He was a great and illustrious example in every stage of life, from His first humble appearance in a manger to His ignominious death upon the cross. Though He was the Son of God, and equal to His Father in all the essential perfections of the Deity, yet He vouchsafed to take our nature upon Him and appear in the contemptible garments of mortality and weakness. Though He was the Lord of Glory, and had dwelt from the days of eternity in the happy regions of light and joy, yet when He pitched His tabernacle among men He wandered about without any settled habitation, and was more destitute of the conveniences of life than the very brute creation. "The foxes have holes, and the birds of the air have nests, but the Son of Man had not where to lay His head." Though thousands of angels ministered unto Him in heaven, and ten thousand times ten thousand stood before Him to worship at His footstool and obey His sacred orders, yet His favorite companions upon earth were chosen from among the meanest of the people, and His most illustrious disciples were poor and despised fishermen. Though heaven was His throne and the earth was His footstool, and the whole creation was subject to His authority and government, yet He appeared in the form of a servant and condescended to be treated not only as the meanest of men, but as the vilest of criminals, to be condemned by the princes of this world and crucified upon an accursed cross. How justly may our thoughts be swallowed up in the consideration of this amazing stoop? How highly should we adore that unsearchable grace that prepared the way for this stupendous abasement!

But it is not enough that we admire and adore the condescension of the Son of God in our nature, but we must imitate His divine and amiable example. This is what our Lord Himself so solemnly enjoined upon His disciples: "Take My yoke upon you and learn of Me; for I am meek and lowly of heart" (Matthew 11:29). And this duty St. Paul, a humble follower of the blessed Jesus, in the most earnest and pathetic manner inculcates in our context: "If there be any consolation in Christ, if any comfort of love, if any fellowship of the Spirit, if any bowels of mercies, fulfill ye my joy. In lowliness of mind, let each esteem other better than himself." To which he adds this powerful and constraining motive: "Let the same mind be in you which was also in Christ Jesus, who, being in the form of God, thought it not robbery to be equal with God, but made Himself of no reputation and took upon Him the form of a servant, and was made in the likeness of men; and being found in fashion as a man, He humbled Himself, and became obedient unto death, even the death of the cross."

How should the pride of man be abased, and the glory of all flesh be covered with shame and confusion, when they reflect upon this great and glorious instance of humility? How cheerfully should we submit to the lowest circumstances of poverty and disgrace when we consider how freely the Son of God incarnate stooped from the height of happiness to the depths of misery? From Him we should learn to despise all the glittering pomp and vanities of this evil world, and to be adorned with that unaffected humility, of which He has given us so beautiful and engaging an example.

We must imitate the example of Christ in His universal charity and kindness to men. This is indeed beyond a parallel, and what can never be fully imitated by any of the children of men. His whole life upon earth was one continued act of the most generous and disinterested love to the most base and unworthy objects. The gospel history everywhere abounds with astonishing instances of His grace and benignity to mankind.

It was love that brought him down from the bright realms of eternal day and fixed His abode for a time in this miserable and benighted world. This animated Him continually to go about doing good to the souls and bodies of men, instructing the ignorant, comforting the sorrowful, healing the sick, and supplying the wants of the poor and needy. This carried Him through a scene of the most distressing sorrows and afflictions in His life, and at last humbled Him to the dust of death and nailed Him to the cursed tree as an expiatory sacrifice for the sins of the world. This is such an instance of love as exceeds the power of language to describe, and the utmost stretch of our imagination to conceive of the height and depth, the length and breadth. "Greater love hath no man than this, that a man lay down his life for his friends" (John 15:13). "But herein God commended His love toward us, that while we were yet sinners, Christ died for us" (Romans 5:8). It is the manner of men to place their affections upon those they apprehend to be the most agreeable and deserving objects; and it is the highest instance of human love to die for a friend. But this is the transcendent excellency of the love of Christ, that it was placed upon the most base and unlovely part of the creation. He laid down His life for His very enemies, who had renounced His sacred authority and were in open rebellion against His laws.

This is certainly a most surprising and unusual pattern of love, and should powerfully dispose us to the most extensive charity and benevolence to our fellow creatures. This is the inference made by St. John, the beloved disciple: "If God so loved us, we ought also to love one another." For this end the example of Christ is frequently proposed for our imitation, and we are solemnly enjoined to copy it. "This is My commandment, that ye love one another as I have loved you" (John 13:34). Nay, He makes it the distinguishing badge of His followers, and the necessary character of His genuine disciples: "By this shall all men know that ye are My disciples, if ye love one another." And what stronger obligations can we be under to this excellent duty, what more powerful motives can be set before us to engage us to the practice of it, than the positive command of our Master and Lord, and the noble example of Him who has given us so many expensive evidences of His wonderful kindness and love.

His heavenly meekness in the midst of unmerited abuses and affronts is a noble pattern for our imitation. Meekness is a virtue of distinguishing excellence and one of the brightest ornaments of the Christian character. But how high and difficult an attainment do we generally find it to be? How apt are our passions to kindle into a flame upon every slight provocation, and to break forth into the most indecent sallies of wrath and revenge at every shadow of offense? But our Lord preserved a happy serenity of soul under the most provoking injuries and affronts, and bore with an unruffled calmness of mind the spiteful reproaches and cruel persecutions of His malicious and implacable adversaries.

He was the brightest example of innocence that ever appeared in the world. He was absolutely free from the least shadow of an imperfection or blemish. He did injury to none, even of the meanest of men, and showed kindness to all without exception who implored His relief and assistance. And yet how this divine and excellent Person, this great and extensive blessing to the world, was treated even by those who enjoyed His heavenly instructions and in whose streets He performed so many wonderful works of charity and love! How He was pursued with restless and unrelenting malice, loaded with the most false and undeserved reproaches, and prosecuted with incessant violence and cruelty until they had arraigned Him at the bar of the Roman governor and brought Him under an ignominious sentence of death!

Nor did even this satisfy their importunate rage and malice, but they aggravated His sufferings by the most abusive and insulting behavior. They smote Him with the palms of their hands, clothed Him with mock signs of royalty and power, and bowed the knee before Him in contempt and ridicule. And yet, with astonishing meekness, He bore these continual insults and indignities. All this contradiction of sinners did not inspire His breast with a vengeful thought, nor extort a passionate expression from His lips. Amidst the most trying provocations He maintained a perfect mastery over His passions and answered the most abusive calumnies, either by soft and gentle replies, calm and moving expostulations, or by a meek and patient silence. When they reproached Him for the meanness of His birth and parentage, and reflected upon the lowness and poverty of His condition in the world, He calmly told them (Matthew 13:57), "A prophet is not without honor, save in his own country, and in his own house." When they charged Him with an undue familiarity with persons of a scandalous character, and upon this account represented Him as a glutton and a wine-bibber, a friend of publicans and sinners, He justified His conduct by the charitable design He had in view, and the peculiar need they were in of His instruction and assistance. When they impudently branded Him with the infamous character of an impostor, and accused Him with the complicated crimes of blasphemy against God and confederacy with the devil, He appealed to His miraculous works which were an unanswerable evidence that He came from God, and to the manifest tendency of His doctrine, which was to destroy the kingdom of Satan. In the end, when their insatiable rage had attained to the most extravagant height and they were preparing to gratify their revenge by inflicting upon Him the most bloody and tormenting death, He quietly submitted to their rudeness and barbarity, and was brought as a lamb to the slaughter. And as a sheep before her shearers is dumb, so "He opened not His mouth." In the extremity of His sufferings, when the fury of earth and hell was united against Him; when the high priest, soldiers, and common people conspired together to aggravate His affliction and insult over His misery, He was so far from breaking out into any intemperate expressions of anger or showing any undue resentment of mind at their inhuman cruelty that He spent his latest breath in extenuating their guilt, and in His expiring moments recommended them to the divine favor and forgiveness.

Here is a most divine and heavenly example of meekness, worthy to be forever admired, to be continually and diligently imitated. What can more powerfully engage the children of men to restrain their tumultuous passions and suppress the first risings of wrath and revenge in their minds? Come hither, you who are apt to take fire at the least affront, who entertain deep resentments of the injuries you have received and are pursuing your enemies with a lasting and bitter revenge. Contemplate the great example of the meek and heavenly Jesus, who when He was reviled did not revile again; when He suffered, He did not threaten. Behold the Son of God hanging upon an infamous cross, suffering the most outrageous insults from the multitude that attended His execution, and yet pouring out His very blood for the expiation of their guilt, and in the agonies of death interceding for their pardon. And certainly this moving spectacle is enough to quench the fire of revenge in the breast of a Christian, to soften our most passionate resentments, and keep our minds serene and composed under the most provoking injuries and affronts.

We must imitate the example of Christ in His invincible patience under the most severe and bitter sufferings. Never was any sorrow like His sorrow, wherewith the Lord afflicted Him in the day of His fierce anger; and never was any patience like His patience wherewith He bore the heat of the divine displeasure. If we view Him in His astonishing agony in the garden, where the anguish of His mind was so great as to force the blood through the pores of His body, we shall find that He did not utter the least impatient word. Though His soul was exceeding sorrowful at the prospect of His approaching sufferings, and His innocent nature recoiled at the terrible appearance of death, attended with so many circumstances of infamy and horror, yet He manifested the most submissive resignation to the counsels of heaven and freely devoted Himself to fulfill the will of His heavenly Father. "Father, if it be possible, let this cup pass away from Me; nevertheless, not My will, but Thine be done." When He came to the finishing scene of life and was about to be offered up a bloody sacrifice for the sins of the world, though He was clothed with all the tender passions of human nature and had the quickest sense of affliction and suffering, yet He bore the lingering pains of the cross and went through the tormenting agonies of death without any complaint or murmuring; and when his nature sunk under the burden of His sufferings, He bowed down His head and gave up the Ghost with the utmost tranquility and composure.

This is that heroic pattern of patience which is so frequently set before us in the gospels, and which by our profession we are engaged to imitate. For even hereunto are we called, because Christ also has suffered for us, leaving us an example that we should follow in His steps (1 Peter 2:21). Therefore the apostle to the Hebrews, after he had given us many eminent examples of Old Testament saints who were illustrious patterns of suffering affliction and of patience, directs us at last unto Christ as the most complete and powerful example of all: "Wherefore, seeing we also are compassed about with so great a cloud of witnesses, let us lay aside every weight, and the sin that does so easily beset us, and let us run with patience the race that is set before us; looking unto Jesus, the Author and Finisher of our faith, who for the joy that was set before Him, endured the cross, despising the shame. For consider Him who endured such contradiction of sinners against Himself, lest ye be wearied and faint in your minds."

And certainly the contemplation of a crucified Savior, who once suffered for sins, the Just for the unjust, should arm us with undaunted courage in the midst of the most shocking dangers, and inspire us with invincible patience under the severest afflictions. Well may the most innocent of the sons of men bear the indignation of the Lord because we have sinned against Him; and the heaviest sufferings of this life are far below the just desert of our crimes. With what cheerfulness does it become us to take up our cross and follow the great Captain of our Salvation through danger, persecution, and death; especially when we consider that the cross is the way to the crown, and the sufferings of this present time are not worthy to be compared with the glory that shall be revealed.

We should imitate Christ in His devotion towards God, His integrity and righteousness towards men, His sobriety and temperance, His weanedness from the world, His heavenly-mindedness, His zeal against sin, His resistance of temptations, and the like.

But I shall sum up all in saying, lastly, we must copy after the example of Christ in His cheerful obedience to the will of His heavenly Father, and His unwearied diligence in accomplishing the work He came into the world to perform. In compliance with the divine will, He became a party in the covenant of redemption and freely undertook to satisfy the demands of offended justice and make atonement for the sins of His chosen people. And when the fullness of time was come for His appearance in the flesh, that He might execute His eternal engagements, He did not start at the difficulties which attended that mighty design, but cheerfully complied with the call of God and answered, "Lo, I come. In the volume of the book it is written of Me, 'I delight to do Thy will, O My God!' "

And during His continuance upon earth, with what amazing diligence He prosecuted the intention of His coming and fulfilled the hardest services required of Him! He sought not His own will, but the will of His Father who sent Him (John 5:30). And it is said in our context that He became obedient unto death, even the death of the cross.

He improved every opportunity to promote the glory of God and the happiness of men. This blessed work was His meat and drink, His continual joy and refreshment. In this He spent whole days and nights, neglecting His ordinary food. In this He persisted with unwearied industry and diligence, with unrelaxed vigor and resolution, with unfainting constancy and perseverance—notwithstanding the ingratitude and malice of men who put the most uncharitable construction upon His actions, and most basely defamed Him for His most generous acts of kindness and love. Here is an excellent pattern for our imitation, which should be a perpetual spur to our diligence, and animate us with the most active zeal in our Master's service. Having this great example in our view, we should break through every difficulty that lies in our way and count nothing too hard to be undergone, nothing too dear to be parted with, that we may glorify God upon earth and finish the work that He has given us to do.

2. I proceed now to the other general heading of my discourse, to consider the obligations we are under to imitate the example of Christ.

His life is the most perfect pattern of universal piety and goodness, and so is highly worthy of our imitation. It was an indelible scandal upon the ancient philosophers of Rome and Athens that their practice so widely differed from their precepts; though they recommended a contempt of the world to their hearers and said many excellent things in praise of purity and virtue, yet they themselves were inordinately ambitious of honor and applause, and were oftentimes shameful examples of vice and debauchery.

It is the lasting reproach of the scribes and Pharisees, those whited sepulchers among the Jews, that all their appearances of sanctity and devotion were only a cover for their hypocrisy and injustice. They bound heavy burdens, grievous to be borne, and laid them on men's shoulders;

but they would not touch them with one of their fingers (Matthew 23:4). And indeed the best of men upon earth are far from being complete and perfect examples; innumerable defects and infirmities continually attend them. They are at best but fallible and uncertain guides; if we follow them too closely, they will oftentimes precipitate us into dangerous errors and mistakes.

But the example of Christ is an absolute pattern of perfection, and affords unerring direction to His followers in every state and condition of life. He exactly fulfilled the law without any irregularity or defect. He did no sin, neither was guile found in His mouth. He was holy, harmless, undefiled, and separate from sinners, as became the High Priest of our profession (Hebrews 7:26). His life was a perpetual comment upon His doctrine, and He practiced the most difficult duties that He enjoined upon others. His piety and devotion to God was constant and fervent, without affectation and noise. His conversation among men was innocent and familiar, without despising the character of the meanest, or unjustly complying with the humors of the greatest of men. His appetites and passions were kept under the severest restraints, and never allowed to transgress the bounds of sobriety and virtue. His zeal for the glory of God did not break forth into any intemperate heats, nor spend itself in a fierce opposition to innocent and indifferent customs of the age, but was perpetually leveled against the pride and hypocrisy, the covetousness and injustice, the unbelief and impenitence, that so universally prevailed among the people of the Jews. In a word, His whole conduct was exact and regular, just and impartial, charitable and inoffensive. And now, what can more powerfully engage and encourage us to our duty than this perfect and persuasive example of our Savior and Sovereign? The best of saints may lead us out of the way, through the darkness of their understandings and the remaining corruption of their natures, but Christ is the way, the truth, and the life. Him we may securely follow, and be assured that our path shall be that of the just, "which shineth brighter and brighter unto the perfect day."

It was one great design of Christ's coming into the world to set this unerring pattern before us, and engage us to copy it. It must indeed be allowed that this was not the principal end of His manifestation in the flesh and of the sufferings which in our nature He endured. It is indisputably evident that the principal thing He had in view was to satisfy the demands of offended justice and make reconciliation for the iniquities of His chosen people; but this does not exclude the proposing of other ends which also contribute to the glory of God and the salvation of men. Accordingly we find the gospel not only recommends the precepts of Christ to our obedience, but also the life of Christ to our imitation. Our Lord Himself expressly enjoined this upon us: "If any man will come after Me, let Him follow Me" (Matthew 16:24). He tells His disciples in John 13:15, "I have given you an example, that ye should do as I have done unto you." And every Christian is predestined of God to be conformed to the image of His Son. What mighty obligations are we then under to comply with the gracious design of heaven, to set this amiable copy forever before our eyes and endeavor after the nearest resemblance to it? With what face can we expect to receive any advantage by His sufferings and death who have no conformity to His Spirit and life, since it is made the inseparable character of everyone who abides in Christ that he walks ever as Christ walked?

And this leads me to say that without this holy imitation of Christ, our profession is but an empty name, and all our hopes of salvation will end in disappointment and sorrow. None are more forward to claim the privileges of Christians than those who are impatient of the yoke of Christ, and will not have Him to reign over them. Multitudes confidently presume upon a title to His merits who impiously reject His authority and government, who live as though the doctrine of godliness were a mystery of iniquity, as if Christ had made the way to heaven so wide that the most profane and dissolute sinners might enter therein. But, alas! These are wild mistakes contrary to the whole tenor of the gospel. The hopes of such empty professors are built upon the sand and will betray them at last into eternal perdition. Christ will own none for His disciples but such as tread in the steps of His example and purify themselves even as He is pure. "Be not deceived, therefore, my brethren, neither fornicators, nor idolaters, nor adulterers, nor effeminate, nor abusers of themselves with mankind, nor thieves, nor covetous, nor drunkards, nor revilers, nor extortioners shall inherit the kingdom of God." Such may please themselves with delusive hopes of the divine mercy, and confidently call Christ, "Lord, Lord," but He will reject their pleas and sentence them to depart from Him, along with the other workers of iniquity.

I shall only add, to imitate the example of Christ is the only way to preserve the honor of religion and adorn the sacred character we profess. Alas! How often is the gospel reproached, and the great Author and Finisher of our faith reviled and blasphemed, through the wicked and ungodly lives of those who name the name of Christ and pretend to be of the number of His disciples? How many walk in direct opposition to His precepts and example, and instead of bearing the resemblance of our Savior in purity and holiness, by their intemperance and debauchery degrade themselves below the character of beasts, and by their pride, envy, and malice transform themselves into the image of the devil!

By these things our sacred profession is brought into contempt and an unbelieving world is filled with dreadful prejudices against the gospel of Christ. If therefore we have any regard to our holy profession, any concern for the honor of our glorious Redeemer, who underwent so much ignominy and reproach for our sakes, will certainly inspire us with a solicitous care not to crucify the Son of God afresh by our iniquities, nor expose His doctrine to open contempt by our loose and immoral behavior. On the contrary, our desire must be to adorn the doctrine of God our Savior by making Him our great pattern and exemplar, and to have the same mind in us as was also in Christ.

To conclude, then, let us adore the divine goodness which has not only given us the most excellent laws for the government of our lives and actions, but has likewise set before us the perfect example of Christ for our imitation. Let us with the deepest shame and sorrow lament all our want of conformity to Christ in the disposition of our minds and the conduct of our lives. Let us realize what need there is of a transforming work of divine grace upon our souls in order to our having the like mind in us as was in Christ Jesus. For we have in us naturally a carnal mind that is enmity against God, and is not subject to His law, neither indeed can be. We must then be born again, be renewed in the spirit of our mind, and have the image of the Son of God by a divine impression deeply fixed and inwrought into all the powers of our souls if ever we hope to succeed in our attempts to copy after the pattern of Christ's heavenly life and to be approved of God as true and genuine imitators of the holy Jesus.

Oh, let this therefore be the subject of our earnest care and prayer, that we may be transformed by the renewing of our mind; that beholding as in a glass the glory of the Lord, we may be changed into the same image, from glory to glory, even as by the Spirit of the Lord. Let the converts in Zion bitterly mourn the remains of indwelling sin, the unhappy source of all those contrarieties to the example of Christ which they find in their temper and deportment. Let us be ever looking unto Jesus, whose blood cleanses from all sin, and whose grace is sufficient for us. Let us continually be acting out that faith which purifies the heart and transforms the mind. Let our love, that powerful principle of imitation, center in Christ and be cultivated by a daily exercise in the pleasing pursuit after Him and communion with Him. Let meditation of Christ be sweet to us; and on His lovely example in particular let us very frequently employ our devout reflections. Upon this let us keep our attentive eye perpetually, for our direction and encouragement; and with invincible resolution let us follow the glorious Captain of our salvation through the most difficult and unpleasant paths of our duty. And though we cannot hope to attain to that transcendent height of perfection which distinguished our blessed Lord, yet let us labor after a growing conformity to Him so that, in some measure, we may be holy as He was holy and perfect as He was perfect, and so be prepared to dwell with Him in the everlasting kingdom of His glory.

O God of infinite mercy, bring us all, through Jesus Christ to Thee, to whom, with the Son and the Holy Ghost, be dominion and praise forever and ever, Amen.

7

The Folly of Losing the Soul for the Gain of the World

"For what is a man profited if he shall gain the whole
world and lose his own soul?" Matthew 16:26

Gain is one of the great and admired idols of the world
which engages the affections and animates the endeavors
of the generality of mankind. For this they rack their inventions, disturb their rest, and hazard their lives. But,
alas! All their care and solicitude is employed in pursuing
after the perishing enjoyments of sense while the incorruptible treasures of heaven are sordidly neglected; all
their thoughts are busied in securing present, visible, and
temporal things while they disregard future, invisible, and
eternal ones. They greedily embrace that which is profitable for the body, which is continually moldering into
dust, but take no care to avoid that which is hurtful to the
soul, which must continue forever.

This is the unaccountable conduct of many who bear
the character of rational creatures, and in the common
affairs of life exercise the greatest sagacity and wisdom.
Therefore our blessed Lord, who is the compassionate
Friend and Savior of souls, who came into this lower world
to enlighten the understanding and correct the mistakes
of the children of men, displays the folly and discovers the
danger of this absurd and unreasonable conduct in the
words of my text.

Here our Savior shows us that the highest pitch of
prosperity which the most aspiring mortal can flatter him-

self with the prospect of bears no proportion to the inestimable value of the soul which is destroyed by the inordinate love of the world; that whatever else may be gained, if the soul is lost, the man makes a most unprofitable bargain and will find himself an infinite loser when he comes to balance the account. Now, that I may treat this point in a practical and convincing manner, I shall (by divine assistance) endeavor to show that it is the too-common practice of the children of men to lose their souls so that they may gain the world, and that such make a most unprofitable bargain and in the end will sustain an invaluable loss.

1. It is the too-common practice of the children of men to lose their souls for the gain of the world. This, I confess, is a melancholy reflection, and, a stranger to mankind would hope, an uncharitable reproach on human nature. Who could imagine that reasonable creatures, endowed with immortal souls and capable of distinguishing between good and evil, who manage their temporal affairs with such ingenuity and prudence, with such circumspection and diligence, should yet be so scandalously negligent in their eternal interests and suffer their nobler part to perish without thought or concern?

But, alas! Our daily observation affords us innumerable instances of this astonishing madness and folly. How many, who once made a visible profession of the gospel, have in times of persecution and distress apostatized from the Christian faith and renounced their God and Savior through their fond attachment to the world? Our Lord has positively assured us in Matthew 10:33 that if we deny Him before men, He will also deny us before His Father who is in heaven. How many, through carnal and ambitious views, have vitiated the great doctrines of religion by impure and erroneous mixtures, and propagated even damnable heresies, denying the Lord who bought them, upon whom St. Jude pronounces a fearful doom and tells us that they are wandering stars, for whom is reserved the blackness of darkness forever? How many, who maintain the purity of the faith and outwardly appear as the children of the kingdom, are yet impatient of the yoke of Christ's authority and government, and practically say that they will not have Him to reign over them? Are not men oftentimes convinced that the service of God is worthy of their highest regard, and that the kingdom of heaven demands their first and most solicitous care, who yet allow their farms and their merchandise, the business and enjoyments of the world, to vanish these things out of their minds and to engage them to neglect the great salvation? How many are so intent upon increasing their estates and managing their worldly employments to the best advantage that they have no time to attend upon the daily devotions of the family and closet, and frequently neglect the public worship of the church? What is more common than to see men break through all the sacred rules of justice and charity, and try all the methods of oppression and violence to advance their secular interests and gratify their insatiable ambition and avarice? How often do we find unthinking sinners shaking off the awful bonds of religion and laying the reins upon the neck of their impetuous lusts, only that they may please an intemperate appetite or enjoy the beastly pleasures of a lascivious moment?

In all these, and too many other instances to be mentioned at present, the children of men lose their souls for the honors and profits, the pleasures and advantages of the world. Therefore the world is represented in Scripture as one of the great enemies with which the Christian has to contend. And St. Paul tells us that the love of money (and, I may add, of all the other pomps and vanities of life) is the root of all evil, which, while some have coveted after, they have erred from the faith and have pierced themselves through with many sorrows (1 Timothy 6:10).

2. I am to show that those who lose their souls so that they may gain the world make a most unprofitable bar-

gain. And this will appear if we consider that the gain they propose is inconsiderable, and that the loss is invaluable.

• The gain they propose is inconsiderable. This the wisest of men in all ages have declared, the most prosperous men have always experienced, and the sinner himself will be obliged sooner or later to acknowledge. And this truth will shine forth in a convincing light if we weigh the following particulars:

The good things of this world are always uncertain, and no man has any assurance that he shall obtain that which he seeks after.

When they are obtained, they afford no solid satisfaction and pleasure.

At best they are but short-lived, and transitory enjoyments.

The good things of this world are always uncertain, and no man has any assurance that he shall obtain that which he seeks after. Our Savior sets the world in the most advantageous view, and supposes a case which never did (and in all probability never will) happen: that a man is so successful in his pursuits as to get the whole world in his possession, and to have all its glories and enjoyments under his command and at his own disposal. This is what few are so vain as to aspire after, or so ridiculous as to flatter themselves with the hopes of obtaining. All that the generality of men can propose to themselves is to gain some empty titles of honor, to make a shining figure upon this earthly stage, and enjoy a larger share of wealth and pleasure than the rest of their fellow mortals.

But how often are men miserably disappointed in that which they so impatiently pursue? How frequently do all their gilded prospects and flattering expectations suddenly end in vexation and remorse? The covetous extortioner, who grinds the faces of the poor and fills his coffers with the spoils of the fatherless and widow, almost always finds the curse of God attending his ill-gotten wealth, who scatters the gains of oppression and injustice. The voluptuous epicure who is fondly devoted to the sinful gratifications of sense is often miserably deceived in his guilty pursuits, and by pampering the flesh lays a melancholy foundation for the most painful and loathsome diseases. The proud and ambitious seldom arrive at that height of honor and authority they aspire after; at best they stand upon a slippery precipice and frequently tumble down into the depths of contempt and obscurity. Such uncertainties as these attend all the admired vanities of the world, which exceedingly depreciates their value.

But let us suppose a man to attain to the height of his wishes, and to possess all the good things of this world that his heart can desire. Yet . . .

When they are obtained, they afford no solid satisfaction and pleasure. They belong only to the body, the meaner part of man, and are so far from being the proper happiness of a reasonable creature that we enjoy them in common with the beasts that perish. They may for a while gratify the senses and please the inclinations of animal nature, but by frequent repetition they soon become nauseous and end in satiety and loathing.

This we find by the example of Solomon, the wisest of men and the most prosperous of princes, who was advanced to the empire of Israel, the greatest and most powerful nation then upon the earth. He enjoyed so vast an affluence of riches that in his time gold was in plenty as iron, and silver as the stones in the street. His fame was so extensive that it brought the Queen of the South from the remote corners of the earth to admire his wisdom and be a spectator of his greatness and glory. Yet he wandered through the wide creation in search of happiness, ran through all the scenes of sensual pleasure to gratify his unbounded appetites, did not keep his eyes from anything which they desired, nor withheld from his heart any joy which it sought after (Ecclesiastes 2:10). And yet, after all his costly and laborious experiments, he wrote "vanity" upon every mortal joy, and declared all the pleasures of earth and sense to be but vexation of spirit.

And we have not only the opinion of Solomon to convince us of this important and affecting truth, but the experience of all ages to establish us in the belief of it. Yea, we daily see that the most prosperous condition of life is so far from securing that peace and contentment of mind, which is the only foundation of true satisfaction and happiness, that, on the contrary, the great men of the earth stand peculiarly exposed to a thousand disquieting accidents, and are generally loaded with a superior weight of anxiety and care. Hence we read of emperors who have voluntarily laid down their crowns and wisely descended from that height of dignity and power to which others climb with such infinite danger and fatigue, and have found that peace and rest in the retirements of a cottage or a cloister, which they have in vain sought after in the splendors of a court or a palace.

And truly, what can all this world afford us beyond a competent supply of our bodily wants and a suitable provision for the comforts and conveniences of life? And these, if our desires are moderate and we do not give the reins to an ungoverned fancy, may be easily and cheaply provided for. Everything else is burdensome and unprofitable.

The rich man has indeed stronger temptations to gratify his fleshly lusts, and has greater opportunities of indulging himself in sloth and indolence, of wallowing in delicacy and wantonness. He may perhaps please his eye by viewing his mighty stores of useless wealth; he may soothe his pride by being attended with a numerous train of flattering dependants; he may increase his vanity by being treated with abundance of unnecessary complaisance and ceremony. But, alas! None of these things will give rest to a discontented mind or ease to an afflicted body. They cannot recover us to health when languishing on a bed of sickness, or reprieve us from the demands of death one moment beyond the appointed hour. Thus narrow and confined, in many circumstances useless, and at all times unsatisfying, are the good things of this world. Therefore the prophet Isaiah, in chapter 55:2, charges those who waste their days in seeking after them with spending their money for that which is not bread, and their labor for that which does not profit.

However pleasant and valuable these things may be in themselves, they are but transitory and short-lived enjoyments. We hold them all by an uncertain tenure and can't secure the possession of them for a single minute. Providence has innumerable ways to humble the pride of man and to impoverish the wealthiest monarch. God can in an instant throw down the most prosperous sinner from the height of human greatness and glory, and plunge him into a state of the most abject poverty and misery. Riches are uncertain, and are exposed to a thousand accidents. They take to themselves wings, and suddenly fly away from our embraces. Devouring flames may consume them; moth and rust may destroy them, or fraud and injustice may deprive us of what we imagined our most durable treasure. Honor is as precarious as riches; for it consists very much in the applauses of the giddy multitude, who are as inconstant as the wind. Pleasure is an airy dream, and depends upon the sprightliness and vigor of the body, which is liable to the continual assaults of sickness and pain. Thus variable and transitory are all the good things of the world.

But let us for once suppose a man so happy as to have all the wealth of the Indies at his command, all the mighty empires of the world subjected to his government, and all the delights of sense continually flowing into his bosom. And let us suppose this happy man to enjoy all this prosperity uninterrupted by any cross or disquieting accidents, to preserve his health unbroken by any painful diseases, and have every thing his heart can desire accompanying him to the end of life. Yet, alas! His life itself is but a vapor which must suddenly disappear; his days are but as a handbreadth which are quickly hastening to an end; his breath soon goes forth; he returns to the dust, and in that very day his thoughts perish. What will all his vast possessions, his envied honors, and his former pleasures avail him in that dark and distressing hour when he must be stripped of all his beloved enjoyments and descend naked into the gloomy retirement of the grave? Lo! This is the end of all earthly felicity; this is the period of every mortal joy. You see then that the world is but of small and inconsiderable value, even under the most happy and advantageous circumstances.

• I proceed now to consider the invaluable loss they sustain who, for the gain of the world, lose their own souls. This will abundantly evidence their astonishing folly. For the sake of these trifling and transitory vanities, they deprive themselves of the favor of God, forfeit the happiness of heaven, and expose themselves to endless and unutterable misery.

The loss of the soul does not consist in the utter extinction of its being (happy would it be for the wicked if this were all they had to fear), but in an everlasting exclusion from all good, and in suffering the most severe and distressing evils.

It consists in an everlasting exclusion from all good. They shall be banished from the presence of God, where is fullness of joy and from a place at His right hand, where are pleasures forevermore. The gates of the New Jerusalem shall be forever barred against them; and they must remain perpetual exiles from the happy mansions of light and love, where God manifests His astonishing glory to the spotless spirits that surround His exalted throne, and communicates His benignity and goodness to their unutterable joy and transport. They must be entirely shut out from the desirable society of saints and angels, and never taste those satisfying pleasures with which the blessed are continually refreshed and delighted. Though these things may at present make but a faint impression upon the minds of ignorant and besotted sinners, yet they will doubtless have a deep and painful sense of their loss when their eyes are opened to discern the inestimable worth of that happiness they have forfeited, and when they come to see and feel that it is irrecoverably lost to all eternity. What incessant rage and fury, what intolerable horror and despair, will fill their guilty and wretched souls when they find themselves cut off from everything that is desirable and delightful to a reasonable creature, and finally separated by an immovable gulf from the regions of immortal bliss? How will the tormenting passions of malice and revenge distract and distress their minds when they behold the patriarchs, prophets, and apostles, and the whole general assembly of the saints, triumphing in eternal felicity, but themselves numbered with the forlorn herd of accursed fiends, and thrust into blackness of darkness forever!

For they who lose their souls not only stand deprived of heavenly happiness, but are exposed to endless misery and extreme torment. They are confined to the gloomy prison of hell where they are continually devoured by the undying worm, and are wallowing day and night in unquenchable fire; where they feel the inexorable wrath of an offended God, the severe reproaches of an accusing conscience, the merciless cruelty of insulting devils, and the unsatisfied rage of their extravagant lusts and passions. And all these miseries they must endure without the least allay of comfort or gleam of hope, not for a short and limited duration, but without intermission, through the boundless ages of eternity. O ETERNITY! How justly may our thoughts be swallowed up in the contemplation of it? How should it chill our blood and fill our souls with trembling and amazement to think of perpetual horror and despair, of weeping and wailing and gnashing of teeth, forever and ever? And yet this is the appointed portion of the wicked; this the miserable and wretched condition of all those who, for the gain of the world, lose their own souls. How foolish and inconsiderate a bargain they make! How sadly will they find by melancholy experience the truth of our Savior's doctrine in the words: "What will it profit a man if he gain the whole world and lose his own soul?"

Application

Hence we see the false opinion which is commonly entertained of the world and its enjoyments. This world puts on a gay and beautiful appearance, and strangely captivates the hearts of the children of men. It contains many things which are agreeable to the body, and which are necessary to our support and convenience, while we dwell upon earth. It was originally designed for our use, and when improved aright has a happy tendency to assist and strengthen us in the service of God. But through the corruption of our nature, the creature is made subject to vanity, and sadly perverted to the service of sin and Satan. Through the idolatrous love of the world, the hearts of men are alienated from God, the Fountain of their being and the only object of their blessedness, and fixed upon deceitful follies which betray them into endless perdition and misery. The world makes large offers of happiness and pleasure to delude us into its embraces; but its performances are never adequate to its promises, and miserably disappoint our expectations. Its most inviting dainties, though agreeable for the present, yet in the end still sting like a serpent and bite like an adder. Its most delicious morsels, though sweet in the mouth, yet turn to wormwood and gall in the belly. While it pleasantly smiles in our face, like a false and treacherous friend, it robs us of our happiness and pierces us through with many sorrows.

How many are there who, in their early youth, had serious impressions of religion, and to all appearances bid fair for the kingdom of heaven, have turned from the way of righteousness through the tumultuous hurries of worldly business, or through the prevailing charms of sensual pleasure? How many are there who, by an unnecessary conversation with the profane and ungodly, have corrupted their virtue and good manners and been enticed into the chambers of wantonness and reveling, where they have impaired their healths, destroyed their reputations, and damned their souls forever?

Thus the world, though it puts on the flattering appearance of a friend, is really one of our most destructive enemies. It becomes us then always to converse with it with circumspection and care, and diligently to guard against too fond an attachment to its profits and advantages. For the Scripture tells us in James 4:4 that the friendship of the world is enmity to God; and if any man loves the world, the love of the Father is not in him (1 John 2:15).

Let me therefore earnestly dissuade you from the inordinate love of the world, which is so dangerous and destructive to the souls of men. By this multitudes of men daily forfeit all title to the ineffable joys of heaven, and expose themselves to the insufferable torments of hell. And may I not without breach of charity suppose that many of you (O my hearers) belong to that unhappy number! Do not reject the thought, I beseech you, with indignation and contempt, but examine whether my fears have not a real foundation. Are there none of you so fond of the inferior satisfactions of sense that, in defiance of the laws of God your Lord and Master, in contradiction to the remonstrances of your own reason and conscience, you frequently indulge yourselves in rioting and drunkenness, in chambering and wantonness? Are there none of you so immoderately attached to the profits and advantages of the world that you are often chargeable with the un-righteous practices of falsehood and deceit, oppression and violence, so that you may increase your estates and make what you call a profitable bargain? Are there none of you so constantly involved in the hurries of your secular employments that you can find no time for the worship of God in your families and closets, no opportunity for the serious exercises of meditation and prayer, and a diligent attendance upon the sacred ordinances of religion? Do not your consciences testify against you that a great part of your time is wasted away in idleness and indolence, without ever seriously considering the state of your souls, or inquiring what preparation you have made for an eter-nal world? Or if these thoughts sometimes spring up in your minds, do you not industriously endeavor to suppress them, and adjourn the solemn affairs of your souls to a more convenient opportunity? Do none of you, through a sinful compliance with the customs of a degenerate day, conform yourselves to the modish extravagancies and vanities of the age, and break over the sacred bounds of sobriety and strict virtue so that you may escape the char-acter of precisianists and appear with applause among the polite and fashionable part of world?

Apply these things to yourselves, O professors of the gospel; critically examine your hearts and ways, and suffer your consciences to bring in a faithful verdict. And if upon examination you find that you fall under any of the aforementioned characters, you are to be ranked among the number of those fools I have been speaking of who, for the gain of the world, lose their own souls.

Oh, how absurd and unreasonable is your conduct! How inconsiderate and unprofitable a bargain you make! Could you gain the whole world, with all its admired glo-ries and bewitching pleasures, it would be an instance of deplorable madness to purchase such transient and momentary satisfactions at such an infinite expense. But, alas! Among the numerous troops of sinners that are continually posting to the kingdom of darkness, not one ever made so wise and advantageous a bargain; not one ever sold his soul for so considerable a price as the whole world. How the generality of men barter away these noble beings for a despicable trifle, an empty shadow, a vanishing dream! How the lascivious and intemperate forfeit the transporting joys of paradise for the extravagant mirth of a drunken frolic, or the brutish pleasures of a wanton hour! How the idolatrous worldling renounces his title to the incorruptible treasures of heaven for those riches which moth and rust may corrupt, or thieves break through and steal! Yea, how many sport away their souls so that they may please their company and go to hell out of mere complacence and ceremony!

But consider, I beseech you, with what infinite remorse and astonishment will you be filled when you come to review your actions by the light of the eternal world and see your shameful and accursed folly described in its proper colors! How tormenting will be the remembrance of your former filthy and detestable sins, for which you have forfeited the favor of God and provoked His almighty displeasure! With what horror and confusion will you reflect upon your past sensual delights which are now fled forever from your arms, and have left nothing but the stings of guilt behind, everlastingly to distress and torment you! With what rage and despair will you look to the happy mansions of the just, and curse your unaccountable madness and stupidity in so cheaply parting with your hopes of obtaining an interest in them! How bitterly will you reproach yourselves and say, "Ah! Are these the celestial joys which I so ungratefully despised and rejected, and which I foolishly exchanged for the momentary pleasures of sense? Is this that invaluable blessedness which I so wretchedly slighted and disesteemed, and which I have irrecoverably lost for the gains of the world? Are these the rivers of pure and unmixed joy, the vast and unspeakable delights, that I have parted with for the fulsome gratifications of lust, and the short-lived pleasures of sinful mirth and extravagance? What has become of the admired enjoyments which I so passionately doted upon, and for which I renounced a heavenly inheritance? Alas! None of them will now stand by me in my distress, nor can the remembrance of them make any amends for the invaluable loss I sustain. None of them will accompany me in these melancholy abodes where I must now take up my everlasting habitation, nor afford me one gleam of light to abate the horrors of eternal darkness. None of them can extinguish these devouring flames in which I am tormented, nor purchase one drop of water to cool my inflamed tongue!"

Such will be the bitter reproaches and self-condemning reflections of the miserable sinner who has lost his soul forever. How passionately will he then wish that God would give him opportunity to revoke his inconsiderate and sinful bargain! How gladly would he give ten thousand worlds (were it in his power) to redeem that precious and undying soul which he has wantonly thrown away in search of vanity and lies!

Wherefore, let us all be persuaded now, while we have opportunity, to secure the salvation of our souls. The soul is our immortal part, the crown of our nature, the glory of our beings, by which we are exalted above the level of the brute creation, and are allied to the angels of light. Nothing then so highly demands our care and concern, as to prevent their ruin and secure their everlasting welfare. Yea, this is a matter of such infinite consequence that the Son of God willingly parted with the pleasures of His Father's bosom, condescended to live a miserable and afflicted life upon earth, and die a shameful and accursed death upon the cross to redeem them out of the hands of revenging justice and make way for their eternal salvation.

Let us then learn to value our souls and use the utmost industry and diligence to secure their important interests.

Blessed be God that a door of hope is yet open before us, and the offers of salvation are compassionately made unto us. Let us therefore seize the present moment and resign our souls into the hands of God, our faithful Creator, and commit them unto the care of Christ, who is an all-sufficient Redeemer. Let us look down with contempt upon all the flattering charms of sin and sense by which so many are daily betrayed into irretrievable perdition.

Let us earnestly implore the almighty influences of the Spirit of grace that we may be delivered from this present evil world, may be made and preserved unspotted from the world, and escape all its dangerous pollutions. Let us be upon our watch and guard perpetually so that neither its alluring smiles nor its frightening terrors may corrupt our fidelity to Christ or influence us to any willful disobedience to His gospel. Let us take to ourselves the shield of faith, and resolutely resist the strongest temptations of an ensnaring world.

Let us never wax weary and faint in our minds, whatever difficulties we may meet with, whatever trials we may pass through in our way to obtain the victory. But let us continue faithful unto the death, and then we shall receive an unfading crown of life, which God, of His infinite mercy, brings us all through Jesus Christ, to whom be glory both now and forever, Amen.

8

The Nature and Necessity of Conviction

"Now when they heard this, they were pricked in their heart, and said unto Peter, and to the rest of the apostles, 'Men and brethren, what shall we do?' " Acts 2:37

Conviction is the first step to conversion. The sinner must see the evil of his ways before he will be persuaded to amend and reform them. He must be convinced of the malignant nature and destructive tendency of sin, or else he will never be prevailed upon to renounce his darling iniquities and forsake those paths that lead down to destruction and misery.

To this end it is the duty of the ministers of the gospel to set before their hearers a faithful catalog of their crimes, and represent to their view the astonishing aggravations with which they are attended—to strip sin of its false and flattering disguises by which it dazzles the eyes of the children of men, and deceives them to their eternal ruin; to expose its loathsome and abominable nature so that men may be no longer captivated with its treacherous charms, nor deluded into its fatal embraces; to display the terrors of God's wrath, which is proclaimed against impenitent transgressors, so that they may be awakened to a deep sense of their guilt and danger and excited to flee from the wrath to come.

This was the method St. Peter took with his hearers, whose happy success is recorded in my text. He does not address them in the enticing words of human wisdom, but in the demonstration of the Spirit and with power. He does not satisfy himself with a few empty flourishes of wit and some general discourses upon the beauty and excellency of moral virtue, but sets their iniquities in order before them and describes their guilt in all its crimson colors, and particularly charges them with the aggravated sin of rejecting the great Savior of the world and crucifying Him whom God had approved among them by a series of the most wonderful miracles. "Ye men of Israel, hear these words. Jesus of Nazareth, a Man approved of God among you by miracles, and wonders, and signs, which God did by Him in the midst of you, as ye yourselves also know; Him being delivered by the determinate counsel and foreknowledge of God, ye have taken and by wicked hands have crucified and slain. Therefore let all the house of Israel know assuredly that God hath made that same Jesus, whom ye have crucified, both Lord and Christ. Now when they heard this, they were pricked in their hearts."

This plain and pungent address was powerfully impressed upon their consciences by the Spirit of God, and immediately startled them out of their security; conscious of their guilt, they were cast into unutterable anxiety and distress and filled with a trembling concern for their eternal salvation. And this is the usual method in which men are prepared for converting grace, and disposed to accept the invaluable blessings of the gospel. A distressing sense of sin inclines them to give joyful entertainment to the glad tidings of a Savior; a deep impression of their amazing danger excites them to lay hold on the hope that is set before them, and to fly to the city of refuge provided for them. And the general security in which the Christian world is involved is in a great measure owing to their not having this sensible conviction. I shall therefore (by divine assistance) in the following discourse on this subject consider what is implied in this conviction, or wherein it consists, evidence the importance and necessity of it, and then conclude with some practical reflections.

1. First, I am to consider what is implied in this conviction. It intends an affecting sense of our sinfulness by nature and practice. That we are all sinners is a truth universally received; we all acknowledge it in our daily confessions, and none are so absurd as to deny it. But, alas! Very few have suitable impressions of this awful truth, or attend to the affecting consequences that flow from it. Some slight thoughts of their sins perhaps now and then spring up in their minds, but they treat them as unwelcome guests, stifle them with all imaginable ease, and quickly banish them out of their minds lest they should disturb them in their worldly business and pleasure.

But when the sinner's eyes are opened to see the corruption of his nature and the innumerable iniquities of his life and conversation, he has quite different views of himself from what he ever before entertained, and is surprised and confounded at the hideous prospect. His sins rise up in judgment against him and are charged upon the conscience with all their dreadful aggravations; the memory of his youthful follies are revived which had long been buried in darkness and oblivion. His secret iniquities are discovered which he had boldly committed in silence and retirement. He now beholds with amazement the corrupt fountain of original sin from whence all the actual transgressions of his life have been derived, and finds that his whole man is deeply and universally polluted, that the whole head is sick, the whole heart faint; from the crown of his head to the sole of his foot there is no soundness in him (Isaiah 1:5–6). He now sees that his early years have been wasted in vanity and folly; his more vigorous age has been employed in the service of sin and Satan, and that all his time hitherto has been trifled away without any serious concern for the glory of God, the great end of his being, and the salvation of his soul, the important business of life.

Sin no longer appears to him a small and inconsiderable trifle which may be committed without thought and concern, but an odious and detestable evil. He is now convinced that it is a daring affront to the authority of God, his only Maker and Sovereign, an ungrateful abuse of His excellent goodness, which is the fountain of our beings and the foundation of all our mercies; a profane contempt of His laws, which represent the unspotted purity of His nature, and are admirably calculated to promote the universal happiness of the world.

He is therefore filled with horror and surprise when he looks back and considers what innumerable indignities he has offered to the eternal Majesty of heaven, his almighty Maker and bountiful Benefactor; what mighty provocations he has been guilty of towards his generous Patron and continual Preserver. He now sees how vilely he has abused the divine mercies which have laid him under the strongest obligations of gratitude, and perverted them to the service of Satan; how boldly he has despised the threatenings of God's Word, which should have frightened him from sin, and how he has ventured upon God's infinite displeasure to gratify a sordid lust. Thus the sinner in the day of his conviction is confounded with the terrible representation of his numerous and aggravated offenses; his guilt stares him in the face, puts an end to all his evasive pleas, and obliges him to lay his hand upon his mouth and confess with the prodigal, "Father, I have sinned against heaven and in Thy sight, and am not worthy to be called Thy son" (Luke 15:21).

This brings me to say that this conviction is attended with a distressing apprehension of the wrath of God, which by their iniquities they have deserved. Once they could hear the terrors of the law proclaimed from Mount Sinai without fear and distress, and stand unmoved, though the thunders of curses from Mount Ebal uttered their voices against them; with the Leviathan they mocked at fear, and laughed at the glittering sword of divine justice which was brandished before their eyes. They vainly hoped that God would not be so strict as to execute the severity of His justice upon them, and flattered themselves that they would have peace, though they persisted in their iniquities and added drunkenness to thirst.

But now the light of conviction shines in upon their souls; they see the unspotted purity of the divine nature, the equity and reasonableness of the divine commands, and the infinite evil of sin, which is a willful transgression of His laws. And so they are made sensible that death is the just wages of sin and eternal damnation the righteous demerit of their crimes. They see themselves as enemies to God through the wickedness of their hearts, and are every moment exposed to His destructive fury. They admire the astonishing patience of heaven that has so long borne with their numberless provocations and waited to be gracious. They esteem it a wonderful mercy that God has not cut them off in the midst of their iniquities, and hung them up in chains as monuments of His everlasting displeasure. They know that in their present state they are under the condemning sentence of the law, and continually tremble lest they be dragged out to immediate execution. These fears continually terrify and torment them wherever they go, and disturb and interrupt them in all the business and pleasures of life. They lie down in disquietment and terror, and awake in anxiety and surprise. They are filled with awful apprehensions of approaching eternity; they startle at every appearance of danger, and are in a continual fright lest death should surprise them in an unprepared state.

I know that these things are treated with contempt and ridicule by those who are at ease in Zion, and are looked upon as no other than the melancholy dreams of enthusiasm and the effects of a terrified imagination. But sure I am that nothing can be more reasonable than a solicitous concern for our immortal welfare; nothing is a more suitable object of our fear than the blessed God, in whose favor is life and whose wrath is more terrible than death;

and it is impossible for the hardiest mortal, who is thoroughly convinced of the danger of a sinful state and finds himself exposed to the heavy displeasure of almighty God, who finds himself tottering upon the dreadful precipice of eternal misery and knows that there is but a step between him and everlasting burnings, not to be filled with unspeakable anguish and distress, and with the trembling jailor cry out, "What shall I do to be saved?" (Acts 16:30).

But this conviction further implies an utter despair of any deliverance in themselves from these dark and disconsolate circumstances. This aggravates the misery of the sinner, and gives the most bitter accent to their grief and sorrows. In the days of their security they imagined that they could at any time repent of their sins, and by a few importunate addresses for mercy secure a title to the divine favor; but they are now convinced that they have offended an infinite God and stand exposed to the demands of inflexible justice. Wrath from heaven is revealed against them, and will be executed without mercy in its appointed time, if they continue in their present state.

To what sanctuary can they flee and be secure from His avenging arm, at whose rebuke the everlasting mountains are scattered and the deep foundations of the earth totter and shake? To what forlorn corner of the earth can they retire and escape beyond the reach of His knowledge, whose diffusive presence extends to the remotest parts of the creation, and who has all things naked and open before Him? What method can they take to avoid His threatened displeasure? Shall they try by soft and moving entreaties to abate the fierceness of His anger, and excite Him to pity and compassion? Shall they pierce the heavens with their cries, and tire the Holy One of Israel with their incessant importunities? Micah 6:6–7: "Wherewith shall they come before God so as to obtain His favor, or bow themselves before the Most High so as to avert His impending vengeance? Will the Lord be pleased with thousands of rams, or ten thousand rivers of oil? Shall they give their first born for their transgression, and the fruit of their body for the sin of their soul?" Alas! These will not answer the demands of the law or quench the devouring flames of hell. Could they fill the air with their sighs, the heavens with their groans, and spend their days in repentance and remorse, it would not satisfy the justice of heaven nor vindicate the honor of God's violated law. Their prayers are mixed with so many imperfections that God may justly reject them and cast back their solemn sacrifices as dung in their faces. Their confessions of sin may be turned into indictments against them, and a holy God may condemn them out of their own mouths; they are dead in trespasses and sins, and while in this melancholy state cannot perform any duty to the divine approbation and acceptance.

Thus they find they are lost in themselves; and it is beyond the power of the whole creation to deliver them. They have none to flee to but that God whom by their iniquities they have so grievously offended; nothing to depend upon but unmerited mercy, which they have times without number forfeited. "It is not of him that willeth, nor of him that runneth, but of God that showeth mercy" (Romans 9:16). They therefore humble themselves in the dust before God, fall prostrate at the footstool of sovereign grace, and acknowledge that if God utterly casts them off, His throne will be clear and guiltless forever, and they must own His justice even in the regions of torment and misery; that if ever they are saved, the grace of God must triumph over the basest unworthiness, and they shall remain the everlasting monuments of undeserved mercy.

This is that conviction which is preparatory to conversion, by which the sinner is disposed to give a joyful entertainment to the glad tidings of salvation.

2. Here I wish to show the necessity and importance of this conviction. This conviction is necessary so that the

sinner may be awakened out of a state of sin and security, and brought to a serious concern for his eternal welfare. Nothing is more evident than that the greatest part of the world is sunk into a deep sleep of security, and persist in the impenitent practice of sin, notwithstanding the most terrible judgments that are denounced against them, and are every moment ready to be executed upon them. Though they are under the critical inspection of the great and terrible God to whom they are accountable for every action, and upon whom they continually depend for all the comforts and conveniences of life, yet they live in a careless neglect of His service and daily provoke Him to anger, as if they were stronger than He. Though they are endowed with immortal souls which must survive the funeral of the body and exist through eternal ages, yet all their care is confined within the narrow bounds of this life, and they spend their days as if they were to die with the beasts that perish. Though the vengeance of eternal fire is set before their eyes as the unavoidable consequence of their unbelief and impenitence, and the terrors of everlasting damnation are continually sounding in their ears to rouse them out of the sloth and indolence, yet, alas, all these terrible representations have no more influence upon them than thunder upon the deaf and lightning upon the blind. Though the immortal glories of heaven are presented to their view as the reward of faith and obedience, and the ineffable joys of the righteous are described in all the pomp and beauty of eloquence to allure and encourage them, yet they slight these invisible realities as unworthy of their notice and prefer the transitory enjoyments of the world before them.

This is that melancholy state of security which has invaded a sinful world and, till they are awakened out of it, it is impossible that they should ever obtain salvation. Their eyes must be opened to see their misery; their hearts must be affected with a sense of their danger before ever they will be persuaded to flee from the wrath to come, and in good earnest engaged to pursue their future welfare.

Therefore, when God is about to execute the designs of His mercy and to convert any of His chosen people, He sends His Spirit to convict them of sin so that they may be sensible of the punishment they have deserved, to show them that by their ungrateful rebellions against God they are brought under the condemning sentence of the law and exposed to the unutterable torments of hell, and that they stand upon the brink of the infernal gulf and may the next moment be tumbled into the lake that burns with fire and brimstone. And once a sense of guilt is powerfully impressed upon their consciences, when their minds are possessed with a suitable apprehension of their danger, then their ears are opened to instruction. They see the worth of their immortal souls and are anxiously concerned to secure their eternal welfare. Then they are willing to sacrifice their most beloved enjoyments that stand in competition with their future happiness, and to submit to the most self-denying terms that they may escape remediless ruin.

This leads me to say that this conviction is necessary so that the sinner may taste something of the bitterness of sin and be made willing to part with his dearest iniquities. An inclination to sin is deeply implanted in our nature since our first apostasy from God; it is common to the universal progeny of Adam, the primitive transgressor. We were shapen in iniquity, and in sin did our mothers conceive us; and from hence we are naturally disposed to commit it with greediness and to roll it as a sweet morsel under our tongues with affection and delight. Now this disposition of mind must be changed, and the heart must be divided from sin and filled with hatred and displeasure against it— otherwise it is impossible that we should come to Christ and be entitled to the invaluable blessings of the gospel. For God, the righteous Governor of the world, is of purer eyes than to behold iniquity; and Jesus, the compassionate

Redeemer of men, is the Author of eternal salvation only to those who obey Him. The gospel is so far from giving the least encouragement to sin that it declares the severest threatenings against it, and strictly enjoins the sublimest instances of purity and holiness upon all its professors.

It is therefore indispensably requisite that there be a separation made between sin and the soul before any man will accept Christ the Savior or submit to the unalterable terms of mercy. To this end God opens the eyes of His people to see the deadly malignity of sin so that they may detest and abhor it. He uncovers the mouth of the bottomless pit and flashes the flames of eternal vengeance in their faces so that they may avoid those ways that lead down to death and hell. He lets loose their conscience to accuse and reproach them so that hereafter they may be afraid to irritate and offend it. He fills their minds with dark and distressing horrors so that they may remember the wormwood and the gall, and know that it is an evil and a bitter thing that they have forsaken the Lord, and that His fear has not been in them.

This conviction is further necessary to endear Christ to the soul, and dispose us to comply with His gracious invitations. Our blessed Lord is proposed in the gospel as an almighty and compassionate Savior who, by the dignity of His person, the depth of His sufferings, and the perfection and excellency of His obedience, atoned the just displeasure of heaven and made full satisfaction for the offenses of His people. He is set forth in the invitations of grace as able and willing to save all those who come to God in and through Him (Hebrews 7:25). Offers of life and salvation are made to all without exception who will humbly and thankfully accept them. "Whosoever will, let him come and drink of the waters of life freely" (Revelation 22:17).

But sinners, before their conviction, are insensible of their misery, and therefore despise the grace of a Savior. They do not see the avenging justice of God that pursues them, and therefore will not be persuaded to fly to the city of refuge. They do not feel the fatal consequences of sin, and therefore do not seek a deliverance from it. Christ Jesus passes before them in His greatness and glory, but they see no form or comeliness in Him wherefore He should be desired. They are earnestly invited to submit to His righteous demands and bow to the scepter of His grace, but they turn a deaf ear to these alluring calls and obstinately reject His offered mercy. "The whole need not a physician, but they that are sick."

But once they are weary and heavy laden with their sins, they will thankfully come to Christ and take His yoke upon them. When they see hell itself laid flaming in their view, and perceive themselves sinking into that fiery ocean of divine wrath, then they will discern the excellency and value of a Savior, and cheerfully comply with the terms upon which He is offered to their acceptance. They will esteem Him as the chief among ten thousand and altogether lovely, and will prefer an interest in His merits to all the enchanting vanities and pleasures that earth can afford them. With the great St. Paul they will count all things but loss and dung that they may win Christ and be found in Him (Philippians 3:8–9).

Finally, by this conviction we are brought to magnify the grace of God and give Him the entire glory of our salvation. It is the great design of God to glorify the riches of His grace in the redemption of the world by Jesus Christ. And it is the unalterable decree of heaven that every son of Adam shall accept salvation as the gift of unmerited mercy or be made a dreadful sacrifice to the demands of inflexible justice. Every knee must bow at the footstool of sovereign grace or fall unpitied victims to avenging wrath.

Now there is a destructive principle of pride in the hearts of unhumbled sinners who oppose these self-denying terms. They imagine that there are so many good dispositions in their souls, so many amiable virtues in their

lives and conversations, that it would be unjustifiable severity in God to everlastingly cast them off and appoint them
their portion with devils and damned ghosts. They fancy
that they have performed so many acts of piety and devotion to God, and have so laudably observed the rules of
justice and charity to men, that they must stand high in the
divine favor and have a valid claim to eternal life. Thus,
with the church of Laodicea, they think they are rich and
increased in goods, and have need of nothing, not knowing that they are wretched, miserable, poor, blind, and
naked (Revelation 3:17).

When at any time they are startled out of their security
and have their sins brought to remembrance by an awakening sermon or some surprising providence, they make
many promises of amendment, resolve upon a stricter
course of obedience, and so silence the clamors of an uneasy conscience and return to their former state of peace
and security. They build their hopes of heaven upon their
own good intentions and resolutions, their frequent attendance upon religious exercises, and their regular and
inoffensive behavior. They do not perceive the necessity of
the atoning blood of Christ to cleanse away their guilt, nor
their inability to do anything that is spiritually good. They
do not discern the loathsome hypocrisy that attends their
best performances, nor the necessity of an almighty power
to create them anew unto good works.

And while men entertain this fond opinion of their
own sufficiency, and vainly imagine that they have anything of their own to entitle them to the divine favor and
acceptance, they will never truly humble themselves before God and resign themselves as prisoners of his justice.
Therefore, the Most High God, who from eternity designed to save a remnant of the fallen race of men and
make them the everlasting monuments of His victorious
grace, sends His Spirit into the hearts of His elect to convince them not only of their sin and misery, but also of

their inability to help and deliver themselves. He destroys the presumptuous opinion of their own strength and power, levels with the dust the carnal confidences in which they formerly trusted, and shows them that nothing which they can do will appease the wrath of an offended Deity or procure them a title to His favor.

And when they are thus emptied of themselves, they will apply to the overflowing Fountain of benignity and goodness. When they see their pollution and impotency, they will betake themselves to the Lord Jehovah, in whom is everlasting strength and righteousness. When they see the justice of God in their damnation, then they will ascribe to Him the entire honor of their salvation and be prepared to join with the devout psalmist, "Not unto us, not unto us, but unto Thy name, O Lord, be the glory" (Psalm 115:1). It is time now to conclude with some practical reflections upon my subject.

Application

1. This shows us the reason why the preaching of the gospel is so generally unsuccessful, and so few in good earnest seek after eternal salvation. Nothing is more astonishing than to look upon the world of sinners and consider how securely they sleep in the midst of the most terrible dangers, how carelessly they play upon the brink of eternal burnings, and with what cheerfulness and vigor they follow their worldly business and sensual pleasures—though they cannot but know, unless their eyes are judicially blinded by the god of this world, that they are sons of death, and may the next moment be hurried out of this world, and turned into hell with the nations that forget God.

The Most High speaks to them in the voice of thunder, but they regard Him not. He addresses them in the soft and gentle methods of entreaty and persuasion, but they

remain obstinate and unmoved. He compassionately ex-
postulates the case with them and asks them why they will
die. But they impenitently persist in their mad career and
resolutely push on to destruction. Have the workers of iniquity no knowledge, no understanding? Are they turned
into insensible stocks and stones, or transformed into stupid and irrational brutes? How else could it be that they
thus sottishly neglect their eternal interest and provoke
the Lord to jealousy, as if they were stronger than He?
This must be imputed to the dreadful depravation of human nature and the want of a thorough conviction. Their
spiritual powers are so darkened and enfeebled that they
do not see the fatal diseases they are laboring under, nor
startle at the terrors of the Lord that on all hands encompass them. Their consciences are so stupid that the loudest
alarms of divine threatenings do not surprise them. Their
hearts are so hard that all the arrows taken out of the
quiver of God's Word do not wound and distress them.
Such a mortal lethargy has seized them that the same voice
that raises the dead must awaken them, or else they will
sleep the sleep of eternal death.

2. This shows us that it is the most useful method of
preaching which enters into the hearts of men, and gives
them a lively discovery of their guilt and danger. Multitudes under the gospel are so fond of carnal ease and
pleasure that they delight to be flattered in their sins, and
say to the seers, "See not," and to the prophets, "Prophesy
not unto us right things; speak unto us smooth things, and
prophesy deceits" (Isaiah 30:10). And when, on the contrary, the ambassadors of Christ faithfully execute their
commission and unfold the secret abominations of their
hearts, they are apt to treat them with contempt and insolence, and speak of them in the language of Ahab to Mi-
caiah, "I hate this man, because he never prophesies of me
good, but evil." They are fond of those preachers who sew
pillows under their elbows and rock them to sleep in the

arms of their beloved iniquities. They can sit contented while they are only exhorted to some outward reformation, and reproved for those enormous vices that are detestable in the eyes of the world and are a public scandal to human nature. But when the necessity of an inward change is insisted on in order to qualify them for the service of God upon earth, and prepare them for the joys of His presence in a future world; when the importance of a thorough conviction is urged to awaken them out of a state of nature and dispose them for an unfeigned compliance with the terms of the gospel; when the hypocrisy of their hearts is detected and their secret iniquities are brought to light; when they are told that they must feel a distressing sorrow for their sins, esteem their own righteousness as filthy rags, and acknowledge that they justly have become heirs of eternal destruction—then they are offended and enraged, and perhaps stigmatize the preacher as a dreaming visionary, and despise his doctrine as enthusiasm and folly.

Thus were the prophets and the apostles derided in the days of old, and thus have many of the faithful ministers of Christ been treated in all ages ever since. Nevertheless, the foundation of the gospel stands sure; the doctrines of deep and sincere conviction for sin, of man's utter impotence to save and deliver himself, and the absolute necessity of almighty and unmerited grace to the conversion of a sinner will remain unalterable truths till the designs of redemption are completed, till the number of the elect are accomplished, and till these heavens and this earth are no more.

It is therefore the part of every faithful minister to declare the whole counsel of God to His people whether they will bear or whether they will forbear. Such will endeavor to dive into the hearts of their hearers to discover the hidden corruptions of their natures, and unfold the misery to which they are exposed. They will not satisfy themselves in some loose and general harangues, to persuade them to reform the disorders of the outward man and lead a sober and regular life, but will endeavor to expose the deceitfulness of sin, the delusions of Satan, and the danger they are in of being fatally ensnared by his devices They will set before them an unflattering glass in which they may behold their guilt and deformity, and discover those refuges of lies to which they fly for sanctuary and safety so that they may feel the mortal wounds of sin, and apply to the great Physician of souls; and then, being broken off from every deceitful bottom, they may build a sure foundation upon Christ, the unalterable Rock of Ages. This is the most practical and useful method of preaching, and has the greatest tendency to fill the church with true believers, and heaven with sanctified and redeemed souls.

3. How melancholy is the state of careless and unhumbled sinners, notwithstanding their seeming peace and prosperity? If we judge them by their present appearance, they oftentimes seem to be the only happy men. They spend their years in mirth and pleasure, their names are adorned with flattering titles of honor, their houses flourish in wealth and plenty, and they enjoy all the good things of this world that their heart can desire. Their days are not darkened with any afflicting sorrows or their nights disturbed with inward terrors; they eat, drink, and are merry, and think of nothing beyond this gay and sensual life. But, alas! This airy vision of happiness will pass away in a moment as a dream when one awakens; and they are in reality poor and miserable in the midst of their treacherous and deceitful comforts. They are, notwithstanding their present peace, children of wrath, and swiftly posting to inevitable ruin. Do not flatter yourselves then with hopes of happiness and safety while you are at rest in sin. Know to your terror that at present you are under the curse of God, which embitters all the enjoyments of life;

you are destitute of an interest in Christ, without which you must perish with the abhorred of the Lord. The sins which now you are so fond of must be renounced with unfeigned sorrow and remorse or else they will sink you into the bottomless sea of God's wrath. You must be humbled and distressed for your misery upon earth or be fearfully destroyed in the prison of hell. You must now bow to the divine sovereignty and grace or be broken to pieces upon the wheel of His everlasting vengeance. This is the unalterable decree of heaven, and this is the misery that awaits every secure and unhumbled sinner.

Surely then it may be said of your laughter that it is mad. Your happiness is but a delusive dream, and your joy the height of distraction and folly. How much better is it to see sinners in agonies of distress, inquiring the way to salvation, than in pomp and pleasure rushing on to remediless destruction?

4. Hence it follows that it is the highest wisdom of unconverted sinners to seek after a deep and thorough conviction. I know that this is contrary to the grain of corrupted nature, and many of you will be apt to say, "This is a hard saying, and who can hear it?" But I think the reasonableness of this conviction, but above all, the necessity of it, should engage you with incessant importunity to seek after it. Consider, I beseech you, is it not better to mourn here than to be eternally tormented hereafter? Is it not more eligible to see your misery while a door of hope is opened, and that a remedy may be obtained, than to feel it at last when the gate of mercy is barred against you and you are shut up in final despair? Show yourselves men, O ye transgressors! Awake, you who sleep; arise and call upon your God, lest you suddenly perish, and that without remedy. Encompass His throne with continual supplication, that He would give you an affecting sight of your sins, and compassionately save you from those terrible storms of vengeance which will certainly fall upon the wicked and

ungodly. Cherish every conviction that at any time you are favored with, and receive it as a messenger of heaven designed for your good. Welcome the divine influences of the Spirit by which God is striving to awaken and reclaim you, and beware of provoking Him to depart from you. Dread nothing so much as going on in carnal security, which is the blackest symptom of approaching ruin. Tremble lest by your delays you provoke a holy God to give you up to final impenitence and pass that tremendous sentence upon you: "Let him that is filthy be filthy still." And surely it is high time to awake out of sleep and work out your salvation with fear and trembling; for there is no knowledge, work, or device in the grave whither you are hastening. Verily, the time is short; a little more sleep, a little more slumber, and you will awake in everlasting burnings, and be fixed in the congregation of the damned, who no longer hope for divine mercy.

5. To conclude, let the awakened sinner magnify the distinguishing mercy of heaven, which has stopped him in his sins and filled him with a solemn concern for his salvation. Are any of you roused out of that general sleep and insensibility in which the world is involved? Are you filled with awful apprehensions of divine wrath, and anxiously concerned for your immortal welfare? Do not murmur at your present state, though full of uneasiness and trouble. Do not think that God is dealing with you in a severe and rigorous manner; but esteem your convictions as an invaluable mercy. Improve this the day of your visitation with thankfulness and diligence; cry to God with earnestness and perseverance so that your convictions may not wear off till they end in a saving conversion. Let nothing pacify an accusing conscience, let nothing content a disquieted mind, till your heart is truly broken for sin, and broken off from every lust; till you are thoroughly humbled and made unfeignedly willing to accept Christ as your Savior and Lord.

Happy are they who thus have their wills bowed to comply with the invitations of grace, and are effectually turned from darkness to light, and from the power of Satan unto God. What if you now weep and lament while the world rejoices! What if you walk in the bitterness of your souls because of your iniquities, while the wicked dwell at ease and put far from them the evil day, banish all sorrow from their hearts, and chase away their fears with mirth and diversion! Such in this life receive good things, and likewise you evil things; but hereafter you shall be comforted and they tormented. The happy time will shortly come (O repenting souls) when your grief shall be turned into joy, and your pensive groans into cheerful hallelujahs; when you shall join with perfected spirits above in that triumphant song of praise from Revelation 1:5–6 : "Unto Him that hath loved us, and washed us from our sins in His own blood, and hath made us kings and priests to God and His Father; to Him be glory and dominion for ever and ever, Amen."

9

The Nature and Necessity of Preparation for the Coming of Christ

"Wherefore we labor that, whether present or absent, we may be accepted of Him." 2 Corinthians 5:9

Of all the affairs that employ the time and captivate the affections of the children of men, none so justly deserve our attention and concern as a preparation for that awful day when we must stand before the impartial bar of Christ and give an account of the things done in the body. This should be the work of our early years, and engage the strength and vigor of our manly age. But, alas! It is commonly delayed to the dark evening of life, till the melancholy decays of nature warn us of our approaching end.

The specious vanities and trifles of the world divert unthinking sinners from a serious application to the one thing needful; they flatter themselves that the vision is for many days, and they shall have time enough hereafter to secure the favor of their Judge.

The deluge of waters broke in upon the old world in the height of their security, while they were eating and drinking, marrying and giving in marriage, and dispatched them in a moment into irrecoverable misery; and this present earth, which is reserved for the fire of the last day, shall be destroyed in as sudden and irresistible a manner. "As it was in the days of Noah, so shall it be in the days of the Son of Man." When the world is drowned in sin and security, and dreams of nothing but peace and safety, then shall sudden destruction come upon them, as travail upon a woman with child.

Therefore our blessed Savior exhorts His disciples to continual watchfulness and diligence. "Take heed, lest at any time your hearts be overcharged with surfeiting and drunkenness and the cares of this life, and so that day come upon you unawares; for as a snare will it come on all them that dwell on the face of the earth." And every wise, considerate man will receive the solemn caution and avoid the danger of a sudden surprise. Now this can only be done by making it the great business of life to prepare for the coming of our Lord. This was the practice of St. Paul, as we find in our text; and his example is worthy of our careful and diligent imitation.

DOCTRINE: It should be the great study and endeavor of every Christian that he may be accepted of the Lord on the Day of Judgment.

In speaking to this point, I shall, first, consider what is required of us that we may be accepted of the Lord in the Day of Judgment; second, why every Christian should make this his great study and endeavor.

First, I shall consider what is required of us that we may be accepted of the Lord in the Day of Judgment. The case is practical and deserves our close and diligent attention. I shall only insist on a few general, comprehensive articles.

1. We must by faith secure a title to the merits and righteousness of Christ. We are all by nature involved in the guilt of sin, exposed to the condemning sentence of the law, and in danger of suffering the vengeance of eternal fire. The holiest of men are encompassed with innumerable imperfections, and their best performances are defiled with so many blemishes, that should God be strict to mark iniquity, who could stand the fiery trial and appear with safety at the enlightened tribunal of heaven? Hence the humble psalmist vehemently deprecates the strict inquiry of justice: "Enter not into judgment with Thy servant, O Lord! For in Thy sight shall no man living be

justified." And the great doctor of the Gentiles, though among the chief of saints and an eminent apostle, renounces all confidence in himself and counts all things but loss that he may be found in Christ, not having his own righteousness which is of the law, but that which is through faith in Him (Philippians 3:8–9). Not one of the sons of men can perfectly obey the divine commands, nor by anything that he can do or suffer appease the infinite displeasure of a holy God. But the expiatory sacrifice of Christ completely answered the demands of justice, and by His unspotted innocence He vindicated the honor of the law and purchased eternal redemption for His chosen people.

Now if ever we would be acquitted at the bar of God and obtain the favor of our impartial Judge, we must plead not any works of righteousness that we have done, but the meritorious obedience and sufferings of our blessed Savior. And that we may have a title to His invaluable merits, we must by faith accept Him as our only Savior and acknowledge Him as our sovereign Lord and owner, with an entire dependence on His all-sufficient sacrifice, and an unfeigned desire to obey His excellent precepts; for He is a priest upon a throne, a Prince as well as a Savior. And none will be saved by the merits of His blood but those who submit to the scepter of His government. And happy are they who thus by faith receive Him upon the terms of the gospel, for they are delivered from the condemning sentence of the law and may approach the sacred tribunal of justice with a humble confidence of approbation and acceptance.

2. Our natures must be sanctified by the almighty influences of the Spirit, and renewed after the image of the blessed God. Man by nature is not only involved in chains of guilt, but sunk into the most deplorable state of deformity and pollution; his understanding is darkened by clouds of error and ignorance, and filled with mighty

prejudices against the divine and supernatural mysteries of the gospel. His will is stubborn and refractory, impatient of the yoke of God's authority, and inclined to continual rebellion against Him; his affections are captivated to the dominion and tyranny of sin, and placed upon the most degrading and inferior objects.

In short, the whole man is perversely alienated from the life and service of God, and strongly disposed to the most abominable evils. This is the unhappy character of man in a state of unregenerate nature. Hence arises the indispensable necessity of a holy change to qualify us for the acceptable service of God upon earth and prepare us for the ineffable glories of heaven. The understanding must be illuminated by the Spirit of God to believe the certainty and excellency of things unseen and eternal, to perceive the beauty of holiness and the equity and reasonableness of the divine commandments. The native enmity of the sinner's heart must be subdued, and every faculty of the soul brought under a consecration to the service of God. Till this mighty change is produced, the sinner is dead in trespasses and sins, and his most perfect services are a stench and abhorrence in the nostrils of a holy God; and therefore he has nothing else to expect but the awful frowns of his incensed Judge and the distressing thunders of His avenging wrath.

The Lord Jesus Christ is of "purer eyes than to behold iniquity; the heavens are not clean in His sight, and His angels He chargeth with folly." None will be acknowledged and accepted by Him in the great Day of Judgment but such as bear the impression of the divine image, who cleanse themselves from all filthiness of flesh and spirit, and are perfecting holiness in the fear of the Lord. Without this inward purification, the most bright and distinguished profession among men will be disapproved and condemned by our all-seeing Judge. Others indeed may have a name in the church upon earth, and pass for eminent saints in the sight of the world, but they will be excluded from the sanctuary above, and ranked among the workers of iniquity in the day of their decisive trial.

3. A sincere and impartial regard to the law of God is necessary to final acceptance with our Judge. Many who boast of a high profession, and vainly triumph in their gospel privileges, are hypocritical in their pretenses and partial in their obedience to the laws of Christ. With the ancient Pharisees, they are strict in their attendance upon the divine worship, and zealously attached to the outward formalities of religion, but are unjust and oppressive in their dealings, carnal and covetous in their conversations. Still others build their hopes upon a moral and inoffensive behavior towards men, though they are sadly negligent of their obligations to God and live in an avowed contempt of His worship and ordinances A third sort calculate their religion for the public view and make a plausible appearance in the temple, but are strangers to the devotions of the closet; they liberally dispense their alms when the sound of a trumpet proclaims their charity, but are sordidly sparing when there is no prospect of gratifying a vainglorious humor. They are zealous for the Kingdom of Christ when it will advance their honor and interest, but are cold and indifferent when the great doctrines of the gospel are fallen under reproach and boldly assaulted by men of figure and estate.

By such hypocritical pretenses as these, multitudes lull themselves into security and vainly imagine to obtain the favor of God. But, alas! His all-seeing eye pierces through every disguise and marks out the painted formalist, however cautiously he may be concealed. A partial obedience to the divine commands will not stand the trial of an enlightened conscience upon earth, nor be approved by the unerring verdict of heaven. If our hearts condemn us of any secret and indulged iniquity, God "is greater than our hearts and knoweth all things; but if our hearts condemn us not, then we have confidence towards God" and may hope for the divine acceptance (1 John 3:20–21).

If therefore we would enjoy the testimony of an un-reproaching conscience and receive the commendation of our Judge, we must have a sacred respect to every duty, without exception or reserve, and be the same in the secret closet, when no eye but that of God and conscience is upon us, as when we stand upon the open theater of the world and are encompassed with a thousand witnesses. We must bear a universal hatred to sin, though dear unto us as a right hand and a right eye; and we must particularly watch and strive against those darling iniquities which the constitution of our bodies, the disposition of our minds, and our company and business most strongly incline us to the commission of. We must not only pay a strict regard to the important duties of piety towards God, but inviolably observe the sacred rules of justice and charity to men. This will afford us a divine support in the darkest hours of distress, and enable us to say with the inspired apostle, "Our rejoicing is this, the testimony of our conscience, that in simplicity and godly sincerity, by the grace of God, we have had our conversation in the world" (2 Corinthians 1:12).

4. A frequent review of our lives and actions, and a judging of ourselves for our sins, is a happy preparative for the great day of trial. It is the wisdom of persons engaged in worldly business to frequently survey their accounts and inquire into the state of their affairs. And it is equally incumbent on the children of light to examine into the state of their souls so that they may know what duties they have omitted, what sins they have been guilty of, and what progress they have made in the Christian course. While we tabernacle in flesh and are surrounded with so many ensnaring objects, the best of men will be sometimes surprised into sin through the remaining corruption of their natures, or be overborne by the strength and violence of temptations. It is therefore highly necessary that we fre-

quently review our conduct and compare it with the law of God, the unerring rule of our duty, so that we may be acquainted with our errors and miscarriages.

This will awaken our repentance for our daily offenses and engage us to a fervent application to the blood of Christ for pardon, that Fountain which is set open for sin and for uncleanness. This will inspire us with unfeigned resolutions of amendment and excite our care and vigilance to avoid those sins for which we have so severely judged and condemned ourselves. And this has a blessed tendency to keep our consciences clear from indulged iniquities, and to prevent that awful surprise that must seize the impenitent sinner when the midnight cry shall awaken him out of his security and summon him to the tremendous judgment seat of Christ.

What an unspeakable happiness will it then be to have our conscience purified from defiling sins, and all breaches made up between God and our souls! Such may hear the sound of the last trumpet with calmness and serenity of mind, and stand secure amidst the shocks of a dissolving world.

5. Continual meditation upon the certainty and solemnity of a future judgment is an excellent means to engage us to a serious preparation for it. There's nothing that more highly deserves our serious and attentive regards, and yet nothing that unthinking sinners so industriously banish out of their minds. What subject of equal importance can employ our thoughts and engage our attention as this great and illustrious event? This will unfold the mysteries of divine providence, clear up the difficulties of His government, and display the perfections of the Deity in their brightest glories. What are all the dazzling triumphs of the mighty princes and generals of the earth but childish and despicable trifles, in comparison with the pompous descent of our almighty Savior, attended with the shining equipage of heaven! If now we are affected with the ap-

pearance of an earthly judge, attended with the ministers of justice, to enforce the execution of the law, is it not infinitely more reasonable to employ our thoughts upon that vast and most affecting scene in which all the posterity of Adam shall stand before the throne of God and receive an irrevocable sentence of happiness, or misery, according to their works! Especially if we consider that we are all deeply concerned in this great transaction, and must bear a part on the joys and triumphs, or in the fears and terrors of that awful day. The neglect of this great duty is one cause of the general impiety and wickedness of the world, and makes them presumptuous and secure in the midst of amazing dangers.

We should therefore call off our thoughts from the contemptible vanities of time and sense, fix them upon a future judgment, and consider its important consequences so that we may be quickened to prepare for that great and terrible Day of the Lord.

I now proceed to consider, second, why it should be the great study and endeavor of every Christian to prepare for the Day of Judgment, and that he may then be accepted of the Lord.

1. It is a work of the greatest difficulty, and requires the utmost self-denial, resolution, and diligence. This our Master and Judge has warned His followers of so that they might not please themselves with vain dreams of carnal ease and pleasure on the way to the kingdom, but might be prepared to encounter the hardships that attend the Christian life. He has assured us that the kingdom of heaven suffers violence, and the violent take it by force. He has commanded us to strive to enter in at the strait gate, for many will seek to enter in and shall not be able (Matthew 11:12; Luke 13:24).

The duties enjoined upon us are contrary to the corrupt inclinations of flesh and blood, and require the deepest mortification and self-denial. The carnal mind is enmity to God, impatient of restraint, and madly bent upon those ways that lead to destruction and ruin. And what can be a greater difficulty than to offer violence to our depraved natures, to subdue our darling lusts, and maintain a continual war against ourselves?

And the difficulty is greatly increased by the external impediments that attend us. Satan, the grand adversary of souls, shoots his envenomed arrows on every side to wound and destroy us, and uses a thousand unobserved and shrewd stratagems to entice us from God and our duty. The men of the world will revile and persecute us for our fidelity and diligence in the discharge of our duty, and practice the most destructive methods to corrupt and defile us. And is it not a laborious task to withstand the rage of earth and hell, to resist the infection of evil examples, and stem the tide of a degenerate age? Is it not difficult to oppose the soft enchantments of vice and escape the corruption that is in the world through lust? What manly courage and resolution is required to subdue the inveterate habits of vice, to conquer our native indisposition to holiness, and to bear up against the subtle insinuations and violent assaults of temptation? Now this must be done by everyone who would be faithful to the cause of Christ and obtain the approbation of his Judge. Therefore we are commanded not to be slothful in business, but fervent in spirit, serving the Lord (Romans 12:11), and are exhorted to give all diligence to make our calling and election sure (2 Peter 1:10).

2. This life is the only season allotted for this great work. The foundation of our future happiness must be laid in this world if ever we expect to receive the reward of future glory. We must now sow the seeds of righteousness if we would rejoice in a plentiful harvest at the resurrection of the just. The divine life must be begun upon earth so that it may receive its last and finishing stroke of beauty

and perfection in heaven. Now we must arise from the death of sin and follow Christ in the regeneration; and then we shall hereafter rise unto glory and be accounted worthy to stand before the Son of Man in the day of His appearance and kingdom. This is the time of trial in which we must engage in the Christian warfare, fight the good fight, and continue faithful unto death, so that in the Day of Judgment we may give up our account with joy and receive a crown of life. For in that day the rewards and punishments will be distributed according to our present spirit and behavior, and the sentence that shall be passed will be final and irreversible. No appeal can be made from this high tribunal; no review can be obtained in the court of heaven; the Judge will then be inexorable and the state of all mankind unalterable.

3. Which leads me to say that if death surprises us in an unprepared estate, the Day of Judgment will be a day of inconceivable terror and amazement. Unutterable anguish and distress will seize upon impenitent sinners when they shall see Him whom they have pierced and remember the innumerable indignities they have thrown upon Him. They will no longer be able to drown the voice of conscience in floods of wine, nor drive away their melancholy thoughts with music and dancing, with gaiety and entertainment. The principles of infidelity which are now so greedily imbibed against the repeated admonitions of conscience and to the reproach of human nature will then afford but a poor and feeble support. Unbelievers will receive a terrible conviction that the great doctrines of the gospel are not the dreams of enthusiasm, nor the subtle inventions of the designing priest and the crafty politician. They will find by sad experience that God is not to be mocked, that His wrath is not to be trifled with, nor the methods of His grace to be insulted and blasphemed.

What excuse will plead for their insolent defiance of heaven, their stupid neglect of the invaluable offers of a

Savior, their obstinate continuance in sin, in opposition to
the convictions and strivings of the Holy Spirit? What defense will they make for their contempt of their baptismal
vows and their preferring the pomp and vanities of this
world to the favor of God and the ineffable joys of His
presence?

How will their countenance be appalled and their
souls filled with terror when they shall see their almighty
Judge, whose authority they have despised, whose laws they
have disobeyed, and whose merits they have blasphemed,
descending in the clouds of heaven, attended with the
dreadful artillery of His wrath, to vindicate the authority
of His laws and punish the contempt of His government!
What confusion and horror will surprise them when they
meet with their sinful and defiled bodies, the ancient
partners of their wickedness, which have been the detestable instruments of their profaneness and impiety, their
oppression and cruelty, their riot and debauchery! With
what weeping eyes, astonished countenances, and trembling hearts will they stand before the tribunal of Christ
when their secret impurities, their hypocritical disguises,
their lewd and wicked intentions, shall be publicly detected and exposed to the contempt and abhorrence of
the congregation of the righteous! What distressing agonies and convulsions must seize them when they shall be
condemned in the day of trial, and their incensed Lord
shall pass that unalterable sentence upon them, "Depart
from Me, ye cursed, into everlasting fire, prepared for the
devil and his angels!"

If the sentence of an earthly judge is so much to be
dreaded, and excites in a condemned criminal such bitter
lamentations, how inconceivably more terrible will be the
final determination of our eternal Judge which condemns
the wicked to endless and intolerable misery! With what
vehemence and importunity will they lift up their cries for
that mercy which now they affront and despise! But, alas!

Their righteous Judge will then be deaf to their loudest entreaties. Once He compassionately called upon them to flee from the wrath to come, and sent His ambassadors to invite them to accept eternal happiness; but they insolently rejected His invaluable offers and ungratefully abused the methods of His grace. They despised His wise counsels and disregarded His awful reproofs; therefore He will mock at their calamity and laugh when their fear comes. Not all the surprising miracles of His love, not all the bitter agonies and sorrows of His death, not the sacred streams of His blood, which was shed for the redemption of a guilty world, could persuade them to forsake their sins and devote themselves to His service; but they obstinately retained their beloved lusts and preferred their sins before their Savior. His abused goodness will therefore be converted into fury, and the door of mercy will be bolted against them forever.

4. But I turn to a brighter scene, and proceed to say to those who are found in a state of favor and acceptance with Christ, the Day of Judgment will be a time of unspeakable joy and refreshment. With what satisfaction and pleasure may they who live soberly, righteously, and godly in the world look for that blessed hope and the glorious appearance of the great God their Savior, who has loved them with an everlasting love, chosen them from among the degenerate mass of mankind, washed them from their sins in the fountain of His blood, and is coming to receive them to His arms and embraces forever!

With what ecstasies of joy and triumph will they salute the happy day when their glorified Redeemer shall descend to this lower world in the pomp and character of an incarnate God, clothed with majesty and strength, and attended with all the honors of His exalted state! How will they rejoice with joy unspeakable to behold Him who for their sakes made Himself of no reputation, became poor, and passed through an amazing scene of the most dismal sufferings, even the Man Jesus Christ, seated upon a triumphant throne of glory, and surrounded with a shining crowd of angels, archangels, and the spirits of just men made perfect!

How agreeable a meeting will they have with their ancient bodies, the companions of their meekness, humility, and self-denial, which have for so many years been confined to the dark and silent grave, and covered with deformity and corruption; but are now raised from the dust of death, clothed with immortal youth and beauty, and fitted for a state of perfect innocence and happiness! How transporting a sight will it be to behold the goodly company of the prophets, patriarchs, and apostles, and all those brave and generous souls who in all ages of the church have sacrificed their lives for the testimony of Jesus, and have followed their Lord and Master in suffering and patience, in purity and heavenly-mindedness, all united in one vast assembly, and shouting forth the praises of their exalted Redeemer! How will it refresh them to have their injured innocence publicly vindicated, their secret piety and charity applauded, and their holy thoughts and intentions proclaimed, to their immortal honor! But what heart can conceive, what tongue can utter, the mighty transports that will possess the saints when their God and Savior shall openly acknowledge them as His friends and favorites, and declare them heirs of eternal glory! With what raptures of joy will they hear that happy sentence pronounced upon them, "Come, ye blessed of My Father, inherit the Kingdom prepared for you from the foundation of the world!" after which they shall immediately enter into the heavenly paradise, and be forever with the Lord.

And now, upon the whole, since preparation for a future judgment is a work of so much difficulty and pains; since this life is the only time allotted for this great work; since the consequences of an unprepared state are so in-

finitely terrible and the advantages of the contrary so inconceivably joyful—surely it behooves every Christian to
make it his great study and endeavor.

"Wherefore," in the words of 2 Peter 3:14, "beloved, be
diligent that ye may be found of your Judge in peace,
without spot and blemish." This is the natural and necessary counsel upon what has now been delivered unto you;
and what is more important than a speedy and unfeigned
compliance with it? Especially if we consider that the time
of this great event is reserved among the secrets of heaven,
and wisely concealed from the most sagacious and inquisi-
tive minds. So that, for all we know, the Judge may be now
standing at the door; and before the dawn of another day
the last trumpet may sound and summon us to the bar of
Christ. And considering the infidelity and profaneness, the
corrupt principles and dissolute manners of the present
age, we have common reason to believe that day hastens
upon us quickly; for "when the Son of Man cometh, shall
He find faith upon the earth?" (Luke 18:8).

These things may now be received with scorn and banter, and the awful warnings of heaven may be treated as
the melancholy dreams of a gloomy and superstitious
mind; the scoffers of the present day may break their impious jests upon religion, and triumph in their present
peace and security. But we are assured from the unerring
oracles of God that the day of the Lord will come "as a
thief in the night, in which the heavens shall pass away with
a great noise, and the elements shall melt with fervent
heat; the earth also, and the works that are therein, shall
be burnt up" (2 Peter 3:10). It is therefore our wisdom
and duty to attend to the advice of our Lord with which
we conclude from Matthew 24:42–46: "Watch therefore,
for ye know not what hour your Lord doth come. Be ye
ready; for in such an hour as ye think not, the Son of Man
cometh; and blessed is that servant whom his Lord, when
He cometh, shall find so doing."

10

The Manner and Circumstances of Christ's Appearance at the Last Day

"For the Son of Man shall come in the glory of His Father with His angels; and then He shall reward every man according to His works." Matthew 16:27

The dispensation of the gospel is admirably calculated to reclaim a sinful world from the paths of error and delusion and to persuade the children of men to consult their duty and happiness. Its doctrines are sublime and excellent, worthy of their heavenly descent, and come recommended to our faith by the brightest evidences of a divine authority. Its precepts contain the noblest rules for our moral conduct and are happily designed to exalt and purify the nature of man and advance the universal prosperity of the world.

And since we are at present in a corrupt and degenerate state, disinclined to our duty and indeed filled with prejudices against it, therefore the wise Author of our beings has seen fit to enforce His laws by suitable sanctions, and engage us to obedience by the most powerful and persuasive arguments. Hence in the gospel there everywhere appears the greatest severity to dissuade us from sin, and the highest condescension and goodness to allure us to holiness.

The Eternal Majesty of Heaven is sometimes revealed in the amazing terrors of His wrath as a consuming fire to the workers of iniquity; at other times He appears in the bright displays of His mercy as a tender and indulgent father to those who serve and obey Him. And the great Savior of souls is represented as one who died a sacrifice for the sins of the world, and compassionately invites the children of men to come to Him so that they may have life; but He will shortly appear in flaming fire to take vengeance on those who do not know God and do not obey the gospel of Christ.

These different representations are wonderfully suited to influence the hopes and fears of men, the two great ruling passions of our nature and the secret springs of our actions, and have a happy tendency to deter us from all ungodliness and unrighteousness, which lead to destruction and misery, and to engage us to a steadfast adherence to our duty, which is the way to immortality and glory. Our blessed Savior having therefore urged upon His disciples the necessity of denying themselves, taking up their cross, and following Him, their Lord and Master, in humility and suffering, enforces all with the awful consideration that the Son of Man shall come in the glory of His Father, with His angels, and then He shall reward every man according to his works. In speaking to these words (by divine assistance), I shall, first, consider the manner of Christ's second appearance, and, second, the work that He will then perform.

1. First, I am to consider the manner of Christ's second appearance. When He first left the mansions of glory and descended into this lower world, He came in a state of humility and meanness, and stooped to numberless hardships and difficulties so that He might answer the design of His manifestation in the flesh and accomplish the great work of redemption. But His second advent will be with surprising majesty and glory, to execute vengeance upon the ungodly and vindicate the cause of His despised gospel.

When God came down upon Mount Sinai to proclaim the law to the children of Israel, the glory of the Lord appeared like devouring fire and the mountain was covered with darkness and smoke. So terrible was the sight that Moses, the friend of God, exceedingly feared and quaked; the whole army of Israel was struck with amazement and cried out in distress, "Let not God speak with us, lest we die." If such surprising terrors attended the first promulgation of the law, with what awful solemnity will the Lawgiver appear when He comes to avenge the quarrel of His covenant, and punish the profane contempt of His authority?

The Scriptures represent this awful event in the most lofty and magnificent language. Amazing prodigies will usher in this illustrious day and proclaim the descend of our almighty Judge; continual tragedies will be acted on the great stage of nature, and this lower world will be involved in universal confusion and disorder. The sun shall be turned into darkness and the moon into blood; the stars of heaven shall start from their exalted orbs and the powers of the heavens shall be shaken; perpetual thunders shall roar from the lower regions of the air, the earth shall tremble and quake, and the foundations of the hills shall be removed (see Joel 2:31; Matthew 24:29; Psalm 18:7). "Then shall appear the signs of the Son of Man in the heavens" (Matthew 24:30), and give the world a convincing evidence of the near approach of the great and terrible day of the Lord. At this amazing sight the inhabitants of the earth shall mourn, and the sinners in Zion shall be horribly afraid.

In the midst of their perplexity and distress, the Son of Man shall descend in the clouds of heaven with power and great glory. He will appear in the pomp and solemnity of an incarnate God, and assume a glory and magnificence suitable to the dignity of His office. His personal glory will be inexpressibly great. His eyes will sparkle like flames of fire, His countenance will shine with dazzling beams of majesty and beauty, and His whole body be bright and luminous beyond the sun in its meridian splendor. Thus He is described in the vision of St. John: "In the midst of the seven candlesticks was one like the Son of Man. His head and His hair were white as wool, as white as snow, His eyes were as a flame of fire, and His countenance was as the sun shining in its strength" (Revelation 1:13–14, 16).

He will also come in the glory of His heavenly Father and be clothed with the authority of the universal Judge of the world. God has appointed Him King upon His holy Zion, and proclaimed an unalterable decree that to Him every knee shall bow—not in scorn and derision, as in the days of His infirmity and suffering, but with the deepest humility and reverence—and every tongue shall confess His royal dignity and power, not with an insulting scoff, but in submissive postures of adoration.

But to increase the glory of His appearance, He will be attended with a splendid and numerous equipage becoming the dignity of His person and the exalted character He sustains. The innumerable host of angels shall leave the mansions of heaven and attend their descending Lord to obey His sovereign orders and adorn the triumph of His justice. The general assembly of the saints, whom He has redeemed by His invaluable blood, and sanctified by His all-conquering grace, shall forsake the celestial paradise and accompany the great God our Savior in His illustrious progress through the skies. Thus the patriarch Enoch prophesied of old: "Behold, the Lord cometh with ten thousands of His saints to execute judgment on the ungodly" (Jude 14–15). And the prophet Daniel assures us that a thousand thousands shall minister unto Him, and ten thousand times ten thousand shall stand before Him (Daniel 7:10). St. Paul tells us that He shall be revealed from heaven with His mighty angels (2 Thessalonians 1:7). Those spotless spirits shall be clothed in their brightest robes of glory, and appear in visible splendor to the inhabitants of the earth. And how vast and surprising a figure will they make! How awful and majestic will be the appearance of our Judge when He shall assume His own proper greatness and be attended with the shining inhabitants of heaven! Who may abide the day of His coming, or be able to stand before His awful tribunal? How will all nations fall prostrate at His footstool and tremble at His presence, who can by a word of His mouth sentence them to the depths of misery, or advance them to the height of glory and happiness?

2. This brings me to the other thing proposed, which is, second, to consider the work that He will perform. Then shall He reward every man according to His works. And this includes three things.

(1) All mankind shall be summoned before Him. No sooner shall the Judge descend to this lower world and erect His throne in the air but they who are in their graves shall be awakened out of the sleep of death, and all the inhabitants of the world be cited to appear before the judgment seat of Christ. The voice of the archangel, the chief of the heavenly host, shall echo through the wide creation and penetrate into the secret caverns of the earth; at this mighty sound the dead shall start out of their dusty beds and all the descendants of Adam shall be compelled to obey the call; those who are alive shall be immediately changed and prepared to make their personal appearance at the bar of their Judge. Thus the Scripture assures us: "We shall all stand before the judgment seat of Christ." Every one of us shall give an account of himself unto God. The universal Father of men, without respect of persons, judges every man according to his work. He does not accept the persons of princes, nor does He regard the rich more than the poor, for they are all the work of His hands (Romans 13:1; 1 Peter 1:17; Job 34:18–19).

Civil distinctions make a mighty sound among men, and persons of superior wealth and power are admired and applauded like so many deities, by their servile flatter-ers; hence they are apt to swell with pride upon the account of their elevated circumstances, and vainly hope that they shall be treated with deference and respect at the future judgment. They flatter themselves that God will not be strict to mark iniquity in men of their dignity and station, but that He will make some favorable allowances for the excesses and follies which are so common among men of figure and estate in the world. But, alas! These are vain imaginations; the sovereign Ruler of the world pays no regard to earthly greatness, neither has He any value for those distinctions which are made by birth and estate. The great potentates of the earth, who are cried up as gods by deluded mortals, are in His sight but contemptible worms of the dust. In that day they will be divested of all their stately ornaments, deprived of the signs of their greatness and power, and stand upon a level with the meanest slave. Death, the universal conqueror, pays no complements to their quality, but arrests them without ceremony or respect, and their impartial Judge will irresistibly summon them to His tremendous bar. The mighty Caesars and Alexanders who have depopulated the earth by their destructive swords, and sacrificed nations to their unbounded lusts, shall tremble at His appearance and curse their ambition and madness. Thus this astonishing scene is represented by St. John in Revelation 6:15–17: "And the kings of the earth, and the great men, and the rich men, and the chief captains, and the mighty men, hid themselves in the dens and rocks of the mountain, and said to the mountains and rocks, 'Fall on us, and hide us from the face of Him that sitteth upon the throne, and from the wrath of the Lamb; for the great day of His wrath is come; and who shall be able to stand?' "

And as none are too great and mighty to be called to an account, so none are too mean and contemptible to be taken notice of. They who have made no figure among men, but have spent their days in want and obscurity, will not be overlooked in this vast assembly, but will be strictly examined whether they have submitted to the wise disposals of providence and improved the talents committed to their trust. Those who are in the morning of their youth, and in the strength and vigor of their age, shall be brought into judgment for their unmindfulness of their great Creator, and their criminal indulgence of sensual pleasures. Ignorant, uninstructed heathens, who have inhabited the wild and desolate corners of the earth, shall be called to account for transgression of the law of nature and their abuse of the divine goodness. The learned and civilized nations, who have been favored with the light of the gospel and early instructed in the will of heaven, must answer for their superior advantages and their neglect of the means of grace and salvation. Such as will not now approach the throne of divine mercy must then appear at the bar of inflexible justice. Thus all mankind of every nation and language, of every quality and condition, of every age and sex, must be judged in the great day. What a grand and solemn sight will this be, to behold all the successive generations of men standing together in their respective orders and waiting for their decisive trial!

(2) This leads me to say that on that day men shall be called to a strict account for all their actions. So the royal preacher informs us: "God will bring every work into judgment, with every secret thing, whether it be good or whether it be evil" (Ecclesiastes 12:14). All the actions of men are recorded in the book of God's remembrance and shall be disclosed to the public view of the world in the great day of the revelation of all things.

Unthinking sinners are apt to imagine themselves secure if they can conceal their crimes from the cognizance of men and commit their sins in darkness and retirement. But, alas! The ways of man are now before the eyes of the Lord, and He ponders all his goings. There is no darkness or shadow of death where the workers of iniquity may hide themselves (Proverbs 5:21; Job 34:21). No secret impurity can escape the knowledge of our Judge, nor any artful hypocrisy deceive His piercing eyes; even the secret motions and inclinations of our hearts are exposed to His critical observation. All proud and vengeful thoughts, all uncharitable and malicious intentions, all the covetous and unjust designs that men have secretly harbored in their breasts, shall then be unfolded before the grand consistory of angels and men. For "there is nothing covered that shall not be revealed, nor hid that shall not be known" (Luke 12:2).

Men frequently imagine that their tongues are their own, that their words vanish into air, and shall not be brought to any future account. But our Savior tells us in Matthew 12:36–37 that men shall give an account for every idle word that they speak. You therefore delude yourselves to your eternal ruin if you think that your vain and filthy communication, your profane and irreligious discourse, your horrid oaths and imprecations, your impious jests upon our holy religion, and your malicious slanders of good men, shall pass unobserved in that day; for "by thy words thou shalt be justified, and by thy words thou shalt be condemned." When our Lord shall come to execute judgment upon all, He will convict the wicked not only of their ungodly deeds which they have impiously committed, but also of all their hard and grievous speeches which they have spoken against Him (Jude 15).

But sinners shall not only be called to an account for their transgressions of the law of God, but also for their omissions of duty and neglecting to improve the various and happy advantages they have enjoyed—their power and estates, their health of body and abilities of mind, their opportunities and capacities of glorifying God and promoting the welfare of mankind. These things shall then be produced against them and be a heavy article in their indictment. Thus we find the slothful servant, who did not trade with his lord's talent, but buried it in the earth, is sentenced into outer darkness where there is perpetual weeping and gnashing of teeth (Matthew 25:30).

All the aggravations of men's sins shall then be enumerated and their guilt shall appear in its crimson colors. If the Gentile world shall be condemned for resisting the glimmering light of nature and rebelling against the law of God so obscurely written on their hearts, how inexcusable will be their guilt, how vast their condemnation, who have shut their eyes against the marvelous light of the gospel and stifled the powerful convictions of the Spirit of grace!

Finally, while the wicked shall be exposed in all their guilt and deformity, and be publicly charged with their numberless transgressions, God will not be regardless of the saints, nor forget their labor of love. Their heavenly Father knows their works, and with pleasure observes their zeal and fidelity in His service. Their secret prayers and tears, their diffusive charity and beneficence, are set down in the sacred records of heaven, and will be mentioned to their immortal honor in the day of the Lord. Their patient sufferings in the ways of their duty will be carefully remembered, and their smallest services to the kingdom of Christ will meet with a vast and unspeakable reward.

(3) Thus I come to the last thing to be considered. The righteous shall be judged to unalterable glory, but the wicked condemned to eternal misery. Those who have accepted the compassionate offers of a Savior, and complied with the gracious demands of the gospel, who have devoted themselves to God without exception or reserve, and made it the great study of their lives to approve themselves to their all-seeing Judge, who have lamented their innumerable defects and infirmities and sincerely endeavored to mortify their most beloved lusts, who have improved the means of grace with fidelity and diligence and abounded in acts of charity and benevolence—these shall be openly acknowledged by Christ in that day and ranked

among the number of His servants and followers. Their Master and Judge, whose authority they have reverenced, whose laws they have observed, and in whose merits they have confided, the Lord Jesus Christ, with indulgent smiles in His countenance and the tenderest accents in His voice, will pronounce that happy sentence upon them, "Come, ye blessed of My Father, inherit the kingdom, prepared for you from the foundation of the world" (Matthew 25:34).

But the wicked, who have despised His sacred authority, trampled under foot His invaluable blood and obstinately persisted in sin, in contempt of all the condescending offers of His grace, shall receive that awful doom from the mouth of their slighted and injured Savior, "Depart from Me, ye cursed, into everlasting fire, prepared for the devil and his angels" (Matthew 25:41).

And according to these different sentences will the final state of the children of men be unchangeably determined. The wicked shall be immediately seized upon by devils and conveyed to the dark abodes of horror and despair; the heavens from above shall shower down torrents of flaming fire upon their guilty heads, and hell from below shall open its mouth to receive them, where they shall be tormented day and night, without any possibility of escape or hope of deliverance. The righteous shall ascend to their enthroned Lord and Savior, and with crowns upon their heads and palms of victory in their hands, make their triumphant entrance into the new Jerusalem, the city of the living God, a place of unspeakable joy and refreshment, where all sorrow shall be banished from their breast, all tears shall be wiped from their eyes, their hopes shall be satisfied, their desires accomplished, and their whole man filled with those divine and transporting pleasures that flow at the right hand of God. Then shall they shine like the sun in the kingdom of their Father, and be immovably fixed in the firmament of immortal glory. They shall no longer complain that they sojourn in Mesech, and are vexed with the filthy conversation of the wicked; but shall be associated with the glorious company of the apostles, the goodly fellowship of the prophets and martyrs, and the general assembly of the church throughout the world. Together with these they shall encompass the throne of God with prostration and praise, and tune their voices to the sacred anthems of heaven, saying, "To Him that hath loved us and washed us from our sins in His own blood, and hath made us kings and priests unto God and His Father, to Him be glory and dominion forever. Amen."

Application

1. What we have heard should be improved as a powerful restraint from the practice of secret sins. For what can be a higher absurdity than for men to encourage themselves in sin when they have the advantage of privacy and retirement, and to imagine that they are safe from punishment if the curtains of night, or any artful disguises, hide their wicked actions from the view and observation of men? Alas! What will it avail you to conceal your wickedness from the eyes of men when your most secret actions are visible to the God with whom you have to do? What little advantage will you receive by avoiding worldly shame and punishment when your secret enormities will shortly be brought upon the public stage and displayed in their most odious colors to your eternal confusion? Though now you cover your transgressions as Adam, and hide your iniquities in your bosom, yet there is nothing so secretly committed but it shall then be brought to light and exposed before the vast and numerous assembly of angels and men.

The firm belief of this awful truth would break the force of many temptations and be a happy preservative from defiling sins; it would make us reject with abhorrence the insinuating charms of vice and say with holy Joseph, "How can I do this great wickedness and sin against God?"

2. This shows us the vanity of hypocrisy. For the eyes of our Judge are as flaming fire, and penetrate into the hidden corners of our souls. In the Day of Judgment, every mask shall be pulled off, every flattering disguise shall be removed, and the secrets of all hearts shall be disclosed. Why then will you put on a form of godliness and engage in external acts of devotion, only to be seen of men and gain the empty applause of your fellow creatures, when your eternal state will be decided not by the charitable opinion of short-sighted mortals, but by the unerring sentence of an all-seeing God! Do not be deceived; Christ is not to be mocked. He sees the pride and hypocrisy of the painted Pharisee under the most amiable and goodly appearance. He beholds the sordid flattery of false and noisy professors who bow the knee before Him with seeming humility and devotion, while their affections are wedded to the world and their lives are stained with abominable impurities. This, therefore, should excite us all to the greatest sincerity in our profession, to be faithful to our solemn vows and engagements, that we may be found the disciples of Christ not only in outward appearance, but in the inward temper and disposition of our minds. So we shall have this for our rejoicing, even the testimony of our conscience, that in simplicity and godly sincerity we have had our conversation in the world.

3. How much does it concern us to hold fast the profession of our faith in the midst of the greatest difficulties and discouragements? We live in a dark day of error and apostasy, in which the distinguishing glories of the gospel are publicly reviled and insulted by men of corrupt principles and licentious morals. Weak and unstable minds are in danger of being carried away by the prevailing torrent of infidelity. It is therefore our indispensable duty to main-

tain our sacred profession in this dangerous hour of temptation, and vigorously to defend the faith once delivered
to the saints, even in the face of its boldest opposers. For
our blessed Savior has made those declarations: "Whosoever shall confess Me before men, him will I confess before
My Father which is in heaven. But whosoever shall be
ashamed of Me or of My words, of him also shall the Son
of Man be ashamed when He comes in the glory of his Father, with His holy angels" (Matthew 10:32; Mark 8:38).

If then we betray the sacred deposit committed to our
trust through covetousness or cowardice; if we corrupt
the purity of the gospel through a sinful compliance with
the humors of the age—what can we expect but that our
Master and Judge will treat us with contempt and abhorrence, and herd us among His abandoned enemies! This
thought should inspire us with undaunted courage in the
cause of Christ, and arm us with a noble resolution to
submit to the greatest hardships and difficulties rather
than make shipwreck of our faith and a good conscience.

4. We should constantly bear in mind the strictness of
our future account, and live as those who expect to be
judged. If the actions of our lives were transient, and there
were no remembrance of them hereafter; if death put a
final period to our being and we were never to be called
to an account for the things done in the body—we might
then loose our sensual inclinations, and eat and drink
without thought or concern, for tomorrow we die. But
since we are candidates for immortality, and our final state
will be determined according to our present behavior, it
infinitely concerns us if we have any true love to ourselves,
any regard to our great and everlasting interest, to keep a
future judgment perpetually in our view; to consider that
every action of life will be scanned with an impartial severity, and an unalterable sentence will pass, according to our
works.

It is for want of this that the unthinking children of

men are emboldened in their sins, and live oftentimes in an allowed course of society and profaneness of rioting and excess, in the habitual neglect of the service of God, and the welfare of their immortal souls. Did men seriously consider the important consequences of their actions, that they are now sowing the seeds of endless and inconceivable joy, or laying the foundation of unutterable horror and despair, it would powerfully excite them to cleanse themselves from all filthiness of flesh and spirit and to be perfecting holiness in the fear of the Lord. This argument is made use of by the wise man: "Fear God, and keep His commandments; for God shall bring every work into judgment, with every secret thing, whether it be good or whether it be evil" (Ecclesiastes 12:13–14).

Let us therefore keep our thoughts fixed upon this great and important day, when the Son of Man shall come in the glory of His Father, with His angels, and shall reward every man according to his works.

This indeed is a harsh and ungrateful subject to the greatest part of mankind. They are so involved in secular business, so solicitous to increase their estates and raise their families, that they have no time to regard the one thing needful, and prepare for an eternal judgment. Therefore they banish the thought of it out of their minds lest it should give a check to their ambitious views and interrupt their worldly enjoyments. But consider, I beseech you, those things which you now so passionately dote on, and for which you sacrifice your eternal all, will not profit you in the day of wrath. They will not appease a stormy conscience nor bribe your impartial Judge. What comfort or satisfaction will it then afford you to reflect that you have had a distinguished name among flattering mortals, that you have been ranked among the great men of the earth, and have been honored with a splendid passage to the grave? Will any of these serve to procure you a favorable sentence at the tribunal of heaven, screen you from the avenging wrath of an offended God, or even abate your punishment and sorrow in the day of perdition of ungodly men? No, verily! Nothing will then support and solace you but the testimony of an unreproaching conscience and the smiles of your almighty Savior, a title to His invaluable merits, and to the great and precious promises of His everlasting gospel.

Let us then be so wise as to foresee the evil, and flee from the wrath to come. Let us now seek and secure the favor of Christ, our supreme Lord and Judge, so that when we come to stand at His awful bar, we may receive a gracious sentence from His mouth, and may appear before Him with joy and confidence in the day when He shall come to be glorified in His saints, and admired in all them who believe.

11

The Salvation Revealed in the Gospel Described

"For by grace are ye saved." Ephesians 2:8

It was the privilege of Adam, immediately on his first creation, to be placed in the delightful garden of Eden. No sooner did he receive his existence but he became an inhabitant of paradise. He entered into a world finished with the most exquisite art, and furnished with everything that could contribute to his happiness. But the children of the second Adam enter into being in very different circumstances: our natures are deeply corrupted, we inhabit a dark and disordered world, and we are born to trouble as the sparks fly upward. Even after we are in some measure recovered from the ruins of the apostasy and readmitted into the family of heaven, it is by slow degrees that we attain to a state of felicity and glory. We must pass through a tedious pilgrimage before we arrive at our destined home; we must endure many sufferings upon earth before we enter into celestial joy.

This is the appointment of God and founded in the nature of men, for the best of saints upon earth are sanctified but in part. Upon this account their happiness is far from complete; these tabernacles of clay must suffer a dissolution before we shall be prepared for the vision and enjoyment of a holy God. When we take farewell of sin, we shall bid an eternal adieu to sorrow.

In the meantime, the most extensive proposals of salvation are made to mankind. Those who cordially accept this salvation are made partakers of its important blessings. These are the interesting truths contained in that passage of Scripture which has now been read unto you, and which by divine permission will be the subject of several discourses. The design of my present discourse is to explain the nature of that salvation which is revealed in the gospel, and the whole will be comprehended under the following headings:

• The salvation revealed in the gospel implies that those who are made partakers of it were in a state of guilt and misery.

• Their recovery is begun in this life.

• Their happiness shall be completed in a future world.

First, it implies that those who are made partakers of this salvation were in a state of guilt and misery. To "save," in strict propriety of speech, is to rescue a person from a danger to which he is exposed, or deliver him from a calamity in which he is involved. Upon this account the eternal Son of God, when He appeared upon earth in the fashion of a man, assumed the character of a Savior. His name was called "Jesus," because He came to save His people from their sins. He assures us the design of His mission was to seek and save them who were lost.

Angels are perfectly happy, but never mentioned among the number of the saved, because they never violated the purity of their nature, but always maintained their primitive innocence. Adorned with the robes of unstained righteousness, they feel no guilt and fear no danger, but taste unmingled felicity and joy. But man is fallen from his original excellence and plunged into an abyss of misery. Having departed from God, he is deprived of the amiable image of the Deity and has become a prey to the most infamous appetites. A deluded understanding leads him into endless mazes of error and folly; he pursues a vanishing shadow and despises the true felicity of his nature. Captivated with the charms of sense, he neglects the purity and perfection of his immortal spirit. Dazzled with a gay appearance, he follows every glittering phantom; corrupted in his moral taste, he rushes into the embraces of the most polluting pleasures; unmindful of his heavenly birth, his affections are chained down to the enjoyments of this inferior earth. Seduced by flattering dreams, he sleeps on securely till the light of eternity discovers the fatal mistake. So strong is the deception while men remain under the power of depraved nature that we imagine ourselves free even when we are the most passive slaves. We hug our chains as if they were the noblest ornaments. With thoughtless gaiety we tread the beaten road that leads to death and hell.

To finish our unhappiness, our Maker is offended. His wrath is revealed from heaven against us; the sentence of His righteous law condemns us to eternal death; to what sanctuary shall we fly in this lost and desperate state? Can we bribe inexorable Justice? Can we resist an omnipotent arm? Can we be concealed from that Being whose all-penetrating eyes survey all nature with a single glance? Can we escape beyond the bounds of His universal empire? Or can we support the terrors of His avenging wrath? Who can thunder with an arm like God? Who can abide the day of his indignation? Our consciences accuse us of innumerable crimes; the law pronounces its awful curses against every transgressor. We live only to increase the number of our offenses, and die to become the victims of divine justice.

In this melancholy situation, a reprieve must be acknowledged a favor and a mitigation of our punishment an unmerited mercy; but the glad tidings of deliverance, one would think, must be received with transports of gratitude! To publish this good news is the design of the gospel; and the whole number of the saved attend to the consolatory message with a humble faith.

Second, their recovery is begun in this life. "Ye are saved," said St. Paul to the believing Ephesians. He speaks of their salvation not as a future event, but as a present privilege. He does not say, "Ye shall be saved in the hour of death, in the morning of the resurrection, or at the illustrious day of the restitution of all things"; but describes it as a happiness which in some good degree they then enjoyed.

But how can this be? Do not true believers inhabit a world of sorrow? Are they not defiled with innumerable corruptions? Is not Satan continually disturbing their peace? Does not the world, with its treacherous smiles, frequently betray men into sin? Do they not groan under the burden of various afflictions? Must they not submit to the empire of death? Are not their bodies, the workmanship of the Almighty, by an irrevocable decree, condemned to become the food of worms? Are these the advantages which the Son of God has purchased for His favorite people? Is this the salvation described with such pomp and magnificence in the gospel?

I grant, my brethren, upon earth we do not receive our perfect consummation in bliss. This event will not take place till the day of Christ's second appearance, in the glory and grandeur of an incarnate God, in the character of Universal Judge of angels and men. Then our adorable Redeemer will manifest the fullness of His saving power, complete the designs of His almighty love, and establish His people in a state of immutable felicity and glory. But upon earth, we receive the first fruits of this joyful harvest; we are favored with delightful foretastes of those rivers of transporting pleasure which flow in the paradise above. We view at a distance the immortal glories of that kingdom where the saints shall live and reign with God forever and ever.

The faithful disciples of Christ were appointed to this salvation in the eternal counsels of God. In the fullness of

time, Jesus the Savior paid the price of their redemption
to the uttermost farthing. By His all-sufficient merits, He
purchased for them the honor and happiness of the sons
of God. As an evidence of this, He has sent His Spirit into
their hearts to turn them from darkness to light, from the
follies of vice to the wisdom of the just, from the labyrinths
of error and delusion to the paths of holiness and happiness. By this we know that we are passed from death unto
life, are united to the Son of God, and interested in His
immaculate righteousness. In consequence of this, we have
now the forgiveness of our sins and shall shortly receive an
inheritance among those who are sanctified. We are no
more considered as aliens and strangers, but fellow citizens with the saints and of the household of God.

How divine a change have these happy souls experienced! Well may they rejoice in their ineffable privileges. If
we are of this happy number, salvation is ours by an unfailing title. Shortly we shall possess all its extensive blessings.
We need not tremble at the condemning sentence of the
law, but may rejoice in the hope of immortal glory. Christ
has endured the punishment due to our crimes, and
wrought out a perfect righteousness in the character of
our Surety. By this we are justified at the tribunal of God
and declared heirs of the kingdom of heaven. We shall be
preserved from the world and its deceitful temptations,
for the great Captain of our salvation has overcome this
dangerous enemy. He will preserve us from being fatally
seduced by its terrors or allurements.

Every Christian has his conversation in heaven while
here upon earth, and is every day aspiring after a more
exact conformity to the maxims and manners of that
blessed world. We shall not be destroyed by the prevalency
of corrupted nature, for an immortal principle of life has
quickened us who were dead in trespasses and sins. We
have a divine assurance that sin, the worst of evils, shall no
more have the dominion over us. Under the conduct of

almighty grace, its influence is continually diminishing; the path of the just, like the morning light, shines more and more unto the perfect day. We shall be delivered from the policy and power of Satan, though described as a roaring lion seeking whom he may devour. Our blessed Lord has triumphed over this inveterate opposer of God and goodness, and will not suffer him finally to prevail against those who are committed to his care. He may disturb their peace by his malignant suggestions, but not destroy their safety. He may tempt them by the most artful methods, but shall not be able to reduce them to a subjection to his detested empire. They are under the protection of One who is able to save unto the uttermost, and may depend on His faithful promise that none shall pluck them out of His hands.

We are indeed exposed to the arrests of the king of terrors, and must, at the appointed time, enter the dark dominions of the grave. But fear not, O Christian! The divine presence will irradiate your passage through the gloomy vale of death. Guards of angels will safely escort you through the territories of the prince of darkness. The Lord of life bears the keys of the invisible world, and death can't remove us beyond the limits of His extensive jurisdiction. It indeed closes our eyes upon the beauties of this material system, but introduces us to the unutterable glories of heaven. It translates us from this obscure corner of the creation to the place of the divine residence, the seat of His eternal empire.

But the illustration of this point naturally falls under the third part of my discourse, which is to show that the recovery of the people of God, which is begun in this life, shall be completed in a future world.

The argument of St. Paul is strictly just and must give full conviction to every attentive mind: "He that spared not His own Son, but delivered Him up for us all, shall He not with Him freely give us all things?" The love of God in delivering up His Son to sufferings and death for miserable mortals is one of the most astonishing mysteries of faith, and will be the perpetual admiration of the sublime intelligences of heaven. But when we are convinced of this fundamental truth by the divine testimony, we may easily conceive that the most excellent favors will be bestowed upon those for whom He made so costly a sacrifice. Accordingly, Christians are adorned with the most honorable titles, invested with the most extensive privileges, and assured of complete and eternal happiness.

But what is their condition while they reside upon earth? Do they appear in the proper dignity of the sons of God, in the genuine character of those who are appointed to inherit all things? No, they are often defiled with sin, disturbed with fears, disfigured with reproach, and oppressed with a variety of temptations and trials. But the hour of darkness is short; very soon the heavenly light will arise. The night of affliction will quickly come to an end and be succeeded with perpetual and unclouded day. Then they shall be freed from every sorrow, purified from every sin, and be made kings and priests unto God.

In the present dispensation, the ways of providence are mysterious; the equity and goodness of the divine government is, in a great measure, concealed from the most diligent inquirers. Vice often receives the rewards of virtue, and virtue is condemned to the punishment of vice. Jesus Christ is confined to a manger while an impious Herod is advanced to the throne of Israel. St. Paul is a prisoner in chains while a bloody Nero sways the scepter of the Roman Empire. The best of men are trampled under foot as the offscouring of all things, and the vilest monsters of human nature are attended with applause and ride upon the high places of the earth. But in the day of the restitution of all things, vice shall appear in its naked deformity and be punished with righteous severity. Virtue shall be publicly applauded at the supreme tribunal and receive a crown of incorruptible glory. The slaves of Satan shall be confined in chains of everlasting darkness, while the servants of Christ shine as the brightness of the firmament forever.

How poor and imperfect is the happiness which the saints enjoy upon earth in comparison to the magnificent promises which are made unto them in the Word of God! In their best estate, their happiest hours, they are far from that purity and perfection to which they ardently aspire. But the day of their redemption is swiftly approaching when they shall awake, arrayed in the Redeemer's righteousness, adorned with the beauties of the divine image, and receive the full satisfaction of all their desires. The everlasting love of God to His people will appear in its richest glory, and the designs of redeeming grace receive their final accomplishment. Then we shall no longer prostrate ourselves before an invisible God, but approach the throne of His glory, behold His unveiled face, and triumph in the joys of His immediate presence. We shall no longer worship Him in temples made with hands, in company with sinful and miserable mortals, but shall enter the undefiled sanctuary above and unite our voices with angels and archangels in the triumphant "hallelujahs" of heaven. We shall no longer be confined to a few refreshing tastes of the divine benignity, but have free access to the Tree of Life, which stands in the midst of the paradise of God; and we shall quench our thirst after happiness at the original Fountain of all good.

I conclude with one or two reflections.

What obligations are we under to the Son of God, who has purchased this salvation for the heirs of guilt and misery? No sooner had the great Creator introduced man into a state of existence but the prince of darkness assaulted his innocence and contrived his ruin. He filled the minds of our first parents with false apprehensions of the Deity, and by this means betrayed them into committing a voluntary disobedience to the divine mandate. Immediately the human nature was defaced and defiled; the favorites of heaven became confederates with the spirits of hell. As we were partakers of their crimes, we were condemned to suffer their punishment.

But the Son of God descended from heaven that He might destroy the works of the devil. He assumed our nature with its innocent infirmities, fulfilled the law which we had violated, and submitted to the punishment which was the just demerit of our crimes. In consequence of this, salvation is preached to all nations; the greatest sinners are invited to return to their offended Maker; free access is opened to the throne of grace and the humble penitent is assured of audience and acceptance.

They who improve these happy advantages and confide in this all-sufficient Savior immediately experience the compassions of His heart and the power of His hands. He abolishes their guilt and constitutes them heirs of the Kingdom of God. He inspires them with His blessed Spirit, which conquers their native corruption and forms them to a divine and heavenly life. He gives them the peace of God which passes all understanding, refreshes them under their various afflictions with the visits of His love, and sometimes gives them transporting earnests of the happiness reserved for them in a future world. Shortly He will descend in all His mediatorial glory and ascend the throne of judgment. This flesh and blood, which is hastening to the silent grave, shall hear His animating voice, shake off the sleep of death, and arise glorious and immortal. Our whole man shall partake of His triumphs and rejoice forever in His love.

And now, my brethren, who of us does not say, "May I be of the happy number! May my portion be with the nations of the redeemed! May I, O adorable Savior, see the good of Thy chosen, and rejoice with the gladness of Thine inheritance!"

Is this our language? Then to obtain this happiness ought to be our principle care. To be happy is the universal desire of all mankind. There are two kinds of happiness that present themselves to our view and court our affections: the one consists in the enjoyment of the pomp and pleasures of this life, the other in the dignity and privileges of the children of God. The men who have their portion in this life choose their happiness in a world that groans under the wrath of indignant heaven. The men who embrace the salvation of the gospel place their felicity in a world that is filled with the lovingkindness of God. This world is the melancholy abode of darkness and disorder; the future is perpetually illuminated with the rays of the divine glory. Everything here below is subject to continual charge, but the felicity of the saints above is free from all vicissitudes. The earth with all its splendors must perish in the flames; but heaven, the throne of God, endures forever.

Detach, therefore, O professors of the gospel, your affections from this scene of vanity; fix your desires on a better country, which is reserved in heaven. Why should we amuse ourselves with dreams of happiness in these regions of darkness when Christ has purchased for us a world of light and joy? Encompassed with so great a cloud of witnesses who have finished their course with joy, we should run with patience the race which is set before us, looking unto Jesus, the Author and Finisher of our faith. Amen.

12

Salvation by Grace

"For by grace are ye saved." Ephesians 2:8

Pride introduced the apostasy of our first parents, and in all ages proves the destruction of multitudes. This animates princes to unsheathe the sword of war, and millions are sacrificed to their aspiring views. This sows the seeds of contention in churches and commonwealths; the public safety is endangered to gratify the pride and resentment of a few individuals. This destroys the peace and good order of private families, and renders those who were united in the tenderest bonds as enemies to each other.

But the melancholy consequences of an arrogant and ambitious mind are not confined to the present life; they extend to a future state and exclude mankind from the only way of salvation that is provided for a guilty world. Vain man would be wiser than God and attempts to regain his forfeited felicity by his own strength. Instead of acknowledging his dependence on sovereign grace, he seeks for something in himself that shall placate his offended Maker. Unwilling to ascribe the entire glory of his salvation to God, he aspires to be, in some degree, the author of his own recovery and happiness. This was the fatal mistake of the Jewish zealots and the pagan philosophers. This influenced them to oppose the progress of the gospel from its first appearance and persecute its professors with inflexible severity.

The Jews, intoxicated with an opinion of their own righteousness, expected to be saved by their obedience to the law. The pagan moralists, puffed up with a vain conceit of their superior wisdom, imagined their happiness was in their own hands, independent of any foreign assistance. Happy would it be for the Christian church if this presumption had not entered its sacred enclosure and infected the minds of those who call themselves the disciples of a crucified Savior.

But every imagination of this nature is fully overthrown by the inspired St. Paul in my text. If there were no other passage in Scripture but this, it would be sufficient to destroy the pretensions of human vanity and direct mankind from whence they must expect all their happiness and safety: "By grace are ye saved."

Every impartial observer must be immediately sensible that these words plainly declare that the salvation of mankind is not the effect of their own policy or power, but an undeserved favor; that it cannot be obtained by the improvement of our natural abilities, but descends from the Father of lights, the Giver of every good gift.

In discoursing on this point, I shall inquire what is intended by grace, and how it appears that the salvation of sinners is entirely of grace.

First, grace signifies a free favor, not granted to merit, not founded on superior excellence, but flowing from unpurchased benevolence. That angels are adorned with the noble perfections of their nature, placed in the heavenly sanctuary, preserved in their primitive integrity, and made the favorite ministers of divine providence must be ascribed to unmerited grace. No creature can challenge any thing of the Creator; all their excellencies flow from His goodness.

Adam was made an inhabitant of paradise, advanced to the government of this lower world, by the same free favor. All the privileges of his nature and the advantages of his situation were the effects of pure goodness. But when man left the glory of his innocence and became a guilty criminal, then the triumphs of grace appeared in the most illustrious point of light. Innocent man had nothing to claim from his Maker but what flowed from His gracious promise, and sinful man had everything to fear from his offended Sovereign whose favors he had abused. When, therefore, God delivers us from the punishment we had deserved and restores us to the privileges we had forfeited, it is not only grace, but the riches of grace. He bestows His favors on those who are so far from having any excellency to recommend them that their guilt justly exposes them to His severest displeasure.

This is that grace which the apostle celebrates in the words of my text. This rescues us from the tyranny of Satan, the dominion of sin, and the punishment of death. This restores guilty criminals to the favor of heaven and gives them a title to the happiness of life eternal.

Second, I will inquire how it appears that the salvation of sinners is entirely of grace. If we examine the various parts of this salvation, if we survey its different degrees, if we pursue its progress in all the periods of the present life, and through the unceasing ages of eternity, we shall be immediately convinced that it cannot be challenged as a claim of justice; it cannot be acquired by the powers of unregenerate nature, nor are we introduced into this happy state as the reward of our good works.

It cannot be challenged as a claim of justice. If the revolved posterity of Adam were to appear at the tribunal of justice, they must be covered with the greatest confusion and inevitably receive the sentence of eternal death. If God should enter into judgment with sinners, all must be condemned to remediless destruction. The honor of the divine government requires that the transgression of the law be punished with impartial severity. The infinite perfection of the Deity renders sin the object of His immutable aversion; this He will forever discover to the view of the whole intelligent creation. If therefore almighty grace had not contrived a way to answer the demands of justice, every sinner of the human race must have fallen a sacrifice to its righteous claims. That justice which expelled the apostate angels from the happiness of heaven would have condemned rebellious man to the torments of hell; angels and men united to reject the authority of the great God, and deserved the same punishment. That men are prisoners of hope, and fallen angels delivered over to final despair, is not the claim of justice, but the work of distinguishing grace. This pities criminals condemned to death, freely forgives their offenses, and restores them to favor.

As salvation is not a claim of justice, neither can it be acquired by the powers of unregenerate nature; for human nature in its present degenerate state is deeply and universally corrupted—not only averse to that which is spiritually good, but fatally inclined to that which is evil. When God descended from heaven to survey the state of the moral world, this is the melancholy report: the thoughts and imaginations of men's hearts are evil, only evil, and that continually (Genesis 6:5). In conformity to this divine testimony, St. Paul, who learned his divinity in the school of heaven, declares that of ourselves we are insufficient for so much as a good thought; if we are insufficient to think a good thought, then we are certainly incapable to perform a good action. Our blessed Savior assures us that a bad tree cannot bring forth good fruit, nor can a corrupt fountain send forth salutary streams.

Upon this plan the most enlightened teachers of the Christian church have always maintained that the performances of unregenerate sinners don't recommend them to the special favor of God, nor give them a claim to the saving gifts of His Holy Spirit. A diligent cultivation of our rational powers, a life conducted by the precepts of moral virtue, adorn the characters of men and render them blessings to civil society. But they cannot be acceptable to God when they flow from a carnal mind, which is enmity to God.

Men who are favored with divine revelation certainly enjoy advantages superior to those who have no other instructor than the light of nature; but these will be ineffectual to our salvation if not accompanied with the internal operations of the Spirit. The Word of God may be found in our ears and not penetrate our hearts. Let the law proclaim its formidable curses, we shall be deaf to its alarming voice; let the gospel publish its gracious invitations, we shall be unaffected with its delightful sound; let the ministers of Christ lift up their voices like trumpets and address their hearers with all the charms of celestial eloquence, they labor in vain and spend their strength for naught if these means are not attended with a divine influence. It is the prerogative of omnipotent grace to open the eyes of the blind, unstop the ears of the deaf, communicate a principle of life to those who are dead in trespasses and sins, and incline them to walk in the way that leads to eternal salvation.

Without this, the light of nature with all its improvements, the law with all its precepts, and the gospel with all its transporting discoveries will be a savor of death unto death. We will remain under the dominion of sin; the advantages we enjoy will only serve to increase our guilt and render us inexcusable at the tribunal of justice.

If the improvement of our natural powers or the advantages of external revelation were sufficient for our salvation, why was the Spirit sent down to enlighten the minds of men and sanctify their souls? We must then certainly conclude the powers of human nature are too weak, and all external advantages insufficient, to produce any saving effect. The grace of God must triumph over the weakness of men or sinners would perish in their corruption and misery.

We are not made partakers of this salvation as the reward of our good works. Many profess a high esteem for the inspired Scriptures and acknowledge that grace is a necessary assistant to frail and fallible man; but they depend on the sincerity of their hearts, the purity of their intentions, and the regularity of their lives to recommend them to this important blessing. They compliment God as the Author of their salvation, but think their own virtuous dispositions are essential qualifications to prepare them for the reception of so great a good. Thus they form a scheme plausible to human reason, soothing to the natural vanity of our minds but subversive of the established order of salvation.

It is universally allowed that all who are saved are created anew in Christ Jesus unto good works, and diligently endeavor to walk in the practice of them. But then this is a certain consequence, not a previous condition, of an interest in the salvation of the gospel. We must be delivered from the dominion of sin before we can perform the duties of acceptable obedience. Jesus saves us from the hands of sin and Satan, our spiritual enemies, so that we may be qualified to serve God in holiness and righteousness. The Giver of all good will not alter His plan to gratify the pride of unhumbled nature and accommodate Himself to the schemes of human invention. The only question to be decided is this: is an interest in Christ and His salvation freely given, or conferred as the reward of some antecedent goodness? Our Master has determined the point, and thinks His authority should silence all disputes.

Let us hear the unerring Teacher of the Christian church and submit to His sacred dictates: "As the branch cannot bear fruit of itself except it abide in the vine, no more can ye, except ye abide in Me." To abide in Christ must certainly imply that we are united to Him, and that this union remains undissolved. This we are assured is a requisite preparation to our bringing forth fruit or performing any good work. If it were needful to add anything further, I might adduce the express testimony of St. Paul: "not by works of righteousness which we have done, but according to His mercy He saved us, by the washing of regeneration and the renewing of the Holy Ghost."

I shall conclude my discourse with a few reflections:

What we have heard affords us a test by which we may examine the truth of the doctrines we receive. It also gives us a rule by which we may determine the value of the duties we practice. It points out to us the only way to secure our future welfare.

We have a test by which we may examine the truth of the doctrines we receive. The great design of God in the salvation of sinners is to display the glory of His grace. He has made us to sit down together in heavenly places in Christ Jesus that He might show the exceeding riches of His grace in His kindness towards us through Christ Jesus. To diminish this grace is to darken the glory of the gospel and deprive the blessed God of that tribute of praise He expects from all His redeemed people.

Every opinion which exalts the powers of human nature in its present degenerate state undermines the foundation of the Christian faith, and prevents us from that resignation to divine sovereignty which becomes the character of apostate creatures. That doctrine which ascribes the entire glory of our salvation to God bears the stamp of divinity and will ever recommend itself to those who have been taught in the school of a crucified Savior.

It has always been the stratagem of Satan to employ the powers of wit and learning to support the fabric of human pride and render men vain in their own imaginations. But it is the constant work of the Spirit to humble the sinner in the dust, convince him that he is absolutely lost, that there is no possibility of his recovery but by a grace to which he has no claim, and which he has forfeited a thousand ways. Unilluminated minds may approach the throne of God with a long catalogue of their good works, but those who are acquainted with their own true character will come before the divine Majesty with no other plea than that of the penitent publican: "God be merciful to me, a sinner." This is the only method to glorify God, and consult our own safety.

If this doctrine which teaches us to renounce all dependence upon ourselves in every form, to place our entire trust on sovereign and unmerited grace, is a mistake, it is a perfectly innocent one. It can't be attended with any dangerous consequences; it will not be displeasing to that Being who assures us He gives grace to the humble. What would be my crime? It can only be this, that I entertain too mean an opinion of myself. I degrade apostate nature too low. I form too favorable sentiments of the riches of divine grace when I suppose God bestows salvation as a free gift, and that He confers His choicest favors without money and without price. Is this my error? Is this the fault I am charged with? I am persuaded that I shall not be ashamed of it at the supreme tribunal, however I may be reproached by the polite reasoners of the day. I shall not repent of it in heaven, whatever inconveniences I may suffer upon earth. Men may ridicule my weakness, but God will approve of every attempt to advance the honor of His cause.

This is the only revenue He receives from all the stupendous designs of His love. All endeavors to deprive Him of this will be condemned as the highest sacrilege and punished with the severest vengeance. I run no risk when I acknowledge my extreme indigence and misery, but I incur the greatest danger when I do not adore God as the Author of all good. This is the language of the inspired oracles: "O Israel, thou had destroyed thyself, but in Me is thy help." Upon every amiable disposition we possess, upon every virtuous action we perform, we should engrave this humble inscription: "This is not of ourselves, it is the gift of God." If there is any real good in us, it is planted by the hand of our heavenly Father, watered by His grace, and flourishes by the influences of His Holy Spirit. Were I, like St. Paul, advanced to the dignity of an apostle, transported to paradise, and favored with the visions of glory, with him I desire to be sensible that I am the chief of sinners, and acknowledge that all the privileges which distinguish me from the vilest of men are the gifts of God.

We have a rule by which we may determine the value of the duties we practice. A great part of mankind cast off all reverence of the deity, are insensible of their immortal interests, and neglect the service they owe to the supreme Lord and Lawgiver. Among many who make a more plausible profession of religion, a fear of the divine displeasure, a dread of future punishment, is the only motive of obedience. But if by grace we are saved, then it is a discovery of this grace that encourages us to engage in the service of God; it is a dependence on its constant assistance that animates us in all the duties of the Christian life.

To serve God only from a principle of fear is not the disposition of His children, but the character of a slave. In this frame of mind all our performances are constrained; we abstain from sin with reluctance; we would indulge every vicious appetite with pleasure if we were not afraid of eternal misery. These services, therefore, though performed to the greatest exactness, can't be acceptable to God; for He demands the obedience of the heart, and receives none by a willing people. All His servants are convinced of the excellency and glory of His character; they are captivated with the discoveries of His free grace which are tendered to the greatest of sinners. They admire that wisdom and love which has provided salvation for those who have no recommending qualities to establish a claim to this blessing. They therefore bow their head and adore this disinterested goodness. With transports of joy they accept the gift of a Savior, looking up to Him for wisdom, righteousness, sanctification, and eternal redemption.

This astonishing grace inclines them to renounce with detestation the practice of vice, and with pleasure to engage in the service of so amiable a Master. His commandments are not a disagreeable task, but their daily business and delight. He loved them when they were nothing but guilt and misery, and shall they not love Him who is worthy of their undivided affection? He has delivered them from the terrors of death, and shall they not devote their future lives to the glory of their great Benefactor?

The doctrine of my text points out unto us the only way to secure our future welfare. It is the most interesting inquiry of all mankind, "Wherewith shall I come before God, or bow myself before the Most High? How shall I appear with safety at the tribunal of infinite purity and obtain that salvation which is provided for the people of God?" If by grace we are saved, then we must apply to this grace as our only resource. If it is the gift of God, then we can only obtain it by a humble and grateful reception.

This way, though appointed by infinite wisdom, is often esteemed foolishness by men; though revealed in almost every page of the gospel, is ridiculed by the disputers of this world. But all who are taught of God are made to renounce every claim and receive salvation in its beginning, progress, and completion as the free gift of God through Jesus Christ. If we reject this, there is no sure foundation on which we can build our hopes of eternal happiness. We must live in perpetual doubt and, if our consciences are not stupefied, die in distressing agonies.

Whatever vain men may pretend, the testimony of their own hearts convinces them that they have sinned against that God with whom is terrible majesty; that they have no righteousness which can stand the critical examination of the supreme tribunal. They may put on a gay appearance in the days of their health, and silence the reproaches of their own minds when surrounded with the smiles and flatteries of the world, but when the king of terrors approaches, and a mortal distemper summons them to appear before their Almighty Judge, when the skill of physicians fails and their friends stand round their dying beds with an unavailing pity; when the immortal spirit is just ready to take its flight into the invisible world; when a few moments must determine their eternal destiny—if now they have no hope but what arises from the purity of their hearts and the righteousness of their lives, what visions of wrath will present themselves to their guilty minds! What fears of future vengeance disturb and distract the departing hour!

But if in the happy days of health we humbly accept the proposals of divine grace and fly to that refuge which astonishing goodness has prepared for the security of sinners, we have a sure foundation for comfort in life and hope in death. We may now possess that peace of God which passes all understanding, and rejoice in the certain prospect of future felicity and glory. We may look down on the splendors of this world with a calm disdain, knowing we have a nobler portion reserved for us in heaven. We may stand upon the utmost verge of the present life with untrembling hearts and welcome the happy day which lands us on the immortal shore.

And now, my brethren, who of us does not think this happiness worthy to be desired with ardor, to be embraced with raptures of gratitude? Behold, I bring you glad tidings of great joy. This happiness will be the portion of all who receive it as the free gift of God, through the merits and righteousness of Jesus Christ.

I am sensible that this is a doctrine hard to be believed, and when believed it is perpetually opposed by the pride and prejudices of human nature. Though it forms the brightest glory of the gospel and gives the greatest encouragement to indigent and perishing sinners, though it contains a truth sufficient to make every heart leap for joy and every tongue celebrate the praises of God, yet nothing is more contrary to the prevailing sentiments of mankind. Nothing has occasioned warmer disputes in the church of God. Our natural dispositions are as averse to receive salvation by free grace as to submit to the laws of the divine government. We seek for some recommending qualities which shall render us proper objects of the divine favor and give us some kind of title to the blessings of His grace. We cannot think we have a right to trust in Christ for privileges so incomparably excellent which will make us happy in time and eternity till we are possessed of some previous righteousness to secure us a welcome reception.

Thus, by a proud pretense of humility, we refuse to give to God the glory of the riches of His grace. By an evil heart of unbelief we keep at a distance from the Fountain of all good; we seek to obtain that in ourselves which can only be obtained from the fullness that is in Christ.

Turn a deaf ear, O my brethren, to the dictates of corrupt reason. Hearken to the Son of God, who descended from the bosom of the Father to instruct a misguided world in the way of happiness. To whom did He dispatch His commissioned messengers? To those whose dignity commanded respect, whose wealth recommended them to favor, whose good qualities required they should be treated with distinction? No, they were sent to those who were in the most forlorn, destitute, and miserable circumstances, who had nothing to invite the esteem, but everything which might provoke the aversion of their generous Benefactor.

What is the message these ministers of heaven are commanded to deliver? That all things are ready, everything that is necessary to free them from the guilt of sin, cleanse them from the pollution of it, justify them at the tribunal of infinite purity, and prepare them for the enjoyment of heavenly happiness. The demands of justice are satisfied; the price of your salvation is paid; you are freely invited to receive the justification of your persons, the sanctification of your nature, and complete happiness.

Is this the language of our adorable Redeemer? Then surely it becomes us not to question His fidelity or diminish the riches of His grace. Does He call us? It is not presumption but a duty to obey His voice and accept His kind invitation. The inestimable privileges purchased by His blood are not for sale, but are the gift of God. They who receive them in the appointed way, freely, give glory to God and secure their immortal welfare.

13

The Nature of Faith

"By grace are ye saved through faith." Ephesians 2:8

There is, in many respects, a surprising correspondence between the means by which we were betrayed into ruin and the methods which infinite wisdom employs for our recovery. By the rebellion of the first Adam, we are made sinners; by the obedience of the second Adam, we are constituted righteous. In consequence of our relation to the primitive transgressor, our natures are universally corrupted and defiled; by a union to our divine Redeemer, we are sanctified in spirit, soul, and body. We lost the glory of our innocence by hearkening to the father of lies; we are restored to the favor and image of God by giving credit to the Word of truth. By trusting Satan we became miserable; by believing in Him who came to destroy the works of the devil, we recover our forfeited happiness. This is that sublime truth which is taught us in the words of my text: "By grace are ye saved through faith."

I shall endeavor to explain the nature of that faith by which we are saved, and give some application.

There is a faith that is common to the children of God and the servants of sin. Faith is often mentioned as the distinguishing character of the saints, and sometimes is ascribed to the worst of beings. It formed the brightest glory of Abraham, the friend of God, and inspires the apostate spirits with fear and trembling. There must then be an essential difference between that faith by which we are saved and that which may accompany us to eternal damnation.

Faith, in a religious sense, is an assurance of those truths which are revealed in the inspired Scriptures. It is founded not on the conjectures of human reason, but on the authority of God, the Revealer. Everything which God has revealed or promised, everything which is contained in the volume of the Old and New Testaments, is the proper object of faith. But the especial object of that faith which is the distinguishing characteristic of the real Christian is Jesus Christ, the eternal Son of God, the appointed Savior of a revolted world. He offered Himself as a sacrifice to divine justice so that we might not be condemned at its awful bar. He fulfilled all righteousness so that we might have a valid title to the reward of life eternal. He is proposed in the gospel in all the glories of an all-sufficient and condescending Savior, to be received as the Gift of God, to be trusted in by all those who are sensible of their guilt and misery, and who desire to obtain the blessings of salvation. Faith is a persuasion that it is the sole prerogative of this adorable Person to restore our lapsed race to the favor of God. To express myself in inspired language, "Neither is there salvation in any other, for there is no other name under heaven given among men whereby we must be saved" (Acts 4:12).

This faith is often described in the gospel to be a firm belief that Jesus is the Son of God, the promised Messiah. Consequently, His doctrine is divine and His promises certain, which shall infallibly be accomplished in their appointed order. We believe what the sacred historians have recorded of His miraculous birth, His unspotted life, His wonderful works, His meritorious death, His glorious resurrection, His triumphant ascension into heaven, and His prevalent intercession at the right hand of the Father. These truths are received as faithful sayings not because they could be discovered by human reason, but because they are authenticated by a divine testimony.

When the Son of God commands us to receive Him as

a Messenger from heaven, He gives the most unquestionable evidences of the divinity of His mission. He declares that He is a Teacher sent from God, and discovers His claim to this character by the demonstration of the Spirit and by power. He practiced the most heroic virtues in every period of His residence among men. He confirmed His doctrine by miracles which could only be performed by an omnipotent arm. He appeared to be the Prince of Life when expiring in the agonies of death. He disposed of the joys of paradise when suffering as a condemned malefactor.

In this critical moment, nature, through all her works, declared His dignity and glory; even the inhabitants of the grave arose to do honor to Him who has the keys of the invisible world. He entered the grave not by necessity of nature, but by voluntary consent. He triumphed over the king of terrors in his own dominions, and ascended like an invincible conqueror to immortal life. This set the seal of heaven to the truth of His mission, justified His highest pretensions, and in the most solemn manner declared that He was exalted to be a Friend and a Savior.

They who yield an unfeigned assent to these truths are frequently said to believe. But when this faith only floats in the understanding and does not descend into the heart, captivate the affections, and regulate the conduct of mankind, it will not evidence that we are true disciples of Christ or secure us a title to the privileges which He has purchased for His people. Simon Magus was made a proselyte by the preaching of Philip; he was baptized into the faith of the gospel, and it is said that he also believed. Yet we have the testimony of an inspired apostle that his heart was not right with God; he was in the gall of bitterness and bonds of iniquity. Daily experience teaches us that men's judgments may be convinced and the will remain obstinate and perverse. We may give credit to the truth of a doctrine and our heart rise up in opposition against it.

But this faith, instead of being acceptable to God, increases His displeasure. So far from being beneficial to men, it adds to their guilt and misery. A professed infidel is not so odious a character as a perfidious traitor. It therefore necessarily follows that the faith which is the distinguishing character of the children of God must be of a more excellent kind than that which we have now been describing.

The faith which saves us always engages us unfeignedly to approve the way of salvation by Jesus Christ, to cheerfully accept Him as our only complete and eternal Savior, to humbly confide in Him for all the promised blessings which He confers on His people. These are the inseparable attendants of a true faith, and distinguish it from the most specious counterfeits. I shall explain them in their order.

1. A true faith engages us to an unfeigned approbation of the way of salvation by Jesus Christ. Men who have been educated in the principles of the Christian faith often receive them as true without any hesitation. When convinced of their guilt, they acknowledge the necessity of an interest in Christ to deliver them from the punishment they have deserved. Animated with a dread of future misery and inspired with the hope of heavenly happiness, they attempt to give up themselves to Jesus Christ. But all is forced—their only motive is to remove the grounds of their present disquietude, for when their distress vanishes they soon return to their former sins, or satisfy themselves with a round of religious performances and a conversation outwardly inoffensive and regular. The name of Jesus is heard with indifference, and persons of this character often prove to be the greatest opposers of the unadulterated doctrine of grace.

To form faith in the heart, a supernatural light must be communicated to us from above to convince us not only of the truth, but the excellency and glory of the plan of salvation revealed in the gospel. We view it not only as divinely true, but supremely good. This conquers our prejudices, captivates our hearts, and produces a cheerful acquiescence in the designs of redeeming love. We admire this method of salvation as the contrivance of infinite wisdom, the product of amazing benevolence. We behold the character of the Deity displayed in its brightest glory and the richest grace discovered to perishing sinners. Awful justice maintains the authority of the law, and mercy triumphs in the recovery of a lapsed world. Sin is severely punished, and the sinner received to favor. Our Surety dies to fulfill the penalty of the law and in His obedience unto death accomplishes a perfect righteousness on behalf of His people.

In compliance with this marvelous plan, the glad tidings of a Savior are preached to rebellious men and all nations are invited to accept salvation through His merits and mediation. When this is clearly discovered to the mind, it puts a final period to all our former contrivances to recommend ourselves to the favor of God. We come to a fixed determination to seek for happiness only through the grace and righteousness of our adorable Redeemer. We believe it to be not only a faithful saying, but worthy of all acceptance, that Christ came into the world to save the chief of sinners.

Incredulous men may form a thousand objections against that way of salvation which strips the sinner of all preparatory goodness, and brings him as a convicted criminal to the footstool of sovereign grace, to expect all his blessedness from the merit and obedience of another. Yet this very view (which is so great an offense to the pride of unhumbled nature) attracts the admiration and gratitude of every enlightened mind. They adore a crucified Savior as the wisdom and power of God. This is the language of their enraptured hearts:

"This is a scheme which secures the honor of the Supreme Governor of the universe and provides for the safety of self-destroyed man. God appears encompassed with the most awful and amiable glory. The pride of all flesh is humbled in the dust. The believer is rescued from deserved misery and raised to immortal happiness. This reveals a Savior exactly adapted to the circumstances of destitute condemned malefactors, who have no good qualities to recommend them; who have nothing but the most abject wretchedness to move the divine compassions."

"Happy they who are interested in this adorable Jesus! They are delivered from their guilt and all its melancholy consequences. To obtain this blessing is my most ardent desire, the center of my hopes. If destitute of it, not all the treasures of earth or the glories of heaven can give me any solid satisfaction."

Thus the heart of man is brought to delight in the gospel salvation.

2. These views prepare us to cheerfully accept Christ as our complete and eternal Savior. The revelation of the gospel discovers to me an all-sufficient Savior; the illuminations of the Spirit represent this Savior as incomparably excellent, the most desirable good, a treasure that will enrich me to eternity. The next question that naturally arises in an awakened mind is this: "May I hope for an interest in this inestimable blessing? Will this illustrious Person accept an ungrateful rebel? Will He bestow life and salvation on me, who deserves nothing but death and damnation?"

These objections are in a great measure removed by the views I have just described; for the freedom and riches of divine grace to the greatest of sinners is an essential part of the glory that is displayed in the gospel. But we are naturally slow of heart to believe; a self-righteous spirit appears in a variety of forms to obstruct our approaches to God through Jesus Christ.

Therefore, the Word of God abounds with universal, unlimited invitations to sinners of every order, character, and degree to accept the blessings of salvation without money and without price. These are bestowed not on those who have any previous virtues to authorize their claim, but on polluted, impoverished, and necessitous bankrupts. They are to be received as a free donation, and are the unfailing portion of all who highly esteem and thankfully accept them.

This good news to a guilty world is not contained in a few obscure texts, tortured by the arts of criticism to serve a favorite system, but is the uniform language of inspiration, clothed in a variety of expressions and repeated with the most affectionate tenderness. When the Son of God opened His divine commission, with what meekness, with what condescension did He address His hearers! "The Spirit of the Lord is upon Me, because He hath appointed Me to preach the gospel to the poor, to proclaim deliverance to captives."

In the public course of His ministry, He declared His compassionate designs in the most expressive terms, to remove every doubt, to dissipate every fear that might arise in the breasts of sinners, and assure them of a welcome reception. He stood in a promiscuous multitude, encircled with numbers of His inveterate enemies, and cried with a loud voice, with affectionate vehemence, "If any man thirst, let him come to Me and drink. Though involved in the deepest guilt, covered with the most loathsome deformity, if he earnestly desires the blessings of salvation, let him repair to Me. I will supply all his wants, deliver him from all his distresses, and quench his thirst after happiness with fountains of living waters."

When our blessed Lord had finished His work upon earth and ascended on high in majestic triumph, He received the most inestimable gifts, to be conferred not on the virtuous and deserving, but for the disobedient and rebellious. Therefore, from His exalted throne in glory, He declared the generous intentions of His heart and closed the canon of the sacred Scriptures with this royal proclamation, "Whosoever will, let him come to the waters of life freely."

Animated by these kind invitations, supported by these reiterated assurances of success, the believer bows down at the feet of Jesus and thankfully accepts the offer of His grace. He does not derive his encouragement from any good he observes in himself, but from the free, universal tenders of divine grace to all, without any exclusive clause, to prevent the most indigent and wretched from a participation of these incomparable benefits. The goodwill of God, the merits of Christ, are the only foundation of his hope. Thus he addresses himself to the adorable Jesus in the language of humble faith: "O! Thou condescending Savior! I acknowledge that by sin I am become a child of wrath, justly condemned to suffer the pains of eternal death. I renounce all hopes of deliverance from any created wisdom or power; but Thou art the Son of God, and by the appointment of the Father the commissioned Savior of an apostate world. I therefore commit my soul into Thy hands, as one who is in every way qualified to provide for its welfare in time and eternity. O Thou heavenly Prophet! Remove the veil from my understanding and enlighten me in the knowledge of the truth; conduct me by Thy Word and Spirit in the way that leads to Thy eternal kingdom. O! Thou great High Priest! Sensible that I am a guilty criminal, I fly to the atoning merits of Thy blood to save me from the punishment I have deserved and plead Thy all-perfect righteousness that I may be satisfied at the tribunal of God. O! Thou immortal King! I bow to the scepter of Thy grace and cordially desire that every passion and inclination may be banished from my breast which opposes the laws of Thy government. O! Thou Captain of our salvation! I trust Thy victorious arm to defend me from the power and malice of my spiritual enemies, to subdue the native corruptions of my heart, to preserve me faithful to thy cause, and finally introduce me to the happiness Thou hast appointed for thy people. Had not astonishing grace allowed, nay, commanded me to receive Thee as the Gift of God, to accomplish these important purposes, I might justly suspect that my present address would be rejected with disdain. But since Almighty Love has provided a Savior for perishing sinners, since unlimited goodness has commanded the most unworthy to look unto Him that they may be saved, to receive this gift, to accept this goodwill, is not unwarranted presumption, but a commanded duty."

3. This acceptance of Christ as our Savior is accompanied with an entire dependence upon Him for all the promised blessings which He bestows on His people. This naturally follows from what I have already declared of the nature and operations of saving faith: If I assent to the way of salvation revealed in the gospel as divinely appointed; if I approve it as the most excellent way; if an almighty Savior is offered to every sinner without distinction; if I have been enabled to accept this blessed tender —then I may safely conclude that He will exert His saving power in my favor and bring me to see the good of His chosen. For this is only to believe that He will maintain the honor of His Word and fulfill His sacred engagements to His people. We have a testimony from heaven that "God so loved the world that He gave His only begotten Son that whosoever believeth in Him should not perish, but have everlasting life." It is written with an immortal pen that whoever comes to the blessed Jesus, He will in no wise cast out. If therefore my eyes have been opened to discern His excellency; if my heart has been persuaded to acquiesce to the designs of His redeeming love; if it is the top of my ambition to be found in Him, clothed with His righteousness, a monument of His grace—the inference is just and the

conclusion unfailing: He is and will be made of God unto me wisdom and righteousness, sanctification and redemption.

These heavens shall vanish as a scroll; this earth shall be dissolved by fire, and all the beauties of this lower creation expire in smoke; but not the minutest article of the divine promise shall fail of a punctual accomplishment.

Jesus is the only hope of the saints in the present age. Nations yet unborn shall be the future triumphs of His love. Nor will He lay aside the endearing character of a Savior till the empire of sin and Satan is destroyed, and all who place their trust in Him are fixed in immutable felicity and glory.

Application

Let us examine whether we have that faith which is the unfailing character of the people of God, a certain evidence that we are made partakers of the blessings of salvation. Each of us must ask these questions:

1. Have I been made sensible of my sinfulness and misery, the corruptions of my heart as well as the numberless pollutions of my life, of the infinite evil as well as destructive consequences of sin? Men may talk of free grace with seraphic eloquence, and flatter themselves with a pleasing dream that they are the favorites of heaven; but till they perceive the condemning power of the law and subscribe to the justice of that sentence which is pronounced against every transgressor, they continue under the dominion of sin and see no beauty and loveliness in the Savior.

2. Have I been convinced of my utter inability to deliver myself from this misery? Have I seen the vanity of all dependence upon the uprightness of my intentions, the regularity of my conduct, my humblest confessions or deepest humiliations, to expiate the guilt of sin and satisfy

the justice of offended heaven? Without this I shall inevitably trust my prayers, tears, and amendments to recommend me to the favor of God. I shall neglect the only Sacrifice that has made complete atonement for the sins of men.

3. Have I accepted the proposals of the gospel? The gospel reveals an almighty Savior to a ruined world, and by the most persuasive arguments invites us to receive Him in that amiable character. Have I heard the joyful sound with gratitude, and been made willing to be saved by Christ in His own appointed way? Is this the unfeigned language of my soul: "Lift up your heads, ye everlasting gates, let the King of Glory descend and take the full possession of all my powers?" Do I not only depend on His justifying righteousness, but welcome the sanctifying influences of His Spirit? Is He precious in my esteem not only as an atoning priest, but a commanding king, to mortify my dearest lusts as well as to deliver me from the miseries of hell, to form me to an entire subjection to His laws as well as dignify me with the privileges of His people?

4. Is Jesus, in all His sacred offices, the supreme object of my affection? Do I prefer Him to all the honors and advantages of this life? Do I count all things but loss that I may win Him?

If these dispositions are implanted in us by the Spirit of God, they are fruits of distinguishing grace, and will terminate in the harvest of glory.

They who pour contempt on the love of God manifested by Jesus Christ neglect their most important interests. Interest is the grand spring of human actions. They who are deaf to the calls of duty, insensible of the obligations of gratitude, are generally influenced by what they imagine to be their interest. But it is the infelicity of mankind that they often confine their views to the present moment and disregard future consequences. They fix their eyes on things which are seen and temporal, but are blind to the excellence and beauty of things unseen and eternal.

We see men engaged in a perpetual hurry, disquieted with perplexing fears. Ask them what the matter is and they will tell you, "My honor or interest is at stake." This awakens their solicitous concern and engages them to incessant activity and diligence. Allow me, my brethren, to inquire, is it not your honor and interest to be delivered from the wrath of God and the unutterable torments of hell, to be admitted into the family of heaven and secure a title to the inheritance of the saints in light? I must rank you among the number of abandoned infidels, or degrade you from the character of rational creatures, to suppose you can hesitate one moment in deciding this important question. None can be indifferent whether they live with God or are eternal exiles from His blissful presence, whether they spend unceasing ages in the triumphant joys of heaven or excruciating pains of hell.

Why is it then that future happiness is so generally neglected? Why is it that men who discover the most exquisite sagacity in securing the interests of this life are so infatuated as to pay little or no attention to the momentous affairs of the world to come? Is it because the supreme happiness of their nature is placed out of their reach? Is it because there is no prospect of success, though they employ their utmost diligence? Blessed be God, this is not the case. Are you excluded from the hope of the gospel? Is the inevitable sentence passed upon you? Are you not invited to return to your offended Sovereign? Does not the Son of God call you by His Word and Spirit to come to Him that you may have life? If then you are excluded from future happiness, it is by your own obstinacy and perverseness. If eternal damnation is your portion, it is because you prefer your sins before your Savior, the pleasures of the world before the privileges of the people of God. Every argument of terror and endearment is employed to persuade you not to receive the grace of God in vain.

The compassionate Father of mercies solicits your compliance with His demands, as if His own honor and interest were connected with your happiness. The great Creator becomes a supplicant to His creature man and beseeches us with bowels of pity to be reconciled to Him. He swears by His own unutterable name that He seeks not our destruction, but delights in our happiness. "As I live (says the Lord), I take no pleasure in the death of the sinner, but that he repent and live. Turn ye, turn ye; why will ye die?"

If you reject these pleas, upon what can you depend? Upon your own goodness? The defects of your duties will forever condemn you! Upon your present health and strength? Your life is a vapor which vanishes in a moment! Every hope will deceive you but that which is built on Jesus Christ. Place your entire dependence on Him. He will give you grace, glory, and every desirable good. To Him be glory forever and ever, Amen.

14

Faith the Appointed Way of Salvation

"For by grace are ye saved through faith." Ephesians 2:8

To glorify God, the great Author of our being, ought to be the uninterrupted employment of every intelligent creature. For this we were formed by His almighty hand and redeemed by His marvelous grace. The first creation proclaims the existence of an all-wise and powerful deity; the new creation discovers the wonders of His love to His apostate creatures.

Therefore, when the Son of God descended from the bosom of the Father to tabernacle in human flesh, a multitude of the heavenly host sang "Glory to God in the highest, peace upon earth and goodwill to men." The design of this mysterious dispensation was to place the benignity of the divine nature in the most amiable and attracting point of light so that the innumerable orders of angels might admire the riches of His grace and all the nations of the redeemed might pay an eternal tribute of praise to Him, who delivered them from the abyss of misery and made them heirs of celestial glory. Upon this account the whole scheme of redemption is wisely contrived, to subdue the pride of man and to advance the honor of the Most High God. Therefore, in the eternal counsels of His will, He determined not only that our salvation should be of grace, but through faith.

First, in what sense are we said to be saved through faith? Every man must either be justified by law or saved by grace, or perish forever. If I expect to be justified by law, my obedience must be perfect, without the smallest blemish; it must be universal, without the least exception; and it must be persevering, without a moment's interruption. We appear before the throne of infinite purity and challenge impartial justice to find anything in us worthy of condemnation and death.

But the man who expects to be saved by grace acknowledges himself to be a guilty criminal, worthy of the most severe punishment. He is sensible that his best performances, if examined according to the purity and extent of the law, must be turned into articles of indictment against him. He therefore appeals from the bar of justice to the throne of grace. Humbly confessing that if God should be strict to mark iniquity, he must be eternally condemned, he pleads the pardoning mercy of God through the mediation of Jesus Christ. The only foundation of his hope is that the Supreme Lawgiver will not deal with him according to his personal demerits, but consider him as united to His dear Son, whom he cordially accepts as his Savior and Lord. Through Him, though he is condemned by the law, he expects to be relieved by the gospel; though deserving the miseries of hell, he hopes to enjoy the felicities of the kingdom of heaven. Christ, and He only, has purchased our salvation by His infinite merits; in His righteousness we must appear if we are to be accepted at the tribunal of God. If Christ had not died for our offenses and risen again for our justification, in vain would we bewail our sins, reform our lives, and employ our most assiduous endeavors to recover our innocence and happiness. Every well-instructed mind will therefore say with St. Paul, "God forbid that I should glory, save in the cross of Christ."

Of consequence, when we are said to be saved through faith, it cannot intend that faith merits our salvation, or that God gives us eternal happiness to reward the excellency and goodness of our faith. But it is the appointed method in which we are made partakers of the blessings which Christ has purchased with His blood. In this sense, and in no other, is faith the condition of our salvation. This the gospel testifies through all its inspired pages: "If thou shalt confess with thy mouth the Lord Jesus Christ, and shalt believe in thy heart that God hath raised Him from the dead, thou shalt be saved." When the awakened jailor made the solemn inquiry, "What shall I do to be saved?" this is the answer given by the ambassadors of heaven: "Believe in the Lord Jesus Christ, and thou shalt be saved." Nor have the refinements of later ages found a more direct entrance into the Kingdom of God.

Faith is that grace which unites us to the Son of God, the Savior of the world. By this union, we become partakers of all His benefits. Our guilt is transferred to Him and His righteousness is imputed to us. To express myself in language dictated by the Holy Ghost, "He was made to be sin for us who knew no sin, that we might be made the righteousness of God in Him."

Let us place this truth in another point of light and make it as intelligible as may be to the meanest understanding. Salvation is frequently represented as the gift of God. Now we all know that there is a wise distinction between that which is bestowed as a free gift and that which is obtained as the reward of services performed. To establish our claim to the promised reward, we must accomplish our task, finish the appointed work, and punctually comply with all the articles specified in the agreement. But to enjoy a gift, nothing is requisite but to realize the kindness of our benefactor and receive his generous offer with gratitude.

This gives us a perspicuous view of the method in which we are made partakers of the salvation revealed in the gospel. Salvation is not bestowed upon us as the reward of our good services. We cannot challenge it as a debt from the hand of justice; it is the gift of unpurchased bounty. Our only part is to accept the goodwill of our heavenly Father and ascribe all our happiness to the riches of redeeming love.

Thus we are saved by faith. Faith accepts the condescending offers of a Savior and gives God the glory of that grace which He designed to magnify in the recovery of an apostate world. What is it to believe? It is to give credit to the report of the gospel, to receive that Savior who is freely tendered to us, to depend on His righteousness to give us a title to the favor of God, and to resign ourselves to His Spirit to prepare us for the enjoyment of life eternal.

Upon this foundation all pretenses to merit are destroyed; all claims established on personal worthiness are disallowed. God gives and faith receives a title to the dignity and privileges of the sons of God. There is no merit in receiving a gift, though it is necessary to enjoying the good which is tendered to me. Thus faith does not give me an interest in Christ on the foot of desert, but by virtue of a divine constitution. The wisdom of the Deity did not see fit that those should have a title to this salvation who were insensible of their want of it or unwilling to receive it. They are forever excluded by an irreversible decree who obstinately despise and ungratefully trample under their feet the inestimable blessing.

I am now prepared, second, to inquire into the reasons of this divine constitution.

The design of man's redemption flowed from the eternal counsels of heaven. Before this universe existed, the Deity foresaw that many of the free intelligences He designed to create would violate the established orders of His government and fall from their original dignity. His unbounded benevolence inclined Him to devise a method of recovery for many of His rebellious subjects. The sinning angels, the first transgressors, are excluded from all hopes of mercy, while the sinful posterity of Adam are appointed to be the objects of distinguishing favors.

Infinite wisdom determined that without vindicating the honor of the law there would be no remission of sin. This the Son of God undertook and voluntarily engaged to save a guilty world. He exhibited Himself in the gospel in the character of a Savior and gave us the highest assurance that all who believe in Him shall experience the blessed effects of His power and grace. But if men willfully refuse the kind hand that is extended for their deliverance, nothing remains but that they perish in their sins.

This is the immutable appointment, not only of the sovereignty but wisdom of heaven. Faith is the appropriated way to life because it brings nothing with it, but receives all from the fullness of Christ. It pleads guilty before God and implores a free pardon. It acknowledges the sinner's inability to all spiritual good and supplicates that grace which must perform all our works in us. Thus God alone is exalted, and human vanity prostrate in the dust. All self-dependence is renounced and holiness and happiness received as a communication from Christ; the crown is placed upon the head of our incarnate God, and the entire glory of our salvation is ascribed to free grace. This forms the excellency of faith and discovers it to be a fit method to save those who are utterly ruined in themselves. Upon this account St. Paul, having declared that we are saved through faith, in the next verse excludes works, and gives this reason: "lest any man should boast."

I think I hear some ask, "How can works be excluded? Are they not necessary to salvation?"

I acknowledge that the faith that saves us is a vital principle of universal holiness. Faith is essentially defective if it does not produce good works. I further acknowledge that purity of heart and a uniform obedience to the divine commandments are necessary ingredients in the character of those who shall be finally saved. It is the irrevocable constitution of heaven that without holiness no man shall see the Lord.

The only controversy between us and those who in this article differ from us is whether good works are the consequences of our union with Christ and an interest in His salvation, or whether they are antecedent conditions of our obtaining this invaluable blessing? We assert the first, and think we are supported not only by the authority of St. Paul in the words of my text, but by the uniform tenor of the inspired writings. Grace and works are frequently put in a direct and formal opposition to each other. That purity of heart, that sanctity of life, that victory of corruption, that unreserved devotedness to God which are the grand essentials of the Christian life are not virtues we bring with us in our first approaches to the Savior, but blessings He bestows on them who come to Him by a humble faith.

This will be incontrovertibly evident if we consider that our most specious performances, before we are brought into this sacred union, are corrupt and vicious. Without faith, said the author of Hebrews, it is impossible to please God. "Without Me," said the faithful and true Witness, "ye can do nothing."

By faith then are we saved, and not by works; for this salvation is begun before we can perform any works that may be truly denominated good. We receive Jesus the Savior; we become members of His mystical body. By virtue of this, His righteousness is imputed to us. His Spirit resides in us; this leads us into all truth, inclines us to all good, and enables us to walk in the way that will finally conduct us to consummate purity and blessedness.

Application

1. This instructs us in the difference between the law and the gospel. The law demands perfect and perpetual

obedience as the condition of life; the gospel requires humble faith as the appointed means of safety and happiness. According to the tenor of the law, we must have a complete and personal righteousness to escape its damnatory sentence; according to the condescending terms of the gospel, the righteousness of our Surety delivers us from death and gives us a title to life eternal. This is the unalterable voice of the law: "Do these things and thou shalt live." This is the alluring language of the gospel: "Believe and thou shalt be saved."

The different terms are wisely adapted to the different states and circumstances of mankind. The law was delivered to man when in a state of unblemished innocence, in all the perfection of his nature, when he had strength to perform his entire duty without defect or deviation. But the gospel considers man as fallen from his primitive integrity, destitute of ability or inclination to do that which is good. It is appointed for his rescue from the condemnation of the law and the tyrannical dominion of sin; therefore it does not call him to purchase life by his obedience, but to receive that grace which alone can enable him to will and to do; not to expect happiness from his own virtue and goodness, but by an humble affiance in the grace and righteousness of an all-sufficient Savior.

Everyone who does not submit to the law of faith must stand or fall by the law of works. This infallibly condemns all the posterity of Adam without distinction, whether Gentile, Jew, or Christian. All have violated its righteous precepts and incurred its dreadful penalty. How terrible is that dispensation to an awakened mind that denounces indignation and wrath, tribulation and anguish, on every soul that does evil! How admirable is that grace which reveals Jesus, the wisdom and power of God, to the salvation of everyone who believes! How alarming is that sentence which curses everyone "that continueth not in all things written in the Book of the Law, to do them!" And how reviving is that voice which declares that Christ Jesus delivers us from the curse of the law, being made a curse for us, and assures us that as many as receive Him have power to become the Sons of God!

2. What reason we have to rejoice in the light and advantages of the gospel. In this dispensation, the grace of God appears in its brightest splendor, its unlimited freeness, to attract the attention of perishing sinners. The Divine Majesty is seated on a throne of grace and we are invited to touch the scepter of mercy and live. Angels are commissioned to publish the good-will of God to men; ministers are appointed to preach peace by Jesus Christ to them who are afar off and to them who are near. The condition of our reconciliation with an offended Deity is not undefective holiness, which must sink us into the deepest despair, but a humble faith, which receives all from the over-flowing Fountain of all good. Happy are we, my brethren, though ruined in Adam, who have a way of recovery revealed by Jesus Christ.

What gloomy fears must arise in the breast of an uninstructed pagan, when conscience accuses him of numberless violations of the law of nature? If he looks up, he beholds the heavens darkened with clouds of wrath and thunders prepared by divine justice, ready to be discharged on his guilty head. If he casts his eyes down upon the earth, he sees the grave prepared to receive him, and has just reason to fear that the pains of a temporal death will transmit him to the miseries of an eternal one.

To whom shall he apply in this melancholy situation? To the altars of his gods? Alas! The superstitious rites, the uninstituted sacrifices with which they are approached, instead of effacing his guilt, serve only to increase the number of his crimes. Shall he implore mercy of the idols he absurdly worships? Alas! They have no eyes to see, no ears to hear, no tongues to speak, nor hearts to pity his distress.

Whichever way he turns, he finds no ray of light to scatter the gloom that surrounds him on every side; no friendly director to show him the path of peace and safety. The light of nature discovers his guilt, but can give no assurance of the divine favor and forgiveness. This is the distinguishing glory of the gospel. Those who hearken to its indulgent voice and trust in its faithful promises may be freed from all disquieting doubts and enjoy that peace of God which passes all understanding.

In Christ we behold God reconciled, guilt abolished, the law fulfilled, death disarmed, the fire of hell extinguished, and the joys of heaven purchased for all who believe and obey Him. These happy souls may, in the full assurance of faith, adopt the triumphant challenge of St. Paul: "Who shall lay anything to the charge of God's elect? It is God that justifieth. Who shall condemn? It is Christ that died; yea, rather that is risen again, who is even at the right hand of God, who also maketh intercession for us."

O God! How kind are Thy dealings unto the children of men! How boundless Thy compassions to ungrateful rebels! How adapted are the methods of Thy grace to Thy destitute creatures! Thou knowest the frailty and inconstancy of our natures, and therefore commandest us to commit the keeping of our souls to an almighty Savior, who is the same yesterday, today and forever.

3. While the gospel establishes salvation by faith, it takes the most effectual care to engage us in the practice of universal holiness. True faith infallibly disposes the mind to an impartial obedience to the divine commandments. If it does not have this influence, St. James pronounces it to be a dead faith; and it is the grossest absurdity to suppose a dead faith can bring us to the happiness of eternal life. Faith subdues the heart to a chosen conformity to the nature and design of the gospel. What is the design of the gospel? Everyone must acknowledge it to be not only to publish an act of indemnity in favor of condemned rebels,

but to deliver them from the dominion of their lusts; not only to dignify them with the title of sons, but enable them to walk as becomes the obedient children of God.

Consequently, to rely on Christ to deliver us from the miseries of hell, and not also to save us from the service of sin and Satan, is not the faith of the gospel, but a vain imagination. Instead of introducing us into the way of life, it opens a spacious but dangerous road which betrays us to the chambers of death. The faith so highly recommended in the oracles of God is always attended with the influences of the Holy Spirit; this divine Agent resides in the heart of the true believer, dissolves his attachment to every sin, and causes him to delight in the law of God after the inward man. The fruit of the Spirit is love, and the various graces which constitute the Christian life. They who do not have this Spirit of Christ are positively declared to be none of His.

None believe in Christ who are not previously convinced of the corruption of their nature, and their exposedness to the wrath of God by their innumerable violations of His laws. When brought to acquiesce in the designs of redeeming love, we receive the blessed Jesus to save us from sin as well as wrath. We ardently desire to be made holy as well as happy. An essential part of that salvation which He bestows on His people is a heart purified from the love of sin and unfeignedly devoted to the service of heaven. He delivers us out of the hands of our enemies so that we might serve Him without fear, in holiness and righteousness all the days of our life.

4. They who perish in their sins under the light of the gospel are, of all men, the most inexcusable. Who would not suppose a guilty world would receive the declarations of divine grace with raptures of joy and with the deepest submission accept the offered favor? But constant experience teaches us that multitudes are inattentive to the joyful sound, while others treat it with a profane contempt.

Whence arises this infatuated conduct? A secret infidelity is, doubtless, the source of that fatal security which prevails among mankind. A wavering assent to the truths of the gospel prevents their cheerful compliance with its benevolent design.

Were the doctrines of religion built on the vain imaginations of men; were the sublime hopes of the Christian unsupported with divine credentials—no wonder the wise and considerate part of mankind should treat it with indifference. Why should we pursue the flattering illusions of a credulous mind? Why should we be captivated with airy prospects, which will probably disappoint our expectations?

But salvation by faith is a doctrine revealed by the God of truth, and supported by every kind of evidence that can be desired by a reasonable, unprejudiced mind. St. Paul tells us that this salvation at first began to be spoken by the Lord, and was confirmed to us by them who heard Him— God also bearing them witness with both signs and wonders, and divers miracles and gifts of the Holy Ghost, according to His own will.

The Son of God descended from heaven and clothed Himself with the infirmities of human flesh to reveal these glad tidings to a revolted world. He evidenced His mission by astonishing miracles which bear the character of infinite wisdom and resistless power. These wonderful works were not done in a corner, in a private retirement or among a few friends, no, but in the streets of Jerusalem, in the presence of multitudes, in the view of His enemies. As the Lord of nature, the winds and sea obey His voice; the most inveterate diseases fly at His approach. His commands are heard in the awful mansions of the dead; the inhabitants of the grave answer to His call and rise to life and vigor. He died and the heavens were darkened, the earth trembled, and the rocks were rent. He raised Himself from the dead; angels descended from heaven to pay

Him homage. His timorous disciples acknowledged their Master and Lord. At length He took farewell of this earth and ascended up to heaven in the public view of His followers. The Spirit descended on His apostles in visible forms; they were immediately endowed with the supernatural gift of tongues, and they also performed illustrious miracles in the name of their ascended Master.

These were public and visible facts acknowledged by the incredulous Jews, and allowed by the most inveterate enemies of the Christian faith in the early days of the church. Authorized by these divine credentials, the apostles propagated the religion of Jesus with surprising success. Without power to awe, without wealth to bribe, and without eloquence to persuade, they triumphed over the prejudices of the vulgar, the reasonings of the philosophers, and the long established idolatry of all nations. Though the princes of the Roman Empire endeavored to stop the progress of the gospel; though priests and politicians made use of all their art and address to expose it to contempt; though the fires of persecution consumed its professors for three hundred years—it took deep root, spread far and wide, and filled the whole earth with its salutary influences.

Was ever a doctrine confirmed with such illustrious attestations? What could support it amidst so many dangers but the divine protection? What further evidence can men desire that the gospel is a revelation from heaven and, consequently, that salvation may be obtained by faith?

If men continue in unbelief, it is to be ascribed to the corrupt disposition of their hearts, a fond attachment to their criminal delights. A perpetual engagement in the business and amusements of life prevents their receiving the truth in the love of it. "If our gospel be hid, it is hid to them that are lost, in whom the god of this world hath blinded the minds of them that believe not, lest the light of the glorious gospel of Christ, who is the image of God, should shine unto them."

From this most terrible of all judgments, may God of His infinite mercy deliver us. To Him be glory forever and ever, Amen.

15

Faith the Gift of God

"And that not of yourselves, it is the gift of God."
Ephesians 2:8

When the posterity of Jacob were rescued from the bondage of Egypt, it was a type of the more important deliverance which God grants to His people from the hands of their spiritual enemies. When the tribes of Israel departed in triumph from the land of their oppressors, it was not in consequence of the battles they fought or the victories they obtained; the Lord of Hosts marched at the head of their armies; an invisible Hand destroyed the power of their enemies. When they passed through the Red Sea, they had neither boats nor bridges to convey them to the opposite shore; but God opened to them a passage through the bosom of the deep. The fluid element, contrary to the established laws of nature, was a defense to them and proved the destruction of their assailants. When they traveled for forty years in an inhospitable desert, they did not cultivate the earth or gather in a harvest; they were fed with the bread of angels; manna descended daily around their camp, and the rock poured out water for their refreshment. When to punish their murmuring God sent fiery serpents among them, their deadly wounds were healed not by the skill of physicians or the virtue of antidotes; a brazen serpent was erected by divine command; they looked to the appointed signal and the camp was restored to health and vigor. When they crossed the River Jordan, they had no conveniences to secure their passage;

the mysterious ark, the symbol of the divine presence, arrested the waters in their course; the numerous host passed over on dry ground and entered the borders of the promised Canaan. When they obtained the peaceable possession of that happy land it was not by their own swords and bow; but the captain of the Lord's host fought their battles for them, inspired them with conduct and courage, and crowned them with victory and success.

This is a lively representation of the conduct of heaven towards His spiritual Israel in all ages of the church. As God's ancient people could not ascribe their triumphs to the number of their armies, the greatness of their exploits, or their own policy and power, but to an almighty Arm which caused all opposition to fall before them, so the redemption of the New Testament saints from the slavery of Satan cannot be attributed to the powers of nature or the success of their own endeavors, but to the aids of supernatural grace, which subdued the strength of their ghostly adversaries and led them on from conquering to conquer.

Therefore, the apostle having asserted that by grace we are saved through faith, to remove all ground of boasting, tells us in the words now read that this faith is not of ourselves, it is the gift of God. I am sensible these words are referred by some to salvation in general, which they acknowledge is not of ourselves but the gift of God; but I think it is plainly the design of the apostle to apply these words particularly to faith. He had before established the honor of divine grace in giving salvation to mankind, and declared that faith was the means of obtaining an interest in it. Now, to destroy all pretensions to pride, he teaches us that this faith is not a grace that grows in the garden of nature, but is the production of God. This is evidently the doctrine of religion: a divine power opened the heart of Lydia to believe the preaching of St. Paul. When St. Peter acknowledged Jesus to be the Son of God, our Lord immediately replied, "Blessed art thou, Simon Bar-jona, for flesh and blood hath not revealed it unto thee, but My Father which is in heaven." These texts, with many others which might be mentioned, establish beyond doubt the doctrine I am considering, that faith is the gift of God.

In my discourse I shall show in what sense faith is the gift of God, and then mention a few particulars which illustrate and confirm this important truth.

First, I am to show in what sense faith is the gift of God. Many profess their assent to the proposition that faith is the gift of God, but mean no more than that God gives a general and sufficient grace to all mankind, by virtue of which they may believe if they please, but all are equally free to remain in unbelief and rebellion. According to this scheme, ability to believe comes from God, but actual faith is properly to be ascribed to man. After all the influences with which he is favored, he determines himself with a sovereign and independent freedom. This destroys the divinity of St. Paul and supports the fabric of human pride; it makes man, after all the compliments paid to grace, the final architect of his own happiness. But those who are taught in the school of Christ are inspired with different sentiments. They are convinced that not only the ability, but the inclination to believe is one of those good gifts which descend from the Father of lights.

By the secret illuminations of His Spirit, He discovers to us the excellency and beauty of a Savior, and the value and importance of the blessings He proposes to our choice. By a gentle but effectual influence He disposes us to accept the condescending offer. If this were not the case, with what propriety could the apostle propose that question, "Who maketh thee to differ from another? What hast thou that thou didst not receive?" The believer might answer with the strictest propriety, "I have made the difference; the good improvement I have made of my free will has distinguished me from the perverse and incredulous part of mankind. I adore the Most High God as the

Father of my spirit. I render Him my devout acknow-
ledgements that He made me with a free intelligence. I
give thanks to His name that He has favored me with the
light of the gospel and the kind assistances of His Spirit.
But these are common favors, equally enjoyed by all the
professors of the gospel; they do not distinguish me from
the hardened sinner. That I believe, while others reject the
Word of Life, is not the gift of God, but must be ascribed
to the wisdom of my choice, the good disposition of my
heart."

Whose heart would not tremble! What tongue would
not falter to utter this presumptuous language! I freely acknowledge that those who remain in unbelief must impute
it entirely to their pride and perverseness, their love of this
world and attachment to their criminal pleasures. But
those who believe must ascribe their faith to the effectual
operations of divine grace.

To illustrate and confirm this truth is what I propose to
do in the second part of my discourse. To this end, let us
consider: our natural inability to that which is good; the
resistance men generally make to the operations of the
Spirit, and the stratagems which Satan employs to keep
them from believing to the saving of their souls.

First, let us consider our natural inability to that which
is spiritually good. This is declared in Scripture in the most
expressive terms, in a variety of forms. The God of truth
declares that the thoughts and imaginations of the heart
of man are evil, only evil, and continually evil. An inspired
pen informs us that the carnal (i.e., the unrenewed) mind
is not subject to the law of God, nor can be; that "the
natural man receiveth not the things of the Spirit of God;
for they are foolishness unto him; neither can he know
them because they are spiritually discerned."

The same mortifying truth is taught by metaphors so
that it may be the more deeply engraven on our minds;
not to discourage, but humble us with a view of our

wretchedness; not to fill us with imaginary terrors, but alarm us to solicitously seek a cure. We are represented as blind to divine truths till a celestial ray shines upon our benighted minds and discovers to us their excellency and importance. We are deaf to the voice of incarnate love till a mighty power remove the obstructions and incline our ears to attend to the inviting sound. Our hearts are like obdurate rocks, impenetrable to every religious impression, till victorious grace softens them into flesh and makes them receptive to salutary impressions. We are dead in trespasses and sins till that irresistible command, which must shortly awake the inhabitants of the grave, causes us to arise and live.

These metaphorical expressions are not the flights of fancy, but they convey a solemn truth. No language can be contrived better adapted to represent our inability, by any inherent power of our own to do anything that is spiritually good. I am sensible that metaphors ought not to be pressed into a service for which they were not originally designed; at the same time, I am sure they ought not to be explained away till all their sense, propriety, and beauty is lost. If this variety of metaphors, so often repeated, does not teach us our spiritual impotence to the acts and exercises of the divine life, they signify nothing; they can be esteemed no better than extravagant hyperboles, which I am persuaded no serious mind will impute to an inspired Author.

Second, I proceed to show that in our state of unregenerate nature, we are not only destitute of all good, but resist the influences of divine grace. When our Lord performed His miraculous works, it was with uncontrolled power, without the aid of means or instruments. In the first creation, He issued out His authoritative fiat and this harmonious system immediately existed; nothing opposed the execution of His will. When the dead are raised, though they can contribute nothing to their own resurrection, yet they form no resistance to the all-quickening power of the Son of God. But when apostate man is created anew, when the spiritually dead are animated with a divine life, they are not only destitute of all previous disposition to faith and holiness, but disaffected to the sanctity of God, the methods of His grace, and the laws of His government. They perversely reject the generous hand which is stretched out to recover them from their guilt and misery. They oppose the operations of the sacred Spirit which are designed to restore them to the favor and image of God to present rectitude and future happiness. Surely nothing short of a divine power can subdue the native enmity of our hearts, change the bias of our depraved inclinations, and reduce us to a compliance with the appointed way of salvation. A heart to renounce our former prejudices and prepossessions, to submit to the grace and government of the blessed Jesus, must be the gift of God.

Third, this will be further evident when we take a view of the innumerable stratagems which Satan employs to keep us from believing to the saving of our souls. This subtle spirit is described in the gospel under the character of a strong man who, having entered into a house, guards it against every assault and uses all manner of arts to maintain the possession. Our victorious Redeemer must therefore bind this strong man before he can establish his empire in the human heart. It must be the work of the omnipotent God, and not of frail and feeble man, to triumph over this terrible enemy, to expel him from the dominion he has impiously usurped, and so obstinately defends. He must be cast out with violence before the sanctifying Spirit can regain the peaceable possession of His temple.

The Israelites were delivered from the tyranny of Pharaoh with a high hand and outstretched arm. But this prince, in all the pride and plentitude of power, was an infirm mortal. It is therefore a more illustrious conquest to rescue mankind from the captivity in which they are detained by the infernal tyrant of hell. He is great in strength, and has legions of mighty and malicious auxiliaries who fight under his standard and assiduously promote the designs of his accursed empire. It is the sole prerogative of the Most High God to dispossess the prince of darkness, and establish the kingdom of truth and righteousness in a revolted world.

Application

From what we have heard we must necessarily conclude that the deepest humility becomes the character of fallen creatures. In every view, we have the highest reason to abhor ourselves, to deplore the universal depravity of our natures, and to place our entire dependence on sovereign mercy for every blessing. Consider, attentively consider, into what a fatal abyss of misery the apostasy has plunged the race of men! What miracles of power and goodness are employed for our recovery! How desirable was the primitive state of man! An enlightened understanding taught him the knowledge of God and his duty; an uncorrupted heart inclined him to pay a perfect obedience to the mandates of his heavenly Father; the way to unfailing felicity was open to his view, and every delightful enjoyment was in his possession.

But, alas! He rebelled against God and a melancholy change immediately ensued. His glory departed from him; the privileges of his innocent nature were forfeited forever; darkness veiled his mind; pride and perverseness took possession of his heart; the love of God was banished from his breast, and self-love advanced to the throne. Man, the lord of this visible creation, became an infamous slave; the favorite of his Maker became a captive of hell. The heavens were armed with thunder, the earth exposed to a lasting curse, and everything conspired to make the ungrateful rebel mortal and miserable.

What prodigies of love prepared the way for our restitution to our former happiness! God became incarnate; the Lord of nature took upon Him the form of a servant; the Prince of Life suffered and died. Salvation is purchased at an infinite price, and freely offered to a lapsed world.

But this is not sufficient. Though the great Teacher of the Christian church has plainly directed us in the way that leads to the joys of paradise, yet our eyes are so dazzled with the glories of this world, our affections so strongly attached to sensual pleasures, and our minds so averse to everything which is spiritual and divine, that the same goodness which discovers to us a Savior must dispose us to accept Him in His sacred offices and characters. An omnipotent Arm must be revealed to conquer our reluctant nature or we shall voluntarily persist in the paths of perdition. If this is the case (as it really is), how vain are all our boasts of the dignity and excellency of our nature in its present depraved state! How ridiculous are all our pretenses to recommend ourselves to God by our own wisdom, power, or goodness!

Prostrate yourself in the dust, O fallen creature! Know that you are not only despicably mean, but inconceivably vile. To the all-penetrating eye of God you appear not only destitute of all recommending qualities, but as a mass of deformity. Let us then approach the supreme tribunal not in the presumptuous language of the Pharisee ("Lord, I thank Thee that I am not as other men"), but with the self-condemning disposition of the publican: "God, be merciful to me, a sinner; to Thee, O Lord, belongs righteousness, but to me shame and confusion of face. I have no plea but the merits of a crucified Savior, no hope but in the boundless resources of this grace."

When the haughtiness of man is obliged to stoop, the excellency of faith is clearly discovered. By this we are recovered from misery, restored to the favor of heaven, and conducted in the way that leads to unfading glory. All the graces which reside in the heart, all the virtues which adorn the life of a Christian, are the offspring of faith. This secures us the final victory over our spiritual enemies; by this we are supported in the most dangerous trials, and enabled to persevere in our attachment to the great Redeemer, till we receive the end of our faith, the salvation of our souls.

It is a maxim of eternal truth that whatsoever is not of faith is sin. We must then inevitably conclude that without it the most expensive charity, the most benevolent disposition, the most assiduous prayers, the severest mortifications, and the most amiable virtues, are essentially defective and destitute of life and Spirit. They may establish a reputation among men, but will be pronounced vain at the enlightened tribunal of God. They may gain the advantages of time, but cannot secure the blessings of eternity. If we are saved by grace through faith, it necessarily follows that they who are destitute of this faith are strangers to that grace which forms the distinguishing character of the heirs of salvation, and consequently must be forever deprived of those privileges which constitute the true felicity and glory of human nature.

With what ardor and importunity should we seek to God for this important gift. Our Lord said to the woman of Samaria, "If thou knewest the gift of God, thou wouldest have asked of Him, and He would have given thee living water." "Ask that ye may receive" was the direction given by the same divine Teacher to the multitude who attended on His ministry. This is the voice of reason as well as the command of God. When surrounded with distressing dangers; when all created help fails; when human policy and power discovers no way of escape—is it not natural, is it not rational, to prostrate ourselves in the dust, lift up our eyes to heaven, and implore those almighty aids which God takes pleasure to communicate to the humble supplicant? If our hearts are too haughty, if our knees are too stubborn to bow at the footstool of sovereign grace and ask the life of our immortal souls, surely our damnation is of ourselves. It is presumption to expect that God will vouchsafe to grant His choicest favors to those who proudly neglect to seek Him in the ways of His own institution. Has He erected a throne of grace in our revolted world? Does He command us by prayer and supplication to make known our requests? And shall we live in the neglect of so plain, positive, and reasonable a duty? Should not a people seek their God, a God who is the supreme Dispenser of happiness and misery, upon whose goodwill depends our eternal destiny? Does not the honor of the Deity require that we look up continually to Him from whom alone our help must come, and ardently implore that mercy, without which we are the eternal victims of inexorable justice?

Ask those who live the life of faith by what methods they were introduced into this state. They will answer with one voice: "I was awakened to a solemn concern for my eternal welfare. I daily waited at wisdom's gates and watched at the posts of her doors. I was convinced of the deep and universal corruption of my nature. I found that I was dead in trespasses and sins, that nothing short of an almighty Arm could subdue my reluctant heart and induce me to a cheerful compliance with the prescriptions of sovereign mercy. I prostrated myself at the feet of the supreme Disposer of life and death. I acknowledged that I had forfeited every favor, and that if He rejected me from His presence forever, justice must approve the conduct. I had no ground to complain that He treated me with undeserved severity. But I ardently implored that grace I had no right to challenge, and earnestly deprecated the execution of that sentence which was the just punishment of my crimes. He viewed me with a compassionate eye. He hearkened to the cries of my distress, and stretched out His arm to deliver me from the depths of misery. He revealed unto me His gracious nature, which revived my desponding heart. He directed me by His Word and Spirit to an all-sufficient Savior provided for the greatest of sinners. He captivated me by the charms of His love to resign myself to be His servant forever."

It is in this way the Father of mercies generally manifests Himself to the sinners of human race. Thus He turns them from darkness to light, from the power of sin and Satan unto God. Their success should encourage us to walk in the same way; their example should inspire us with unfainting diligence to pursue the same methods. Never should we desist till we experience that power from on high which alone can form us into the character, and entitle us to the privileges, of the sons of God.

What gratitude should inspire the breasts of those who are made partakers of the gift of faith! It was a pure favor that brought us into existence; but it is greater kindness that bestows upon us faith. Redeeming love demands a higher song of praise than creating goodness. How should we adore the greatness of that power which not only made us at first, but designs to make us happy forever! When we look up to Jesus, who is the Author and Finisher of our faith, our hearts should overflow with love, and our tongues be perpetually employed in thankful "hallelujahs."

When God delivered His people from Egypt, this instance of the divine favor was to be commemorated in every succeeding age; a festival was appointed to perpetuate the remembrance of it to the most distant posterity. But the believer has a nobler deliverance to commemorate. God has saved us not from a temporal bondage, but an eternal prison. He gives us His laws, not inscribed on tables of stone, but on the living tables of our hearts. He directed the marches of His ancient people through an inhospitable desert by a pillar of fire; and He conducts His saints in the present day, by the illuminations of His Spirit, who brings them safely not to an earthly Canaan, but to the celestial one.

Let us follow our divine Leader with undaunted courage, with cheerful perseverance. It is God who works in us both to will and to do. This, instead of encouraging indolence, should animate our zeal and diligence. The teachings of the divine Spirit show us the path of holiness and incline us to walk in it. The allurements of grace captivate our hearts and give us life and spirit to run the way that leads to the Kingdom of God.

To animate us in this blessed course, we are assured that He who has begun a good work in us will carry it on to the day of the Lord. He who has given us faith will increase and perpetuate it. He will receive our discouraged hearts and support our tottering steps. Though weak in ourselves, we shall be strong in the power of His might. His grace will be victorious in the midst of the fiercest opposition.

Neither present enjoyments nor future prospects; neither the malice of men nor the subtlety of the principalities and powers of darkness; neither the charms of life nor fears of death shall detach us from Him in whom we have believed. We may triumph in the assurance that He will keep that which is committed unto Him till faith shall be turned into vision, and the work of grace completed in the regions of glory. To Him be glory forever and ever, Amen.

16

The Salvation We Receive by Faith Is Unspeakably Great

"How shall we escape, if we neglect so great salvation?"
Hebrews 2:3

It is a just reproach to human nature that men are so
solicitous to secure the interests of the present life and so
unconcerned for their happiness in a future world. With
what art and address do they pursue their temporal affairs! What zeal and diligence do they employ to accomplish their designs! New plans are continually formed to
increase their estates and aggrandize their families. If they
fail of success, it is not for want of inclination, but power.

Would to God, my brethren, we were equally zealous
in the things which concern our immortal welfare. But,
alas! To the eternal infamy of a great part of mankind, the
body engrosses all their thoughts; their nobler spirits are
treated with astonishing indifference; transitory vanities
confine their views, and eternal realities are comparatively
despised. This unhappy conduct degrades the dignity of a
reasonable creature and makes us resemble the inferior
animals that are under the entire dominion of sense. We
do not wonder that those beings that are only governed by
instinct have no views beyond the present moment. But
that men, to whom the Almighty has given understanding
and designed for a future existence, should be wise only
for this perishing world, and disregard the supreme happiness of their nature, is truly surprising, and could not be
believed did not constant experience evidence it to be a

melancholy truth.

This conduct of mankind is highly criminal because it is voluntary and chosen; and it is as foolish as criminal because it is attended with the most fatal consequences. If not altered, it inevitably involves us in extreme and eternal misery. A fool is generally esteemed one of the most contemptible characters; but when it is involuntary it does not merit any punishment. But foolishly to neglect the ultimate end of our being that we may gratify our inferior passions, of choice to sacrifice our immortal happiness for a few transitory advantages, involves us in aggravated guilt and exposes us to the most severe punishment.

This is that awful truth which is taught by St. Paul in the words of my text: "How shall we escape, if we neglect so great salvation?" The words contain two propositions which demand our solemn attention: the salvation provided for sinners in the gospel is unspeakably great, and they who neglect this great salvation must inevitably perish. I shall confine myself to the first of these in my present discourse.

DOCTRINE: The salvation provided for sinners in the gospel is unspeakably great. To evidence this let us consider that the plan of salvation was formed in the eternal counsels of heaven. It was purchased with the blood of the Son of God. The mission of the Holy Ghost is peculiarly designed to make us partakers of this salvation. When this happy event takes place with respect to any of the children of men, it gives joy to the angels of light. When others are excluded from it, the spirits of darkness triumph in their ruin. Thus God and His elect angels, as well as the devil and his malicious associates, conspire to evidence the greatness of that salvation which is revealed in the gospel.

First, the plan of salvation was formed in the eternal counsels of heaven. Man was originally the favorite of His Almighty Creator. God gave him the first place of dignity in this visible world. He united heaven and earth, matter and spirit, in the composition of human nature. He introduced our first parents into being in the most agreeable circumstances, and bountifully provided for their happiness in a state of innocence. But the all-seeing eye of God, which penetrates into the most distant futurities, beheld the ungrateful apostasy of man and formed the design of His recovery. He determined that Satan should not triumph in his success, nor the human race be irrecoverably ruined. Though perfectly happy in the enjoyment of Himself, He did not behold with indifference the misery of man. Though millions of worlds must have started into being at His authoritative command, yet He looked with compassion on this revolted earth and determined to disappoint the devices of the devil.

But the most sublime spirits in heaven would have been eternally at a loss to find a way in which this benevolent design could be accomplished and the honor of the Deity preserved. The demands of justice must be answered so that mercy may triumph in the salvation of the guilty. The threatening of the law must be fulfilled so that the transgressor of its righteous precepts may be pardoned. The dignity of the divine government must be maintained so that condemned rebels may be restored to favor. The righteous Governor of the universe will evidence His abhorrence of the crime while He receives the criminal to the embraces of His love.

Infinite wisdom has reconciled these difficulties and formed a plan, which gives the brightest discovery of all the perfections of the Deity, sacredly maintains the majesty of His government, and displays the riches of His grace to His apostate creatures. In conformity to this plan, the Son of God descends upon earth in a human form, fulfills the law which we had violated, submits to bear the punishment of our crimes, and thus prepares the way for our approach unto God as a compassionate and reconciled Father. Here we have the most admirable display of divine love and the clearest evidence of His hatred for sin. The transgression of the law is punished with awful severity, and the transgressor is graciously forgiven. This is that mighty projection which is the astonishment of angels and the joy of the redeemed.

This gives us an affecting view of the inestimable value of salvation, especially if we consider, second, that it was purchased by the blood of the Son of God. In all ages, God has done great things in favor of His chosen people: for their sakes He exercised His patience to a revolted world and delayed that important period when this visible creation shall be consumed by fire; for their sakes He has counteracted the established laws of nature and performed stupendous miracles in the sight of angels and men; for their sakes He will shortly descend from heaven with a shout, with the voice of the archangel and the trump of God. From His radiant throne He will publicly pronounce them His friends and favorites and receive them to a kingdom prepared for them from before the foundation of the world.

But that which raises the value of all these signal favors is the inestimable price with which they are purchased. I know of nothing so incomprehensible to human reason as the sacrifice of the Son of God for a guilty world. If this mystery of divine love had not been predicted by a succession of inspired prophets, confirmed by numerous and unquestionable miracles, attested by heaven and earth, and by angels and men, it could never be received as a truth by any impartial inquirer. It is difficult to conceive that God would do so much for miserable man. But since He has given us this surprising discovery of His love, we may justly infer the greatness of that happiness which He designs for His redeemed people.

Elevate your thoughts, my brethren, above these regions of sense; ascend in your devout contemplations to the throne of the eternal Deity; behold the Son of God shining in the brightness of His Father's glory, surrounded with myriads of adoring angels. Then view Him descending upon earth, covered with wounds, bathed in blood, nailed to the cross, and expiring in death. From the dignity of His Person, learn the value of His sacrifice. From the severity of His sufferings, learn the greatness of His purchase. For us men and our salvation, He appeared upon earth in the form of a Servant, passed through the miseries of life, and submitted to the pains of death. That salvation, then, must be pronounced great which was procured at so great a price. Our blessed Lord would not have forsaken the pleasures of His Father's bosom, parted with His heavenly glory, and passed through this dark and distressing scene of sufferings were it not to answer the most important designs. He knew the just value of things and esteemed the happiness of His people an equivalent for all the sorrows of His life and the agonies of His death. Therefore we are assured that He shall see the travail of His soul and be satisfied.

But to further confirm this point, we may consider, third, that the mission of the Holy Ghost is designed to make us partakers of this salvation. When our blessed Lord finished His work upon earth and ascended to the court of heaven, according to His promise He sent down His Holy Spirit to convict the world of sin, to deliver them from its fatal dominion, and form them to a meetness for the kingdom of glory. Every faithful subject of our adorable Redeemer is justified in the name of Jesus and sanctified by the Spirit of our God. This divine Agent not only favors the church with an external revelation, but secretly influences the minds of men to attend to the truths delivered in the inspired Scriptures. He awakens them to a sense of their danger while they continue in a state of sin and animates them with a salutary concern to flee from the wrath to come. Though inconsiderate sinners often resist His sacred operations and, through a fond attachment to their lusts, reject the indulgent methods of divine grace, He does not immediately abandon His work, but waits upon them with admirable patience, repeats His faithful warnings, continues His friendly offices, and strives with them from day to day, from year to year.

This is His general conduct to mankind under the dispensation of the gospel. Multitudes, for their ungrateful opposition to the agency of the divine Spirit, are at last rejected of God and left to consume away in their iniquities. But with respect to the elect, He continues His influences, does not cease to strive with them till their rebellious hearts are conquered in the day of His power, and they are made the triumphs of divine love, the heirs of immortal glory.

Having produced this happy change, He watches over them with affectionate care, enlightens them in darkness, supports them in weakness, recovers them from their relapses, defends them in dangers, and finally makes them victorious over all their spiritual enemies. The work which He has begun He will never forsake. The seed of grace which He has implanted in their hearts He will cherish and increase till it produces the fruits of immortality and glory. Who can imagine the Holy Spirit would be so sedulously employed to secure the salvation of mankind were it not an affair of the greatest importance? That must be of inestimable value which is accomplished at such an infinite expense. It is dishonorable to suppose that God should send His Son from the regions of glory, that the Son should humble Himself to the dust of death, and that the Spirit should employ His almighty energy, and not have in view the noblest designs?

Fourth, when any of the children of men are made partakers of this salvation, it gives joy to the angels of light. These benevolent spirits, with a disinterested joy, congratulated the first appearance of a Savior in this lower world; they attended Him through all the sorrows of life;

they comforted Him at the approaches of death; they appeared in robes of celestial glory to adorn the triumphs of His resurrection, and they accompanied Him with joyful acclamations in His ascent to the kingdom of His Father. Though they are illustrious courtiers of heaven, they do not think the inhabitants of this earth beneath their notice; though they are the most exalted part of the creation, they do not disdain to maintain an intercourse with worms of the dust. When a sinner is converted from the error of his ways, the glad tidings are propagated through the heavenly mansion. There is joy in the presence of the angels of God that an addition is made to the happy society above. They cheerfully forsake their thrones of glory to become ministering spirits to those who are appointed heirs of salvation. They encamp about the dwellings of the saints, deliver them from numberless dangers, and by a thousand offices of kindness support and encourage them in their passage through the wilderness of this world. When the people of God have finished their work upon earth, they surround their dying beds, receive their departing spirits, guard them from the malignant powers of darkness, conduct them through the regions of the air, and safely introduce them into the paradise of God. Thus the soul of the despised Lazarus was carried by angels into Abraham's bosom. Thus the soul of every faithful servant of Christ, when delivered from the body, becomes the charge of these heavenly ministers. Nor do they desist from their care, till they have fixed it in these happy abodes where it is secure from every danger. Surely that salvation must be great which these exalted beings so affectionately desire to promote; they would not willingly leave the rapturous employments of heaven to secure a trifling advantage. Inconsiderate mortals may despise this salvation, but it is highly esteemed by those wise and holy beings who live in the light of the divine countenance and cannot be mistaken in the true value of things.

Fifth, while the angels rejoice when any are made partakers of this salvation, the devils triumph when any by their fault and folly are excluded from it. The devil is always represented as the enemy of God and goodness. Having deserted his exalted station, he envies the happiness of mankind. Condemned to the punishment of eternal death, he seeks with incessant malice to involve others in the same irremediable ruin. To accomplish this accursed design, he employs every art and exercises indefatigable diligence. While men go on securely in the ways of sin, he flatters them with hopes of impunity and rocks them asleep by a thousand deceitful suggestions so that they may be insensible of their misery and danger. If at any time their guilty fears are alarmed, he hurries them into the business and amusements of life so that they may divert their uneasy thoughts. He employs their gay companions by banter and ridicule to erase all serious impressions from their minds. If a sense of guilt abides upon their consciences, he terrifies them with unreasonable fears that the day of grace has ended, or that, if they give way to their present impressions, they must bid adieu to every pleasant employment and condemn themselves to perpetual melancholy. If all these attempts are in vain, and we are effectually persuaded to give up ourselves to our compassionate Savior, even then he does not abandon his malicious designs. When he cannot prevent our happiness, he endeavors to disturb our peace; when he cannot regain the empire of our hearts, he industriously strives to pollute our persons and performances. He follows us to the altar of God, and by a variety of temptations interrupts our communion with heaven. He pursues us to the gates of paradise and never ceases to distress us till we enter that blessed world from which he is forever excluded.

Now, what is it that animates Satan and his confederate hosts to employ all their power and policy to destroy mankind? They envy us the enjoyment of that heaven from which they are righteously banished; their malice is so great that it increases their torment to behold others rejoicing in the favor of God when they are condemned to an eternal departure from Him.

Thus I have endeavored to give you some view of the greatness of that salvation which is revealed in the gospel; it is great in the judgment of heaven and hell. The goodness of God and malice of Satan, the angels of light and the ministers of darkness, all conspire to proclaim its excellency and value.

Application

Is it not then astonishing madness to forfeit this salvation for the meanest trifles? And yet, O my brethren, to the disgrace of the Christian name, this is a common practice. We daily behold souls capable of the ecstatic joys of heaven confining their pursuits to the defiling pleasures of this degenerate earth. We daily behold souls formed for the society of angels deserting the throne of reason and transformed into the likeness of savage brutes. They renounce the happiness for which they were originally designed, and think and act as if they were made for no higher an end than to delight their eyes with splendid prospects; to gratify their ears with the harmony of sounds; to please their taste with the flavor of meats and drinks; and after having spent a few years in these sensual pleasures, to retire off the state and be insensible forever.

Is this to act agreeable to the character of man, whom God appointed lord of this lower creation, who was formed after the image of the Deity; who was placed upon earth to glorify his Maker and be eternally happy in the enjoyment of His love? Are we capable of the joys of angels, and shall we associate with the beasts that perish? Were we designed to imitate the moral perfections God, the best of beings, and shall we degrade ourselves to a resemblance of the devil, the most hateful of creatures? Awake, O man, from this state of infatuation! Arise and consider the greatness of your folly. You are indeed fallen from your primitive excellency, and your nature is corrupted in all its powers. But God has formed a plan for the recovery of the apostate race of Adam. Christ has died for their salvation; the Spirit is sent down to operate on the minds of men and transform them into new creatures. Shall the love of God be despised, the merits of Christ undervalued, the influences of the Holy Ghost be resisted, and you perish at last, notwithstanding the miracles of divine grace for your recovery? Would you rather have devils triumph in your ruin than saints and angels rejoice in your salvation?

You will doubtless say, "God forbid this should be my case!" But allow me to assure you, this must be your inevitable destiny if you neglect your immortal concerns, spend your time in the vanities and diversions of life, disregard the service of your Maker and Sovereign, and live in those sins against which the wrath of heaven is denounced. There is no medium. Everyone of you must be persuaded to give up yourselves to the compassionate Jesus, experience His saving power rescuing you from the dominion of sin, and be made partakers of the sanctifying influences of the Holy Ghost, or remain under the wrath of God and suffer the damnation of hell through immortal ages.

For what does mankind neglect their eternal interest? A stranger to human nature must suppose it must be for something of inestimable value. No, it is for the pleasures of an intemperate hour, for the joys of a lascivious moment, for the sordid gains of avarice, for the childish amusements which take place on this theater of vanity— for these heaven is renounced and hell is chosen.

O my brethren, do not allow the God of this world to blind your eyes; attend to the one thing needful. Were we condemned to perish without remedy, it would be cruel to attempt to disturb your present repose. Were the great salvation unattainable by the children of men, all exhortations to secure it would be impertinent and absurd. But this world is the region of hope; while we reside upon earth we are candidates for a heavenly inheritance. Proposals of grace are made to sinners of every order and character; they are both invited and commanded to accept the great salvation. Those who are involved in the deepest guilt, and are pining away in indigence and misery, are to be compelled, by all the persuasive charms of divine grace, by every argument that can gain the attention and influence the choice of a rational creature, to accept life and happiness. It was our wants and not our worthiness that engaged our heavenly Father to form the plan of our redemption. It is to extricate us out of misery, and not to reward our virtues, that a Savior is provided for us. The only qualification a sinner can have antecedent to a union with Christ is a deep sense of his misery, a despair of all relief in himself, and a willingness to receive a supply of all his wants from the Fountain of all good. Therefore, "whosoever will" is the language of eternal love. It is an undoubted truth that none perish under the advantages of the gospel but by consequence of their own voluntary choice. By a positive act of their wills they reject Christ and the important blessings He offers to their acceptance. He refuses none who rely on His power and grace, but affectionately calls all weary and heavy-laden sinners to come to Him. He kindly promises, "I will give you rest."

The whole number of believers on earth, and the radiant assembly of glorified saints in heaven, bear their united testimony to this consolatory truth. In the character of guilty creatures they cast themselves down at the feet of an Almighty Savior; encouraged by the unlimited calls of His Word, they committed their future welfare to His care. He extended the scepter of His mercy, and said unto them,

"Live!" Their example should revive the spirit of every trembling sinner and encourage them, from the depths of distress and misery, to confide in that Savior who is the same yesterday, today, and forever.

With what gratitude should we embrace this great salvation! If the King of kings has published a royal proclamation inviting His rebellious subjects to return to their allegiance and receive not only a free pardon, but the dignity and privilege of favorites, we may be assured, without danger of deception, that those who obey the call shall obtain the promised mercy. It is beneath the character of the Deity to amuse His creatures with imaginary hopes, or disappoint the expectations of those who rely on His faithful Word. The Strength of Israel will not lie; the immutable Jehovah will not repent of the purposes of His love.

To confirm our faith, we may take a view of the conduct of our divine Master, when He condescended to be an inhabitant of this inferior earth. None were rejected who applied to Him in their distress; all were relieved who came to Him in the language of humble faith. The most despicable objects were received with condescending goodness and restored to health and vigor by the greatness of His power. The vilest sinners were delivered from the dominion of their infamous lusts and assured of the forgiveness of their aggravated crimes. He is now the same mighty and compassionate Savior He ever was; the dignity to which He is advanced has neither diminished His power nor abated His generous concern for the welfare of mankind. He is equally willing to hearken to the supplicating voice of His distressed creatures, equally willing to deliver them from their guilt and danger.

Who can dispute His power, when all nature obeys His laws and the most perfect orders of creatures are governed by the discretion of His will! Who can question His readiness to apply His power to relieve those who confide in Him! Behold! The sufferings He endured, the blood He shed, the death He underwent for the salvation of a guilty world, and every wound discovers the compassions of His heart. His expiring agonies purchased eternal redemption for all who place their trust in Him.

He was once lifted up on an infamous cross, and is now exalted to a throne of glory, to evidence that He is able to save to the uttermost all who come to God by Him. Those therefore who look unto Him, and receive salvation as His gift, are sure of a welcome reception; their safety is deposited in almighty hands. Neither human weakness or folly, or the opposition of the powers of darkness, shall be able to effect their ruin. Here is the great security of every true believer: the power and fidelity of Christ is engaged for their protection. They may bid adieu to all uneasy fears and banish all disquieting suspicions from their minds, for their hopes are built on the Rock of Ages. The sun shall grow dim with age, the bright luminaries of heaven be extinguished, and the earth we inhabit evaporate in smoke; but the Savior lives, enthroned in majesty and might, to support the hopes and perpetuate the happiness of those who are committed to His care. To Him be glory forever and ever, Amen.

17

Those Who Neglect This Great Salvation Must Inevitably Perish

"How shall we escape, if we neglect so great salvation?"
Hebrews 2:3

The most generous medicines, if they do not answer the end for which they were administered, often exasperate the disease and render the circumstances of the patient more dangerous. In like manner, if the gospel, which is designed to restore mankind to spiritual health, does not produce the desired effect, it is attended with the most prejudicial consequences. If the methods of divine grace are despised, they involve us in aggravated guilt and end in irrecoverable misery. The punishment of infidels who enjoy the light of revelation will be infinitely more terrible than that which shall be inflicted on uninstructed pagans. The Son of God whom they despise no longer resides upon earth in a state of poverty and meanness, but is ascended above the visible heavens and sways the scepter of the universe. The once-despised Galilean is seated on a throne of light; angels prostrate themselves at His feet, and devils tremble at the terrors of His wrath. He has crowns of glory to reward His faithful subjects, and a glittering sword to destroy His implacable enemies.

Therefore, we find the misery of the wicked was never painted in more terrible colors than by that divine Messenger who came "not to condemn the world, but that the world through Him might be saved." The apostles, who imitated their blessed Master, persuaded men by the terrors of the Lord not to receive the grace of God in vain.

The inspired author of my text represents those who neglect the great salvation as being condemned to inevitable destruction: "How shall we escape?" These words are an inference from the severity which attended the legal dispensation. If the word spoken by angels was steadfast, and every transgression and disobedience received a just recompense of reward, how shall *we* escape? The reasoning is conclusive; the threatening it contains should inspire us with awful fear lest it be executed upon us. The law pronounced the sentence of death upon the presumptuous transgressor. The man who violated the sanctity of the Sabbath was immediately stoned; many thousands of Israelites were destroyed in one day for their idolatrous practices. The apostle assures us that severer punishments are appointed for the profane despisers of the gospel: "How shall *they* escape?" This method of expression declares that to escape is a vain expectation, an impossible attempt.

DOCTRINE: Those who neglect the great salvation of the gospel must inevitably perish. To evidence this I shall show that this is the sentence pronounced upon them by impartial justice, that God has power to execute this sentence, and that mercy has provided no way of relief.

First, the sentence of inevitable destruction is pronounced upon the despisers of the gospel by the justice of God. It is the positive determination of the supreme and uncontrollable Sovereign of the world: "He that believeth not shall be damned." This sentence is fixed in the immutable decree of God and will be executed in the appointed time. By sin man has become an enemy to God, and, if he persists in his rebellion, justice must triumph in his final destruction. God beholds His unhappy offspring with pity. He proposes terms of peace. He sends His ambassadors to proclaim the glad tidings to a guilty world. Astonishing love! Is it not daring impiety to refuse the great God a hearing? Is it not inexcusable insolence to reject His proposals? This is the practice of multitudes: they presumptuously despise His grace. This is plainly to declare that they do not value His friendship, nor fear the terrors of His wrath. It is fitting that such obstinate rebels should abide by the consequence of their own choice; they judge themselves unworthy of life eternal, and are justly condemned to suffer the pains of eternal death.

Had divine goodness signified His intention to mitigate the sentence of His righteous law, or grant a temporary suspension of the deserved punishment, it must have been acknowledged a favor and ought to be received with gratitude. But He proclaims complete deliverance to the captives of hell, a deliverance not to be purchased by us, but thankfully received. This contains a freedom from all the miseries we feel or fear, a perfect and perpetual enjoyment of every desirable good. Now, must not they perish who are unwilling to be saved? Should not they remain under guilt who refuse the offer of a pardon?

Men may please themselves with ungrounded surmises, but God will not suffer His laws to be violated, His grace abused, His justice insulted, or His glory eclipsed just so that obstinate transgressors may escape with impunity.

Second, if impartial justice pronounces the sentence, the sovereign Ruler has power to put it in execution. This none can dispute who believe the existence of a God. He who made the world by a command can destroy it in a moment with a frown. His power is supreme and independent; nothing can alter His purposes or resist the execution of His will. His smiles diffuse life and joy through all the inhabitants of heaven. His wrathful presence fills the regions of hell with darkness, terror, and despair.

Men often escape the stroke of human justice by art and address; they may fly from the power of the mighty monarchs of the earth and find a retreat beyond the limits of their jurisdiction. Death always removes us out of their reach; the effects of their anger cannot enter the repository of the grave. But where shall we flee from God? To what part of the universe can we escape and be free from His arrests? Death itself conveys us into His immediate presence and delivers us up, the helpless victims of His vengeance.

If indeed the dissolution of the body was the destruction of the soul, we might neglect the salvation of the gospel and escape all future punishment. But to suppose this is to contradict the voice of reason, the testimony of conscience, and the unerring oracles of truth. That the soul of man is immortal is a doctrine of natural and revealed religion. The ancient philosophers were inspired with this hope. Jesus Christ has confirmed it by express declarations and astonishing miracles. The soul is not formed of the dust, but immediately derived from the great Father of Spirits. The body is a beautiful fabric, finished with consummate art, but animated, directed and moved by the immortal mind. The body is composed of different parts and may be destroyed by innumerable accidents; but the soul is a simple uncompounded substance not liable to a dissolution. These are strong presumptions in favor of this important truth. But that which reason pronounces probable, revealed religion declares to be certain. The system of the gospel is built on this foundation; they who deny it not only reject the religion of Jesus, but are enemies to the peace and good order of civil society. They oppose those sentiments which are common to all except the most abandoned of the human race, and level themselves with the beasts that perish. Not only the philosophers of Rome and Athens, but barbarians and Scythians will rise up against them and condemn them.

If the soul exists in a future state, it perceives and acts, for these are essential to its nature; and therefore it is capable of rewards and punishments. The God of Truth assures us that when the body descends into the dust, the soul returns to God who gave it—to God, either to triumph in His love or to experience the effects of His displeasure. While those who embrace the great salvation enter into the joy of their Lord, they who despise and neglect it must suffer eternal destruction from the presence of the Lord and the glory of His power. If the justice of God has pronounced sentence against them, if He has power to execute this sentence, there can be no hope of escape unless some method is appointed for their deliverance.

This brings me to say, third, that mercy has provided no way of relief for those who neglect this salvation. Divine compassion has instituted a way of recovery; this they reject; and the consequence is that they are deprived of all hope and must perish without remedy. After man had violated the law, the grace of the gospel was revealed. Otherwise the mercy of God must have been forever concealed; the most illustrious triumphs of unlimited goodness could never have been displayed. The sufferings and sacrifice of the Son of God in the place of condemned man was the highest evidence of the divine benevolence, and will be celebrated with transports of gratitude through unceasing ages. But if this love is undervalued, if mercy is insolently despised and the great Sacrifice for sin rejected, there remains no resource; the criminal is placed beyond all possibility of pardon. To what sanctuary will he fly? The law pronounces the terrible sentence; justice demands immediate execution, and insulted mercy increases the severity of the punishment.

Shall Christ again descend from the throne of glory and tabernacle in flesh? Shall the Prince of Life again submit to the stroke of death so that the despisers of His merits and righteousness may be saved? No. The Scriptures positively assure us that henceforth He will die no more. He has finished His work, and they who do not believe must perish forever.

Now is the accepted time; but death finishes the day of

grace. When this event takes place, repentance will be impossible, God inexorable, and the misery of the wicked extreme and eternal.

Application

What multitudes deceive themselves with ungrounded hopes of salvation! Ask them, "Do you expect to be saved?" They answer without hesitation, "Yes." Upon what foundation is your expectation built? Is the salvation revealed in the gospel the most desirable blessing in their esteem? No. They have a greater affection for the pomp and pleasures of this life. Do they seek after an interest in this salvation with unremitting diligence? No. They spend their days in worldly cares and diversions. Have they received power from on high to mortify their dearest lusts? No. They go on securely in the prohibited paths of vice. Do they aspire after that holiness, without which the Scripture declares no man shall enter into the New Jerusalem? No. This would lay too severe a restraint on their nature and deprive them of their chief joys. What reason have you then to hope for future happiness? You flatter yourselves that God is merciful, and will not be so strict as He is represented in His Word.

Ah, fatal delusion! Prodigious folly! Would you venture your estate or reputation on chimerical hopes, destitute of all foundation either in reason or Scripture? If there was any other dispensation of grace besides that which is revealed in the gospel; if there was any other sacrifice for sin than that which the Son of God finished on the cross; if there was any other way to heaven than that which is traced out by the precepts and example of our blessed Savior—there might be some foundation for hope. But if there is no other name given under heaven by which men can be saved but the name of Jesus; if none are accepted at the supreme tribunal but through His all-sufficient righteousness; if the everlasting state of mankind must be determined according to the gospel—then your expectations of future happiness are an imaginary dream. In the end you die a fool, and must lie down in everlasting sorrow.

Do you dispute this? Then you raze the foundations of religion and treat the gospel as if it was a cunningly devised fable. Do you believe Moses and the prophets, Christ and His apostles? I trust, without paying a compliment to my hearers, I may address them as St. Paul did King Agrippa: "I know that you believe." What then remains but that you bow to the authority of divine revelation, and receive the most mysterious doctrines with humble submission.

If our corrupt reason is to be advanced to the infallible chair, and the articles of religion are to be explained according to its dictates, many of its most sublime truths will be pronounced false, and its self-denying precepts accommodated to the genius of a degenerate age.

Men of pleasure cannot conceive that God will be so severe as to punish them for the gratification of their sensual appetites and inclinations. My brethren, if I only consult my reason, I cannot conceive that He should be so indulgent to His guilty creatures as daily experience evidences He is. Nothing can be more incredible to our finite reason that that the Monarch of the universe should send His Son to give His life a ransom for His rebellious subjects; that the immaculate Jesus should bear the punishment of our sins in His own body on the tree; that He should be wounded for our transgressions, bruised for our iniquities, and the chastisement of our peace be upon Him. But God speaks, and let every mortal ear attend; let human reason be silent, and devoutly acknowledge its incapacity to comprehend the depths of the divine counsels. My faith adores this mysterious love; my heart acquiesces with joy in the salutary truth. I receive it as a faithful saying and worthy of all acceptation.

But why should it be esteemed unreasonable that men who obstinately persist in their crimes should reap the fruit of their own doings? What is more equitable than that they who will not accept mercy should fall by the sword of justice?

Every enlightened mind, instead of complaining of the severity of God, will adore His patience to a revolted world. While sinners continue in arms of rebellion against Him, He visits them every morning with His refreshing light, provides for them every day with paternal care, showers down blessings upon them with an unsparing hand. Why do not the thunders of heaven destroy those insolent mortals who defy their omnipotent Maker! Why does not the earth open its mouth and transmit to unquenchable flames those audacious rebels who will not submit to the government of the King of kings! It is because His ways are not as our ways, neither His thoughts as our thoughts. He is long-suffering to us, not willing that any should perish, but that all should be brought to repentance.

How greatly is it to be lamented that the bulk of mankind pays so little attention to that which ought to engage their principal concern! Let us view the conduct of men: how carelessly they spend their time in the fatigues of business or the pursuit of pleasure! They dissipate their thoughts upon a thousand objects and live without retirement or reflection. They contemplate these visible heavens and measure the magnitude and calculate the distance of the stars, but give themselves no concern to secure an entrance into the heaven of heavens, the habitation of God's favorite people. They descend into the depths of the earth to discover the treasures which are concealed in its bloom, but never seriously prepare for that decisive hour when they shall have no more connection with this material system, but become inhabitants of

the invisible world of spirits. Borne on the wings of ambition or avarice, they fly from pole to pole in search of that
wealth and honor that vanish in a moment, but profanely
despise that honor which comes from God, those treasures which would enrich them forever.

This careless and sensual course of life might perhaps
admit of some excuse, if attended with no hurtful consequences; but since it is inconsistent with all regular hopes
of salvation; since, if not awakened out of it, we remain the
children of wrath, every considerate mind must condemn
sinners of this order as the greatest of madmen. What
would you think of a prisoner, confined in chains, who
knew the day of his trial was approaching, that sentence of
death was ready to be pronounced upon him, and when
once pronounced could never be recalled but would certainly be executed, if in this melancholy situation he was
assured that a way of escape was provided. But instead of
improving the opportunity afforded him, he disregarded
the message and spent his time in sports and diversion till
the fatal hour arrived which excluded all hopes forever!
Would not every impartial observer pronounce his conduct the extremity of madness? This is but a faint image of
the madness which possesses the hearts of secure sinners.
As much as the punishment of hell is to be dreaded above
the momentary miseries of this life, so much greater is the
folly of those who neglect the day of their visitation.

Their folly will be still more manifest if we consider
what motives induce them to so fatal a procedure, motives
so mean and contemptible that it is astonishing they have
any influence upon men endowed with the powers of reason and reflection. The true happiness of our nature is
sacrificed for a few sordid delights, which become insipid
by custom, are impaired by the infirmities of age, and will
certainly be lost in death. Doubtless the angels of light are
astonished at the stupidity of men who for a painted toy, a
little heap of glittering dust, or a sensual pleasure which

they enjoy in common with their kindred brutes, part with heaven and its unceasing joys, expose themselves to hell and all its dark and despairing horrors. In the meantime, in perfect consistence with the hopes of eternal happiness, we might enjoy every rational pleasure. The enjoyments of this world, when regulated by the precepts of religion, are attended with peculiar sweetness. We review them without reproach and receive them as earnests of superior joys.

Let us then be persuaded to renounce this inconsiderate conduct, and with unfainting vigor and resolution pursue those blessings that constitute our happiness in time and eternity. Have you hitherto neglected to walk in the way that leads to life? Have you spent your time in those things that the wise Solomon pronounces vanity of vanities? Have you to this day been inattentive to the great concern of a rational and immortal being?

Yet, O indulgent goodness! Yet you live; you hear the voice of a compassionate God, inviting you to return unto Him. He addresses you as He did His ungrateful people in the days of old. "How shall I give thee up Ephraim! How shall I deliver thee Israel! My heart is turned within me; my repentings are kindled together."

Attend, O my brethren, to the heavenly voice; it speaks particularly to you who are in the morning of life, the flourishing bloom of youth. This is the noblest opportunity you will ever enjoy to lay a sure foundation for future safety. Your hearts are not prepossessed with the distracting cares of life, nor your consciences rendered insensible by inveterate habits of vice. Nature is now in her prime and grace is more frequently bestowed upon young persons than on those who are grown old in sin.

But in what language shall I address those who are bowed down under the weight of years and infirmities, and have grown gray in the service of Satan? Must I say your day is past, your doom irreversible? God forbid that I should be sent on so terrible a message. Your case is dangerous, but not desperate. Through the patience of heaven, you are yet commanded to seek the Lord while He may be found. Let your vanishing breath be employed in constant and ardent prayer to that Being who not only permits you to live in this world, but invites you to draw near to the throne of His grace. In a few days more your doom will be fixed, and hope, the relief of the miserable, will forsake you forever.

May a gracious God convince you of your dangerous situation and excite you to fly for deliverance to Him, whom God has exalted to be a Prince and a Savior, to give repentance and remission of sins! To Him be glory forever and ever, Amen.

18

The Joy of Faith

"Whom having not seen ye love, in whom though now
ye see Him not, yet believing ye rejoice with joy
unspeakable and full of glory." 1 Peter 1:8

To rejoice is agreeable to all mankind, though there
are but few who have a just foundation for it. None have a
claim to this privilege but those who are in friendship with
that adorable Being who is the Fountain of felicity to all
His creatures. All the human race have become enemies
to God through the depravity of their natures and the
voluntary transgressions of their lives. A reconciliation
must take place, otherwise the enmity will be perpetual
and the misery of man irrecoverable.

In Christ, God is reconciling the world unto Himself;
none can rejoice in God but those who are interested in
His dear Son. He has made satisfaction for the sins of a
guilty world, but those who do not receive Him as their
Savior are deprived of the advantages that flow from His
merits and mediation. He has purchased every blessing for
His people, but those who are not united to Him by faith
"are aliens and strangers from the commonwealth of Israel
and the covenants of promise."

St. Peter, in the words of my text, describes the character of true Christians and declares their privilege. That
Savior who was once an inhabitant of this inferior earth,
but is now seated at the right hand of the Majesty on high,
is the object of their undissembled affection. They view
Him by faith in all the glories of His person and character,

and believing they rejoice. The words of my text teach us this truth, which shall be the subject of our present meditation.

DOCTRINE: All true believers have a just foundation for rejoicing.

To illustrate this, let us take a view of some of their important privileges: their sins are forgiven, their persons and performances are accepted; their natures are sanctified; they are the care of a distinguished providence; nothing can do them any essential hurt; all things will conspire to promote their real good, and they have the assured prospect of immortal glory.

First, they may rejoice that their sins are forgiven. This is the covenant that God establishes with them through Christ, their exalted Head: "I will be merciful to your unrighteousness; your iniquities will I remember no more." To learn the value of this privilege, let us consider the number and aggravation of our sins; but who can understand his errors? Who can recount his continual deviations from the law of God, the unerring standard of our duty? In many things we all offend; in everything we fall short. The defects that attend our best performances are highly criminal; the defilements which accompany our purest services are justly offensive to the unspotted Majesty of heaven. What shall we say of our presumptuous violations of the divine commands? These are committed against light and love; not through involuntary surprise, but deliberate rebellion. They are peculiarly displeasing to God, and call aloud for vengeance.

How astonishing is that grace which pardons all these sins of every order and degree, with all the heinous circumstances that attend them! With what admiring gratitude must we rejoice in that God who declares that He is "merciful and gracious, abundant in goodness and truth, forgiving iniquity, transgression and sin!"

To increase our gratitude we may consider the pardoning mercy of God is not barely a present benefit, but attended with the most lasting and salutary effects. It assures us of immediate safety and preserves us from future condemnation. The sentence of absolution is passed in favor of every true believer in the court of heaven, and will never be revoked through the varying scenes of the present life or the unchanging ages of eternity. Well might the psalmist triumph in his happiness, and pronounce a blessedness on the man whose iniquities are forgiven.

Let us suppose a malefactor condemned to suffer an infamous death; the day is come; the appointed hour approaches, in which he must deliver himself into the hands of the executioner. He beholds with weeping eyes and a trembling heart the solemn preparation made for his punishment. If in the critical moment a pardon arrives which delivers him from all his distresses and fears, will not his heart leap for joy and his nature sink under the excessive transport? But God bestows a more inestimable favor on the true believer. He delivers him not from the pains of a moment, but from unceasing torments. He restores him not to a temporal life, but to an eternal one.

Second, to increase the kindness, He admits them to friendship; their persons and performances are accepted. A prince may pardon a criminal and not enroll him among the number of his acquaintances; he may open the doors of his prison and not advance him to the dignity of a favorite. But God manifests His love to those who receive forgiveness through the blood of Jesus. He not only obliterates the remembrance of their guilt, but embraces them in the arms of favor. He not only admits them among the train of His menial servants, but exalts them to the honors and privileges of His children. His anger is removed. He beholds them with complacency and delight, and through His dear Son graciously accepts their poor imperfect services.

Who can comprehend their dignity and blessedness!

They have free access to the throne of grace and may approach His presence with filial confidence. They may implore His aid in every exigency and take shelter under the shadow of His wings in every danger. He gives them a sacred assurance that He is their God, and that all His awful and amiable attributes shall be exerted for their advantage.

This is a perpetual source of the most refined and transporting joy. "This God is my God," may the believer say, "not barely by an external title, but by a firm and indissoluble covenant. He not only honors me with the name, but affords me the happiness of His children." Surely this is an all-sufficient Portion; we may rejoice in it though destitute of all other comfort. "Although the fig tree shall not blossom, neither shall fruit be in the vines, the labor of the olives shall fail and the fields shall yield no meat, the flock shall be cut off from the fold and there shall be no herd in the stalls; yet will I rejoice in the Lord, and joy in the God of my salvation."

Third, this restoration to the divine favor is always accompanied with the sanctification of our nature. No change in our nature can make us happy while we remain the servants of sin. Our discordant appetites and passions must keep us in perpetual disquietude. The breasts of the wicked are like the tempestuous ocean, in constant agitation. But the divine Spirit who resides in the heart of the true believer rectifies the disorders of our corrupted nature and introduces peace and harmony instead of lawless riot and confusion. He implants a heavenly principle that inclines us to revere the authority of the great God, to obey the unerring dictates of His Word, and regulate our various appetites and passions by the laws of reason and religion. By the benign influences of this blessed Agent, light succeeds darkness, order succeeds confusion, and beauty replaces deformity. The storms of passion subside; the savage disposition is softened and subdued. The proud become meek, the morose become benevolent, and monsters of vice become examples of the most amiable virtues. The tyrannical empire of sin is conquered, and that kingdom set up in the souls of men that consists in righteousness, peace, and joy in the Holy Ghost.

Fourth, believers being thus restored to the favor of God and brought to submit to His equitable government, they become the distinguishing care of divine providence. That all-comprehending eye which with a single glance surveys the whole creation is fixed upon them as the objects of His complacent regards. That unerring wisdom that directs the stupendous revolutions of nature is their unfailing companion and guide. That omnipotent arm which nothing can resist is their guard and defense: He who makes His angels spirits, and His ministers flames of fire, gives these benevolent beings charge concerning them, to keep them in all their ways.

Well, then, may they rejoice, though surrounded with darkness, difficulty, and danger. God is their Sun to direct their way. He is their Shield to defend them from their numberless enemies. They are conducted through the wilderness of this world by His Word and Spirit. They are preserved in safety by His guardian care. The faithful may therefore triumph in their almighty Protector and Friend, and say with the psalmist, "Because He is at my right hand I shall not be moved. Though I walk through the valley of the shadow of death, I will fear no evil."

Fifth, in consequence of this distinguished care of divine providence, I proceed to say that nothing can do them any essential hurt. Their security is founded on their union to the Son of God, and confirmed by an unalterable promise that nothing shall separate them from His love. In this situation they may possess their souls in peace amidst the tempests that disturb the repose of the rest of mankind. The basis of their happiness remains unshaken in all the revolutions that take place in this lower world.

Attached to their exalted Head who holds the reins of universal empire, they shall finally overcome the power and policy of their enemies. They may be serene in the greatest dangers, secure in the severest trials, and happy in the most afflicted condition.

The edicts of princes may banish them to uncultivated deserts, and the fires of persecution consume all their earthly enjoyments, but if we belong to Christ, our happiness is out of the reach of accidents and disappointments. Secure of an invincible Friend, we need not fear the lightnings of heaven, the shakings of the earth, nor the flames that shall consume this habitable globe. Let the sun be covered with darkness, the moon withdraw her light, and this material universe sink into ruin; let these tabernacles of clay be destroyed by the stroke of death and this beautiful arrangement of flesh and blood return to its original dust; let the illustrious day appear when the Son of God shall descend from heaven in radiant majesty and summon the trembling nations to stand at his impartial bar—the true believer will lift up his head with joy amidst these astonishing scenes, and with a voice of triumph congratulate the appearance of his God and Savior. Clothed with His righteousness, he fears no condemnation; animated by His Spirit, he is sure to be found among the number of His friends. If the judge is his Friend, what can prejudice his happiness?

Sixth, all these great revolutions shall conspire to promote his real good. The destruction of the universe prepares the way for the descent of his adorable Redeemer; the dissolution of the body introduces him into the joys of the divine presence. Death is a messenger sent from heaven to convey him into a state of immortal existence. When the heavens vanish away, the veil is removed that conceals the ineffable glories of the kingdom of God.

While we reside upon earth, we necessarily partake of those miseries that are inseparable from a state of mortality; but when removed from this valley of tears, we enter on the true felicity and glory of our natures. As the children of the first Adam, we are subject to the empire of sin and death; by our relation to the second Adam, we are heirs of a heavenly kingdom, where all His people shall live and reign with Him forever.

Seventh, and finally, they rejoice in the prospect of immortal glory. Their joy is not confined to the narrow boundaries of time, but extends through eternal ages. This makes it full without any defect, complete without any alloy. The happiest condition on earth is not equal to the magnificent promises of divine grace, nor answerable to the sublime hopes which God has implanted in the breasts of His people. Though their joys are superior to those of the most fortunate worldling, yet they do not satisfy the immensity of our desires; we only perceive the dawn of a heavenly day. The fruits of grace are but foretastes of the harvest of glory. We are refreshed with a few drops which flow from the unbounded ocean of blessedness. We have a transient glimpse of that amiable countenance which diffuses life and joy through the celestial regions. Even these imperfect enjoyments put gladness into our hearts, and enable us to rejoice more than when corn and wine are increased. In the destitution of all things, we may adopt the language of the psalmist, "Thou O Lord art my Portion in the land of the living! Whom have I in heaven but Thee? And there is none upon earth that I desire besides Thee."

In some favorite moments, the faithful servants of God experience those divine consolations that change this earth into a paradise of delights. Filled with the transporting views of a Savior's excellency and beauty, the world vanishes from their sight. Inspired with love of the supreme Good, all creatures appear as comparative nothings. To forsake the pleasures of sense for the enjoyment of God gives them greater satisfaction than to possess them in their highest perfection.

"If, O my God, to behold Thy face in this land of exile, through a glass darkly, is so inexpressibly delightful, how ecstatic will be my joy when I shall enter Thy heavenly habitation and see Thee as Thou art, in all Thy unveiled glory! If the refreshments I receive in the place of my pilgrimage are so agreeable, how vast will be my felicity when I shall eat of the Tree of Life, and drink of those rivers of pleasures that flow at Thy right hand! If the visits of Thy love make me happy in these regions of sorrow, what may I not hope for in the mansions of bliss!"

Well may the voice of rejoicing be heard in the tabernacles of the righteous! Have I received Jesus as my Savior? Has a view of His glory inspired me with unfeigned love to His person and character? Is His salvation more precious in my esteem than the dearest earthly enjoyments? Do I value His favor as life, and His loving-kindness as better than life? Then let me rejoice that God has opened my eyes to discern the true value of things, and directed me to choose that good part that can never be taken away. After a few struggles more with a corrupted heart, a few more self-denials in an ensnaring world, I shall enter upon a state of existence in which my nature will be perfected, my joys sincere, my happiness complete, without interruption and without end.

Application

This discovers the excellency of true religion and evidences that it is not an enemy to human happiness. Deluded mortals are prejudiced against the ways of Christ; they imagine they are beset with thorns, and that those who walk in them must bid adieu to every agreeable enjoyment—but this is a fatal mistake. Our amiable Master consults the present comfort as well as future welfare of those who enroll themselves under His banners. He indeed prohibits those sensual excesses that pollute the body, degrade the mind, and ever prove bitter in the end. All His laws are admirably adapted to make us happy in ourselves, and blessings to all around us.

The pleasures of sin are indeed inconsistent with the character of a disciple of Christ. All who follow Him are strictly enjoined to keep themselves unspotted from the world, its dangerous and polluting manners. But they are introduced into a new scene of delights, superior in their kind and more lasting in their duration. We renounce that false and delusive joy which, like a blazing meteor, makes a gaudy appearance, but soon vanishes into empty air. In the room of these disguised trifles we receive spiritual and divine joys which are continually refining and will increase more and more till they do not leave one unaccomplished wish, not one unsatisfied desire. The pleasures of religion may be compared to the path of the just, which shines more and more to the perfect day.

These joys are discovered in the gospel to those who, without its irradiating beams, must have remained in the regions of the shadow of death. They are offered to those who, without these glad tidings, must live in perpetual fear, die in unutterable distress, and after death be involved in blackness of darkness forever.

How consolatory are the discoveries of the gospel! They present to our view a God reconciled through the atoning blood of Jesus, a Savior sufficient to supply all our wants, and ready to relieve us in all our necessities. To those who thankfully receive these revelations of divine grace, it makes the most precious promises and assures them the possession of every desirable blessing through every period of their existence.

When we rejoice in any created good, our joy may be innocent, but it cannot be enduring; earthly joys may delight for a moment, but are like the crackling of thorns under a pot; they form a sudden blaze which soon expires. But to rejoice in the Lord Jesus Christ is to build the fabric of human happiness on an immovable basis, which neither the tempests of life nor the depredations of death can diminish or destroy. This is to possess a joy that will not decay with age, but survive the funeral of universal nature and flourish through all eternity. Well may the believer rejoice with joy unspeakable and full of glory.

This should be improved as a mighty argument to persuade us to accept the great salvation. This is the design I have been carrying on in these several discourses; and certainly nothing can be more worthy the attention of a being in a state of trial and designed for an eternal existence. If this is despised and neglected, the wrath of God attends you in all your ways; it lies down with you at night; it rises with you in the morning; it accompanies you through all the business and diversions of the day. A secret curse is mingled with all your enjoyments; you are every moment exposed to the arrests of death. This delivers you over to unceasing torments. To rejoice in these circumstances is the most thoughtless stupidity. The joys of the sinner may be compared to the revels of a condemned malefactor, who in the height of his folly goes dancing to an infamous execution.

Think, O my brethren, how full, how free, how unlimited are the calls of sovereign mercy? With what authority does God command! With what compassion does He invite! With what earnestness does He beseech you not to refuse the offers of His love!

Review the unspeakable blessings that will be the immediate portion of those who receive this great salvation with humility and gratitude, and labor to obtain it with indefatigable zeal and diligence. Being justified by faith in Jesus, they become members of His sacred family; they enjoy the privileges of the children of God, and in the relation of children are heirs of His heavenly kingdom. Compared to this, what are crowns and scepters? What are all the glories of created nature? They are glittering phantoms, disguised nothings.

But if men bar their hearts against the impressions of incarnate love and give the blessed Savior a final refusal, God, His elect angels, and the assembly of perfected spirits will rejoice in their damnation. May infinite mercy prevent this terrible event! Perhaps you have lived long under a dispensation of grace, but have entertained no thoughts of preparing for eternity. Perhaps you are full of gay expectations of pleasure in the ways of sin; in the pride of life captivated with the enjoyment of your lusts and immersed in earthly cares, you pour contempt on the solemnities of religion. But pause and think with yourselves before it is too late. You have no time to trifle. Your life is as a vapor, and may expire before the dawn of another day. Or, if your time upon earth is lengthened out, a provoked God may swear in His wrath that you shall never enter into His rest. Consider this, you who forget God. Kiss the Son lest He be angry, when His wrath is but kindled. Blessed are they who trust in Him, to whom be glory forever and ever, Amen.

19

The Duty of Ministers

(A sermon preached at the ordination of David Brainerd
in Newark, June 12, 1744)

"And the lord said unto the servant, 'Go out into the
highways and hedges, and compel them to come in,
that my house may be filled.' " Luke 14:23

God erected this visible world as a monument of His
glory, a theater for the display of His adorable perfections.
The heavens proclaim His wisdom and power in shining
characters, and the whole earth is full of His goodness.
Man was, in his original creation, excellently fitted for the
service of God, and for perfect happiness in the enjoyment of the divine favor. But sin has disturbed the order
of nature, defaced the beauty of the creation, and involved man, the lord of this lower world, in the most disconsolate circumstances of guilt and misery.

The all-seeing eye of God beheld our deplorable state;
infinite pity touched the heart of the Father of mercies
and infinite wisdom laid the plan of our recovery. The
Majesty of heaven did not see fit to suffer the enemy of
mankind eternally to triumph in His success; nor leave His
favorite workmanship irrecoverably to perish in the ruins
of the apostasy. By a method which at once astonishes and
delights the sublimest spirits above, He opened a way for
the display of His mercy without any violation of the sacred claims of His justice; in this way the honor of the law
is vindicated and the guilty offender acquitted; sin is con-

demned and the sinner eternally saved. To accomplish this blessed design, the beloved Son of God assumed the nature of man, in our nature died a spotless sacrifice for sin; by the atoning virtue of His blood He made reconciliation for iniquity, and by His perfect obedience to the law of God brought in everlasting righteousness.

Having finished His work upon earth before He ascended to His heavenly Father, He commissioned the ministers of His kingdom to preach the gospel to every creature. He sent them forth to make the most extensive offers of salvation to rebellious sinners, and by all the methods of holy violence to compel them to come in and accept the invitations of His grace. We have a lively representation of this in the parable in our text.

The evident design of the parable is under the figure of a marriage supper, to set forth the plentiful provision which is made in our Lord Jesus Christ for the reception of His people, and the freedom and riches of divine grace which invites the most unworthy and miserable sinners to partake of this sacred entertainment. The first invited guests were the Jews, the favorite people of God who were heirs of divine love, while the rest of the world were aliens from the commonwealth of Israel and strangers from the covenants of promise. But these, through the power of prevailing prejudice and the influence of carnal affections, obstinately rejected the invitation and were therefore finally excluded from these invaluable blessings.

But it was not the design of infinite wisdom that these costly preparations should be lost and the table He had spread remain unfurnished with guests. Therefore He sent forth His servant into the streets and lanes of the city, and commanded Him to bring in the poor, the maimed, the halt, and the blind, i.e., the most necessitous and miserable of mankind; yea, to go out into the highways and hedges, to the wretched and perishing Gentiles, and not only invite, but even compel them to come in so that His house might be filled.

The words of the text represent to us:

1. The melancholy state of the Gentile world. They are described as being in the highways and hedges, in the most perishing and helpless condition.

2. The compassionate care which the blessed Redeemer takes of them in these their deplorable circumstances. He sends out His servants to them to invite them to partake of the entertainments of His house.

3. The duty of ministers of the gospel to compel them to come in and accept His gracious invitation.

These I shall consider in their order, and then apply them to the present occasion.

1. I am to consider the melancholy state of the heathen world while in the darkness of nature, and destitute of divine revelation. It is easy to harangue upon the excellency and advantage of the light of nature. 'Tis agreeable to the pride of mankind to exalt the powers of human reason and pronounce it a sufficient guide to eternal happiness. But let us inquire into the records of antiquity; let us consult the experience of all ages, and we shall find that those who had no guide but the light of nature, no instructor but unassisted reason, have wandered in perpetual uncertainty, darkness, and error. Or let us take a view of the present state of those countries that have not been illuminated by the gospel, and we shall see that, notwithstanding the improvements of nearly six thousand years, they remain to this day covered with the grossest darkness, and abandoned to the most immoral and vicious practice.

The beauty and good order, everywhere discovered in the visible frame of nature, evidences beyond all reasonable dispute the existence of an infinite and almighty Cause, who first gave being to the universe and still preserves it by His powerful providence. The apostle to the Gentiles said in Romans 1:20, "The invisible things of God, from the creation of the world, are clearly seen, being understood by the things that are made, even His eternal power and Godhead."

And yet many, even among the philosophers of the Gentile nations, impiously denied the eternal Deity from whose hands they received their existence, and blasphemed His infinite perfections when surrounded with the clearest demonstrations of His power and goodness. Those who acknowledged a deity entertained the most unworthy conceptions of His nature and attributes and worshiped the creature in the place of "the Creator, who is God blessed forever." Not only the illustrious heroes of antiquity and the public benefactors of mankind, but even the most despicable beings in the order of nature, were enrolled in the catalogue of their gods and became the object of their impious adoration. "They changed the glory of the incorruptible God into an image made like to corruptible man, to birds and four-footed beasts and creeping things" (Romans 1:23).

A few of the most sublime geniuses of Rome and Athens had some faint discoveries of the spiritual nature of the human soul, and formed some probable conjectures that man was designed for a future state of existence. When they considered the extensive capacities of the human mind and the deep impressions of futurity engraven in every breast, they could not but infer that the soul was immortal, and at death would be translated to some new and unknown state. When they saw the virtuous oppressed with various and successive calamities, and the vilest of men triumphing in prosperity and pleasure, they entertained distant hopes that in a future revolution these seeming inequalities would be rectified, these inconsistencies removed, the righteous distinguishly rewarded, and the wicked remarkably punished. But after all their inquiries upon this important subject, they attained no higher than some probable conjectures, some uncertain expectations. And when they came to describe the nature and situation of these invisible regions of happiness or misery, they made the wildest guesses and ran into the most absurd and vain imaginations. The heaven they contrived for the entertainment of the virtuous was made up of sensual pleasures, beneath the dignity of human nature, and inconsistent with perfect felicity. The hell they described for the punishment of the vicious consisted in ridiculous terrors, unworthy of the belief of a rational and religious creature.

Their practices were equally corrupt with their principles. As the most extravagant errors were received among the established articles of their faith, so the most infamous vices obtained in their practice, and were indulged not only with impunity, but authorized by the sanction of their laws. They stupidly erected altars to idols of wood and stone, paid divine honors to those who in their lives had been the greatest monsters of lust and cruelty, yea, and offered up their sons and daughters as sacrifices to devils. The principles of honor, the restraints of shame, and the precepts of their philosophers were all too weak to keep their corruptions within any tolerable bounds. The wickedness of their hearts broke through every enclosure and deluged the earth with raping and violence, blood and slaughter, and all manner of brutish and detestable impurities. It is hardly possible to read the melancholy description of the principles and manners of the heathen world given to us by St. Paul without horror and surprise. To think that man, once the friend of God and the lord of this lower world, should thus deny the God who made him, and bow down to dumb idols; should thus by lust and intemperance degrade himself into the character of the beast, which has no understanding; and by pride, malice, and revenge, transform himself into the very image of the devil, who was a murderer from the beginning.

This was the state of the Gentile nations when the light of the gospel appeared to scatter the darkness that overspread the face of the earth. And this has been the case, so far as has yet appeared, of all nations ever since, upon whom the Sun of Righteousness has not arisen with healing in His wings. Every newly discovered country opens a new scene of astonishing ignorance and barbarity, and gives us fresh evidence of the universal corruption of human nature.

2. I proceed now to consider the compassionate care and kindness of our blessed Redeemer towards mankind in their deplorable circumstances. He sends out His servants to invite them to come in and accept the entertainments of His house. God might have left his guilty creatures to have eternally suffered the dismal effects of their apostasy without the last imputation of injustice or violence of His infinite perfections. The fall was the consequence of man's criminal choice, and was attended with the highest aggravations. The angels that sinned were made examples of God's righteous severity, and are reserved in chains of guilt to the judgment of the great day. Mercy, that tender attribute of the divine nature, did not interpose on their behalf to suspend the execution of their sentence, or avert God's threatened displeasure; their punishment is unalterably decreed, their judgment is irreversible; they are the awful monuments of revenging wrath, and are condemned to blackness of darkness forever. Now justice might have shown the same inflexible severity to rebellious man and have left the universal progeny of Adam to perish in their guilt and misery. It was unmerited mercy that distinguished the human race in providing a Savior for us, and the most signal compassion that revealed the counsels of heaven for our recovery.

But though justice did not oblige the divine Being to provide for our relief, yet the goodness of the indulgent Father of the universe inclined Him to show pity to His guilty creatures who fell from their innocence through the subtlety and malice of seducing and apostate spirits. It was agreeable to the divine wisdom to disappoint the devices of Satan, the enemy of God and goodness, and recover the creatures He had made from their subjection to the powers of darkness.

He therefore gave early discoveries of His designs of mercy to our first parents, and immediately upon the apostasy opened a door of hope for their recovery. He revealed a Savior to the ancient patriarchs under dark types and by distant promises; and made clearer declarations of His will as the appointed time drew near for the accomplishment of the promises, and the manifestation of the Son of God in human flesh. "And when the fullness of time was come, God sent forth His Son, made of a woman, made under the law, to redeem them that were under the law, that we might receive the adoption of sons."

This divine and illustrious Person left the bosom of His Father that He might put on the character of a servant. He descended from the glories of heaven that He might dwell on this inferior earth. He was made under the law that He might fulfill all righteousness. He submitted to the infirmities of human nature to the sorrows and sufferings of an afflicted life, and to the agonies of a painful ignominious death on a cross, that He might destroy the power of sin, abolish the empire of death, and purchase immortality and glory for perishing man.

While our Lord Jesus resided in this lower world, He preached the glad tidings of salvation and published the kingdom of God. He confirmed His doctrine by numerous and undoubted miracles, and recommended His instructions by the charms of a spotless life and conversation. He sent forth His apostles to pursue the same gracious design of gospelizing the people, and furnished them with sufficient powers to proselyte the nations to the faith. He also appointed a standing ministry to carry on a treaty of peace with rebellious sinners in the successive ages of the church, to continue till the number of the redeemed is completed and the whole election of grace placed in circumstances of spotless purity and perfect happiness.

These ministers are called the servants of Christ by way of eminence; they are in a peculiar manner devoted to the service of their divine Master; from Him they receive their commission; by Him they are appointed to represent His person, preside in His worship, and teach the laws of His kingdom. To assume this character without being divinely called and regularly introduced into this sacred office is a bold invasion of Christ's royal authority, and an open violation of that order which He has established in His church. These not only derive their mission from Christ, but it is His doctrine they are to preach, and not the inventions of their own brain; it is His glory they are to promote, and not their own interest or honor. Their business is not to propagate the designs of a party, but the common salvation, and to beseech all, in Christ's name, to be reconciled unto God.

The apostles, the primitive heralds of the everlasting gospel, were sent to make the first tender of salvation to the lost sheep of the house of Israel; they were commanded to begin at Jerusalem, the center of the Jewish commonwealth. But when the Jews obstinately persisted in their impenitence and unbelief, the apostles were commissioned to preach the gospel to every creature under heaven. The sinners of the Gentiles were invited to come in and accept the offers of salvation.

The prophets pointed out a Messiah that was to come, and proclaimed the joyful approach of a Redeemer, at the time appointed in the sovereign counsels of heaven. The ministers of the gospel now are sent to declare that the prophecies are accomplished, the promise fulfilled, justice satisfied, salvation purchased, and all who will come in shall receive the blessings of the gospel. They are not only freely to invite sinners of all orders and degrees, of all ages and nations, but to allure them that all things are now ready, and to use the most powerful and persuasive methods that they may engage them to comply with the heavenly call.

3. And so it is the great duty of the ministers of the gospel to compel sinners to come in and accept the blessings of the gospel. This is so plainly contained in my text that I shall not multiply arguments to confirm it. My only business shall be to explain the nature of this compulsion, or show in what manner sinners are to be compelled to come in. To speak negatively, it is not by the deceitful methods of fraud and disguise, nor the inhuman practices of persecution and violence. This text indeed has often been alleged by the persecuting bigots of all ages and applied to support the cause of religious tyranny, to the infinite scandal of the Christian name and the unspeakable detriment of the Christian interest. By this means the enemies of our most holy faith have been strengthened in their infidelity, the weak have been turned aside from the truth as it is in Jesus, and the peaceable kingdom of the Messiah transformed into a field of blood, a scene of hellish and horrid cruelties. If this were the compulsion recommended in the gospel, then absolute, unrelenting tyrants would be the proper and most infallible teachers; then racks and tortures would be the genuine and most successful method of propagating the faith. But surely everything of this kind, every violent and driving measure, is in direct opposition to the precepts and example of our blessed Savior, and contrary to the very genius of His gospel, which proclaims, "Glory to God in the highest, on earth peace, *good will* towards men" (Luke 2:14).

The princes of this world exercise a temporal dominion over mankind, and by fines levied on their estates and punishments inflicted upon their bodies, force men to an outward subjection to their authority and government.

But the kingdom of our Lord is a spiritual nature. He erects His empire in the hearts of men and reigns over a willing people in the day of His power. External violence may necessitate men to an external profession of the truth and procure a dissembled compliance with the institutions of Christ, but can never enlighten the darkness of the mind, conquer the rebellion of the will, nor sanctify and save the soul. It may transfigure men into accomplished hypocrites, but will never convert them into real saints.

The gospel was originally propagated by the powerful preaching of Christ and His apostles, by the astonishing miracles which they wrought in confirmation of their doctrine, and the exemplary lives by which they adorned their profession and character. Instead of propagating their religion by the destructive methods of fire and sword, they submitted to the rage and cruelty of a malignant world with surprising patience, and sacrificed their very lives in the cause of God, without any intemperate discoveries of anger and resentment. Instead of calling for fire from heaven to destroy their opposers, they compassionated their ignorance, instructed them with meekness, counseled and exhorted them with all long-suffering and doctrine, and even spent their dying breath in praying for their conviction and conversion so that they might be saved in the day of the Lord Jesus.

Now in imitation of these primitive doctors of the Christian church, these wise and successful preachers of the gospel, it is the duty of the ministers of the present day to use the same methods of compassion and friendly violence. A disinterested zeal for the glory of God, a steadfast adherence to the truth, and unshaken fidelity in our Master's cause, with universal benevolence to mankind, must constantly animate our public discourses and be conspicuous in our private speech and behavior. We must diligently endeavor to convince the understandings, engage the affections, and direct the practice of our hearers.

Upon this heading, it may not be amiss to descend to a few particulars:

• Ministers are to compel sinners to come in by setting before them their guilty and perishing condition by nature. Sinners are naturally fond of carnal ease and security; they are delighted with their pleasant and profitable sins; they even drink in iniquity like water, with great greediness, with insatiable thirst and incessant gratification, but without fear or remorse. Upon this account there is the highest necessity to sound an alarm in their ears so that they may be awakened to see and consider their dangerous state, or else they will never be excited to flee from the wrath to come. The secure sinner is insensible of his want of a Savior; the whole do not need a physician, but they who are sick.

To this end, the ministers of the gospel are to set the terrors of the Lord in array against the sinner and let him hear the thunder of divine curses that utter their voice against the unbelieving. They are to represent in the clearest light, and with the most convincing evidence, the evil of sin and the danger it exposes men to; that wrath from heaven is revealed against all ungodliness and unrighteousness of men (Romans 1:18); that the flaming sword of incensed justice is unsheathed, and the arm of the Almighty ready to destroy such as are going on still in their trespasses, impenitent and secure. They are not only thus to show them their danger, but to set before them at the same time their wretched and helpless circumstances: that there's no human eye can successfully pity them, nor any created arm can bring them effectual deliverance; that, while in a state of unregenerate nature, they are destitute of strength to perform any acceptable service to the blessed God and are unable to make any adequate satisfaction to His offended justice; that indeed they can neither avoid the divine displeasure nor endure the punishment that is due to their crimes.

Thus, by a faithful application of the law and its
threatenings, we should endeavor, by God's blessing, to
make way for the reception of the gospel and its promises.
This was the wise method observed by our blessed Savior,
the first Preacher of the gospel, and by the apostles, His
inspired successors. So John the Baptist, who served as the
morning star to usher in the appearance of the Sun of
righteousness, thus prepared the way of the Lord by en-
lightening the minds of men in the knowledge of their
guilt and misery, and inciting them to flee from the damnation of hell. The three thousand who were converted to
the faith at one sermon in the infancy of the Christian
church were first awakened with a sense of their aggravated guilt in crucifying the Lord of glory, and brought in
agony and distress to cry out, "Men and brethren, what
shall we do?" (Acts 2:36–37).

This method, I confess, is disagreeable to the sentiments and inclinations of a secure world, and may expose us to the reproach of those who are at ease in Zion,
but is agreeable to the dictates of an enlightened mind,
conformable to the plan laid down in the sacred Scriptures, and has in all ages approved itself the most successful method of promoting the interests of real and vital religion.

• They are to compel sinners to come in by a lively representation of the power and grace of our almighty Redeemer. All the thunder and terror of curses from Mount
Ebal, all the tremendous wrath revealed from heaven
against the ungodly, and all the anguish and horror of a
wounded spirit in an awakened sinner, are unable to produce an unfeigned and effectual compliance with the
gospel terms of mercy. The ministry of the law can only
give the knowledge of sin, rouse the sinner's conscience,
and alarm his fears; it is the dispensation of grace that
sanctifies and saves the soul. Nor is the former needful but
in order to the latter. So much conviction as gives us a

sight of our sin and misery, as inclines us to flee from the wrath to come, and disposes us to submit to the gospel method of salvation by grace through faith, by sovereign mercy through the Mediator, so much is necessary; and more is neither requisite, nor useful, nor desirable.

It is not the office of preachers to be perpetually employed in the language of terror, or exhaust their strength and zeal in awakening and distressing subjects. No, but as it is their distinguishing character, they are ministers of the gospel, so it is their peculiar business to preach the unsearchable riches of Christ—the Person and offices and love of the great Redeemer, the merits of His obedience and purchases of His cross, the victories of His resurrection, the triumphs of His ascension and prevalence of His intercession, the power of His Spirit, greatness of His salvation, the freeness of His grace, and so on. These are to be the chosen and delightful subjects of their discourses.

They are to represent Him as one who has completely answered the demands of the law, rendered the Deity propitious to the sinner, and upon this account is able eternally to save us from the vengeance of an offended God, who is clothed with almighty power to subdue the inveterate habits of sin, sanctify our polluted nature, and restore us to spiritual health and purity. This Christ is Lord of the visible and invisible worlds, who knows how to defeat the most artful devices of Satan, and will finally render His people victorious over their most malicious and implacable adversaries; who, having made reconciliation for iniquity upon the cross, is pleading the merits of His blood in heaven and powerfully interceding for all suitable blessings on behalf of His people; who is there exalted as a Prince and a Savior to give repentance and remission of sins (Acts 5:31), and is able to save unto the uttermost all those who come to God in and through Him (Hebrews 7:25). Christ, from His illustrious throne in glory, stoops to look down with pity upon guilty and perishing sinners,

stretches forth the scepter of grace, and opens the everlasting arms of His mercy to receive them. These peculiar
doctrines of the gospel ministers are frequently to teach;
upon these they are to dwell with constant pleasure so that
sinners may be persuaded to hearken to the inviting voice
of divine love and put their trust in this almighty and compassionate Savior.

• In order to accomplish this, ministers are to show
sinners the mighty encouragement that the gospel gives
them to accept Christ, and salvation through His merits
and righteousness. As for ignorant presumers, these hear
the glad tidings of the gospel with a fatal indifference and
say in their hearts that they shall have peace, though they
go on in their evil way, stupidly neglecting so great salvation, and regardless of eternal things. But awakened minds
are rather apt to draw the darkest conclusions with respect to their case, and to judge themselves excluded from
the invitations of the gospel. Sometimes they imagine that
the number and aggravations of their sins exceed the designs of pardoning mercy; at other times, that they have so
long resisted the heavenly call that now the gate of heaven
is irrecoverably barred against them. And Satan further
suggests that it would be the height of presumption in
them to lay claim to the blessings of the gospel till they are
better prepared for the divine reception. Upon such
imaginary and false grounds as these, multitudes of the invited guests make excuses and exclude themselves from
the marriage supper of the Lamb. It is therefore the business of the servants of Christ to show that there is yet room
even for the greatest and vilest sinners to come in and partake of the gospel festival; that all things are now ready for
their welcome entertainment; that the door is still open
and there is free access, not only for those who have escaped the grosser pollutions of the world, but even for the
chief of sinners whose guilt is of a crimson color and a
scarlet dye; that neither the number nor aggravations of

their iniquities will exclude them a share in the divine mercy if now they submit to the scepter of grace; that whatever their condition and circumstances may be, it is of present obligation upon them to accept the gospel call, and their instant duty to come in. The Master invites them to come to Him so that they may have life; and whosoever does so, the Master of the house has assured them that He will in no wise cast them out (John 6:37).

• They are to exhibit the unspeakable advantages that will attend a compliance with the gospel call. I know indeed that the religion of Jesus, by its enemies, is often represented in the most frightful and hideous colors, particularly as laying an unreasonable restraint on the liberties of mankind and sinking them into melancholy enthusiasts. It becomes us, therefore, who are set for the defense of the gospel, to endeavor to remove this groundless prejudice and to convince mankind by the light of reason and Scripture that the ways of wisdom are ways of pleasantness, and all her paths are peace; that verily a life of faith in the blessed Redeemer is the way to be happy, both here and hereafter.

Oh, what is more honorable than to be a child of God, an heir of the kingdom of heaven? What is more pleasant than to look back and behold our past iniquities all buried in the depths of eternal oblivion; than to look forward and view our dear Savior acknowledging us to be His friends and favorites, and judging us to a state of unperishing glory? What is more advantageous than to have the divine favor engaged for our protection, the promises of divine grace for our consolation, and an assured title to an inheritance undefiled, incorruptible, and eternal? This is the portion of the true believer; these the privileges that attend a compliance with the gospel call.

These things are to be represented in such a manner as may tend to captivate the hearts of men and engage them in a solicitous care and resolution to renounce the degrading servitude of sin and resign themselves to the power of redeeming grace. Thus, by the most effectual and persuasive methods, the ministers of Jesus are to compel sinners to come in so that His house may be filled.

It was not my design to consider the duty of the ministry in its just extent, but only to insist upon those things that more properly belong to my subject and lie directly in the view of my text.

It will now doubtless be expected that I apply my discourse more immediately to the present occasion. And suffer me, dear sir, in the first place to address myself to you, who are this day coming under a public consecration to the service of Christ; to bear His name among the Gentiles, to whom the Master is now sending you forth, to compel them to come in so that His house may be filled. We trust you are a chosen vessel, designed for extensive service in this honorable, though difficult employment. We adore the God of nature who has furnished you with such endowments as suit you to this important charge. We adore the great Head of the church for the nobler gifts and graces of His Spirit by which, we trust, you are enabled to engage in this mission with an ardent love to God, the universal Father of mankind, with a disinterested zeal for the honor of Christ, the compassionate Friend of sinners, and with tender concern for the perishing souls of a people who sit in darkness and in the shadow of death; who have for so many ages been wandering out of the way of salvation, without Christ, and without God in the world.

The work of the ministry, in every place, has its difficulties and dangers and requires much wisdom, fortitude, patience, and self-denial to discharge it in a right manner with an encouraging prospect of success. But greater degrees of prudence, humility, meekness, mortification to the present world, holy courage, and zeal for the honor of God our Savior are necessary where any are called to minister the gospel unto those who, through a long succession of ages, have dwelt in the darkness of heathenism, who have from their infancy imbibed inveterate prejudices against the Christian faith, and from time immemorial have been inured to many superstitious and idolatrous practices, directly opposite to the nature and design of the gospel.

What heavenly skill is required to convey the supernatural mysteries of the gospel into the minds of uninstructed pagans, who are a people of a strange speech and hard language? What deep self-denial is necessary to enable you cheerfully to forsake the pleasures of your native country with the agreeable society of your friends and acquaintance, to dwell among those who inhabit not indeed the highways and hedges, but uncultivated deserts and the remotest recesses of the wilderness? What unwearied zeal and diligence is needed to proselytize those to the faith of the gospel who have quenched the light of reason and, by their inhumane and barbarous practices, have placed themselves upon a level with the brute creatures?

I think I hear you crying out, "Who is sufficient for these things?" And indeed, if you had no strength to depend upon but your own, no encouragement but from human assistance, you might justly sink down in a disconsolate despair and utter the passionate language of Moses, "O my Lord, send, I pray Thee, by the hand of him whom Thou wilt send. Thy servant is insufficient for so great a work." But it is at the command of Christ, the great Head of the church, that you go forth; who by a train of surprising providences has been preparing your way for this important embassy. And therefore you may be assured that He will support you in the faithful discharge of your duty, accept your unfeigned desires to promote the interests of His kingdom, and finally reward your imperfect services with His gracious approbation. You have His divine promise for your security and consolation, "Lo! I am with you always, even to the end of the world." This will afford you light in every darkness, defense in every danger, strength in every weakness, and a final victory over every temptation. If Christ is with you, in vain do the heathen rage, in vain will their confederated tribes unite their forces to obstruct and discourage you. Infinite wisdom will be your guide, almighty power your shield, and God Himself your exceedingly great reward. The presence of your divine Master will make amends for the absence of your dearest friends and relatives. This will transform a wild and uncultivated desert into a paradise of joy and pleasure, and the lonely huts of savages into more delightful habitations than the palaces of princes.

Let not then any difficulties discourage or any dangers frighten you. Go forth in the name and strength of the Lord Jesus, to whom you are now to be devoted in the sacred office of the ministry. Do not be ashamed of the gospel of Christ, for "it is the power of God unto salvation to everyone that believeth, to the Jew first, and also to the Gentile." Let zeal for the honor of God and compassion for the souls of men animate your public discourses and private addresses to the people committed to your charge. Always remember that your character is as a minister of Jesus; and therefore, with the inspired doctor of the Gentiles, you are to know nothing among them save Christ and Him crucified.

Frequently consider that the gospel is a divine discipline to purify the heart and set up the kingdom of the Redeemer in the souls of men. And therefore it is not sufficient to bring sinners to a profession of the name of Christ and an outward subjection to the institutions of divine worship. You are sent to turn them from darkness to light, and from the power of Satan unto God, so that they may receive forgiveness of sins and an inheritance among them who are sanctified by faith that is in Christ. Unless this is effected (whatever other improvements they gain), they are left under the dominion of sin and exposed to the wrath of God; and their superior degrees of knowledge will only serve to light them down to the regions of death and misery. This then is to be the principal design of your ministry; for this you are to labor with unwearied application, and with incessant importunity to encompass the throne of that God whose peculiar prerogative it is to teach us to profit; whose grace alone can make them a willing people in the day of His power.

And for your encouragement I will only add, when I consider the many prophecies in sacred Scripture of the triumphant progress of the gospel in the last ages of the world, I cannot but lift up my head with joy in a humble expectation that the day draws near, yea, is even at hand, when the promises made to the Son of God shall be more illustriously fulfilled; when His name shall be great among the Gentiles, and be honored and adored from the rising of the sun to the going down of the same. But if the appointed time is not yet come, and if the attempts made to introduce this glorious day fail of its desired success, your judgment will be with the Lord, and your reward with your God. If the Gentiles are not gathered in, you will be glorious in the eyes of the Lord, who accepts and rewards His servants according to the sincerity of their desires, and not according to the success of their endeavors.

I shall conclude with a few words to the body of the people.

God our Savior, in infinite condescension, has sent His servants to invite you to come in and receive the blessings which infinite wisdom has contrived and astonishing grace prepared for your entertainment. And surely, my brethren, it is your important duty and incomparable interest not to despise the salvation of God sent unto the Gentiles, nor make light of the gospel message to you.

God has been pleased to employ us as the messengers of His grace, men of like passions with yourselves, subject to the common infirmities of human nature. But the message comes from Him who is King of kings and Lord of lords; whom you are under the strongest obligations to hear and obey, in point of interest, gratitude, and duty.

What gracious and condescending methods has He taken to assure and invite you! Has He not descended from heaven to earth, from the boundless glories of eternity to all the sufferings and afflictions of this mortal life, that He might purchase and reveal salvation; that He might engage your love and persuade you to comply with His saving designs! Does He not send His ambassadors to beseech you in His stead to be reconciled to God!

What excuses have you to make that will stand the trial of an enlightened conscience or justify you at the awful tribunal of God? Will the vanishing enjoyments of sin and sense, or the perishing riches of this transitory world, make amends for the loss of the divine favor, or support you under the terrors of eternal damnation?

Are there any honors comparable to the dignity and character of a child of God, a title to the privileges of His house and family? Are there any pleasures equal to the smiles of God's reconciled face, the refreshing visits of His love, and the immortal joys of His salvation?

But how deplorable, how desperate will be your case, if you finally refuse the gospel invitation and perish in your natural state of guilt and misery? The compassionate Jesus, who now addresses you in the inviting language of love, will then speak to you with the voice of terror, and swear in His wrath that you shall never enter into His rest, that you shall never taste of His supper, the rich provision which He has made for the eternal entertainment of His guests. Once the Master of the house has risen up and has shut the door, you will in fain stand outside and knock for admission.

In a word, now He declares by His servants that all things are ready, and all who are bidden shall be welcome upon their coming in to be partakers of the benefit. The blood of Christ is now ready to cleanse you from all your guilt and pollution. His righteousness is now ready to adorn your naked souls with the garment of salvation. His Spirit is now ready to take possession of you and make you eternal monuments of victorious and redeeming grace. The Spirit and the bride say, "Come; and whosoever [of the lost and perishing sons of Adam] will, let him come," and participate in the blessings of the gospel freely, without money and without price. The arms of everlasting mercy are open to receive you; the treasures of divine grace are open to supply your wants. And everyone of you who now sincerely accepts this gracious invitation shall hereafter be admitted to sit down with Abraham, Isaac, and Jacob in the kingdom of heaven.

For which, may God of His infinite mercy prepare us all through Jesus Christ, to whom be glory and dominion world without end, Amen.

20

Heaven the Residence of the Saints

(A sermon occcasioned by the sudden and much lamented
death of the Reverend George Whitefield)

"To an inheritance, reserved for you in heaven."
1 Peter 1:4

The desire of happiness is common to all intelligent beings; it is so interwoven in the constitution of human nature that it can never be separated from it. It animates the
prince upon the throne and the peasant in his humble
cottage. It springs up in our breasts in the early dawn of
life; it attends us in our maturer age; it does not desert us
at the gates of death, but accompanies us through every
period of our existence.

We all desire to be happy, but the greatest part of
mankind does not know where this blessing is to be obtained. They erect their altars to imaginary idols and seek
satisfaction in sensual indulgences, which inevitably disappoint their expectations.

The complaints of all ages are sufficient to convince us
that this earth is not the place where happiness is to be
found. Its brightest days are shaded with melancholy
clouds; its sweetest enjoyments are infected with many bitter ingredients; its highest pleasures afford only a transient
flash of delight, and frequently end in satiety and disgust.

We find by constant experience that the scenes of the
present life are perpetually varying; a succession of hopes
and fears, of joys and sorrows attend us from the cradle to

the grave.

Must we then renounce all hopes of happiness forever, and resign ourselves up to a dark and inconsolable despair? No! The Creator and Father of the universe has not consigned man, His favorite offspring, to unavoidable misery. He is the Reward of them who diligently seek Him. He has provided a happiness for them beyond the dominion of death! The present life is the infancy of our being; if we improve it aright, we shall shortly attain to the stature of perfect men in Christ Jesus, and enter upon a nobler state of existence. While upon earth we inhabit a valley of tears; but in heaven is the seat of unmingled felicity and joy.

This hope the apostle set before the primitive Christians to support them under their distinguishing trials, to animate them to the zealous discharge of the various duties of the Christian life. "Blessed be God, the Father of our Lord Jesus Christ, which according to His abundant mercy, hath begotten us again to a lively hope by the resurrection of Jesus Christ from the dead; to an inheritance incorruptible and undefiled and that fadeth not away, reserved in heaven for you."

In speaking to the words of my text, I shall show that heaven is the appointed residence of the people of God in a future world, and then take a view of some of the magnificent descriptions that are given of heaven in the Word of God.

First, I am to show that heaven is the appointed residence of the people of God in a future world. They have here no continuing city. Heaven is the place designed for their eternal abode. Into this place the penitent thief was translated immediately after he expired upon the cross; our blessed Lord, amidst the agonies of dissolving nature, addressed him in language becoming the Prince of Life: "This day thou shalt be with Me in paradise." Into this delightful abode the spirit of departed Lazarus was conveyed by ministering angels. No sooner was he delivered from the sorrows of this mortal state than he was admitted to the refreshments of Abraham's bosom.

The spirits of just men, while on earth, reside in tabernacles of clay, which must shortly be resolved into their original dust. But they have a building not made with hands, eternal in the heavens. Even while they dwell in this land of their pilgrimage, they seek a better, even a heavenly country. God, who condescends to call Himself their Father and their Friend, will not disappoint those hopes which are founded on the promises of His Word, but will exceed their largest expectations.

The enlivening prospect of an entrance into this happy place caused St. Paul to think of his approaching dissolution: he desired to be absent from the body so that he might be present with the Lord.

When our divine Master took an affectionate farewell of His favorite apostles, He comforted them with this kind and condescending promise: "I go to prepare a place for you. . . . I will come again and receive you to Myself, that where I am, ye may be also."

We know that when our blessed Lord had finished His work upon earth, He was received into the highest heavens. In the view of His astonished disciples, attended with a radiant guard of angels, He entered into the courts above to appear for us in the presence of God. The heaven of heavens must receive Him until the times of the restitution of all things (Acts 3:21). If then the souls of departed saints are to be with Christ, as we are assured by the unerring oracles of truth, they must be received into heaven. For this is the place where our blessed Redeemer resides; from thence He issues out His authoritative orders and governs the worlds of nature and grace for the advantage of His church.

Second, we now proceed to take a view of some of the magnificent descriptions that are given us of heaven in the Word of God. We are indeed, at present, too distant from this superior world to form an adequate idea of its excellency and glory. It is in a great measure an unknown country; its glories are covered with a veil; they are only discovered by an eye of faith. Let us extend our view to the utmost limits of our present capacity, and we shall form as defective conceptions of these exalted regions as a man confined all his days to a solitary dungeon will conceive of the pomp and grandeur of the most magnificent palace. But, blessed be God, though we are not capable of a full view, we may take a distant prospect of the heavenly world. We are not left entirely in the dark; we may form some faint conception of the happiness of those who are admitted into it.

The Son of God, descended from heaven to bring life and immortality to light. He has given us such an account of this unseen state as is adapted to our present situation and circumstances. Enough is discovered to inspire us with ardent desires after it, and engage us to the most active and earnest endeavors to prepare for it. Though we must pass through the shades of death before we enter into this land of life and light, yet we may view it as described in the sacred Scriptures. While traveling through this dark and uncomfortable desert, we are permitted to behold as in a landscape the promised Canaan.

The strongest images are employed to shadow out its invisible glories. The charms of nature and art are described in strains of the sublimest eloquence, to give us the most lively prospect of the happiness of its glorified inhabitants.

It is represented as a city, not like those erected by human hands—which are often disturbed by intestine divisions and destroyed by hostile neighbors—but a city founded upon an immovable basis whose Maker and Builder is God. Its citizens are forever exempted from the assaults of pain, the ravages of war, and the fury of the elements. It is free from those melancholy accidents which have often depopulated the most flourishing communities and transformed the superb palaces of princes into heaps of ruin. Into this city enters nothing that defiles or distresses its inhabitants; there is no night, for the presence of the Lord God Almighty enlightens it. The beams of His blessed countenance form a perpetual and unclouded day.

But further, to give us the most exalted idea of the dignity and privileges to which the righteous are advanced, they are represented as possessing a kingdom. A kingdom is the utmost wish of ambitious and aspiring mortals. To enjoy this, they form the most artful intrigues, encounter the most formidable dangers, wade through fields of blood, and often sacrifice the lives of their dearest friends. If they succeed to the extent of their wishes, how often are earthly kingdoms undermined by secret treachery or overthrown by open violence? The crowns of princes are lined with thorns; their distinguished heads become the marks against which the shafts of envy and malice are perpetually discharged. Their administration is rendered uneasy by popular discontents, and the public tranquility is destroyed by schemes of ambition and avarice.

But the kingdom of the just is at all times free from these disagreeable circumstances. There the Lord God Omnipotent reigns; there the most consummate wisdom, impartial justice, and condescending goodness are displayed in every part of the divine government. Universal love reigns in every breast. The laws of peace, order, and harmony are invariably observed through all the heavenly mansion.

Heaven is called "the Kingdom of God" because it is the chosen residence of the supreme Monarch of the universe. Here He has erected His throne and fixed the seat of His eternal empire. Here He appears in the grandeur and majesty of a God and displays the awful and amiable perfections of His nature. His smiles perpetually irradiate these regions. A sense of His love diffuses unutterable joy to all the subjects of His extensive dominion. Myriads of adoring seraphs surround His throne and, with the voice of triumph, celebrate the honors of their King. Clothed with the charms of unfading beauty, possessed of angelic strength and vigor, they stand before Him in shining ranks, and with quick obedience perform His sovereign orders.

The spirits of departed saints immediately become members of this pure and perfect society, are admitted to the same dignity, partake of the same joys, and with unutterable transport join in the same "hallelujahs." The rays which continually proceed from the Son of Righteousness spread life and joy through every part of this holy community. All who die in the faith of God's elect are appointed to dwell in this kingdom and are the favorites of the King of kings. They all share in its honors, riches, and delights; they are adorned with the title of kings and priests unto God. In this character they stand before the throne of God and serve Him day and night. Clothed with the unspotted robes of the Mediator's righteousness, they shine with transcendent glory. Each wears a crown upon his head to intimate the honor to which he is advanced. All have palms in their hands as signs of victory and triumph. What is the splendor of an earthly court when compared with the dazzling luster in which the sons of God appear in the kingdom of their Father!

I add, the habitation of the righteous is not only described as a place of dignity, but pleasure. To guard against the imaginary dream of a Mohammedan paradise, its pleasures are represented as pure and spiritual, such as exalt our natures and form us to a resemblance of the Great Father of our spirits.

In this celestial paradise ample provision is made to supply the wants, satisfy the desires, complete the happiness of the illustrious residents. They are freed from those disorders of body, those distresses of mind which attend us through every state of our pilgrimage upon earth. None of the inhabitants say they are sick; they flourish in immortal youth and vigor. The reviving presence of God banishes all sorrow from their breasts, and His own kind hand wipes all tears from their eyes. The Lamb, which is in the midst of the throne, feeds them with the heavenly manna, and leads them to fountains of living waters. Then shall be fulfilled in the most sublime sense that consolatory promise. Behold the tabernacle of God is with men. He will dwell with them, and they shall be His people, and God Himself shall be their God (Revelation 21:3). This contains everything that is requisite to complete and perpetuate our happiness, a happiness superior to our largest desires, a happiness that surpasses our highest imaginations.

Application

This discourse will naturally lead us to many profitable reflections, but time will permit only two.

1. Hence we see the astonishing folly of those who attach their affection to the vanities of the present life and neglect the glories of a future world. Who can behold without a mixture of compassion and grief, inconsiderate mortals seeking happiness where it is not to be found, and after a thousand disappointments pursuing a deluding phantom? Captivated with pleasing dreams, they despise the only felicity of a rational and immortal mind. With unceasing toil, they ransack the whole creation in search of something which will satisfy their desires and in every place they meet with vanity and vexation. To use the language of inspiration, they "spend their money for that which is not bread, and their labor for that which satisfieth not" (Isaiah 55:2). To increase their unhappiness, often they mistake a fatal poison for an agreeable enjoyment. With eager haste

they take down the intoxicating draft that consigns them over to death and misery. They vainly expect to be happy in a world that lies under the curse of the Almighty, and stupidly neglect that world where blessedness flows in an uninterrupted stream and makes glad the city of God. Happiness is purchased for us by the Son of God; and the gospel invites us to secure this inestimable gift. But, alas! Men are so infatuated that they choose to walk in the prohibited paths of vice, though they lead to hell, and are unwilling to observe the appointed road of duty, though it conducts us safely to the glories of heaven. They remain the voluntary slaves of Satan, when they might appear in the character of the sons of God. They wallow in those sordid lusts which they enjoy in common with the beasts that perish, and despise the dignity and blessedness of the angels of light.

How awfully is human nature degraded from its primitive rectitude! How astonishing is the madness of mankind! The service of God is neglected that we may follow the dictates of appetite and passion. Heaven is undervalued for the transitory delights of earth. The man who loses a kingdom that he may spend his time in trifling amusements, the man who forfeits an immense estate for a momentary pleasure, is not as guilty of that extremity of folly as the wretch who forfeits the favor of God that he may enjoy the smiles of the world, and excludes himself the joys of paradise that he may live without restraint in the pomps and delicacies of the present life. What is the grandeur of a monarch! What is the wealth of the Indies! What is the pleasures of the most prosperous sensualist when compared with the unfading honors, the incorruptible treasures, the transporting delights which are reserved for the people of God! What darkness veils the understanding! What stupidity possesses the minds of men that they prefer the things that are seen and temporal to the things that, though unseen, are eternal!

Consider, O sinner! Though the objects of sense may now captivate your heart and render you inattentive to the most important interests, in a little time your folly will be manifest before the assembled world of angels and men. Covered with unutterable confusion, you will be obliged to confess the absurdity and extravagance of your conduct. With what amazement will you view this earth, the seat of all your joys, becoming a sacrifice to the wrath of an avenging God! What agonies must you feel when those brutal satisfactions for which you have forfeited the joys of the divine presence shall escape your embraces forever? With what terror must you behold a despised and insulted Savior descending from heaven, in the majesty and glory of an Almighty Judge! With what regret will you see the Patriarchs and Prophets, and all the saints and servants of God, rejoicing in the Kingdom of their Father while you are condemned to blackness of darkness forever!

Let the consideration of these things awaken you out of your security and excite you to flee from the wrath to come. Give all diligence to be found of your Judge in peace so that when this lower world shall be enwrapped in flames and all its admired glories vanish into smoke, you may possess "an inheritance, incorruptible and undefiled, that fadeth not away, reserved for you in heaven."

2. How unbecoming is it for the heirs of heaven to imitate the manners of this corrupted earth. Shall the sons and daughters of the Most High God act and live like the children of this world? Shall they who are appointed to inherit all things incessantly toil for those enjoyments which perish in the using? Is it not below the dignity of a Christian to judge the least attachment to the criminal pleasures of sin and sense? Is it not a disgrace to our character to pursue the honors and advantages of this life by the low and unmanly acts of fraud and falsehood? Shall not the candidates for an unfading crown look down with

a generous contempt upon the infamous practices of insincerity and ingratitude? Shall they who are destined to enjoy a kingdom be solicitous to obtain the favor and applause of mistaken and misguided mortals? Shall they who have an unperishing treasure in heaven meanly stoop to grovel in the dust of the earth to obtain those riches which are destroyed by a thousand accidents? Shall they who expect shortly to be admitted into the pure and perfect society of saints and angels be fond of those glittering trifles, those defiling amusements, which form the happiness of men who live without God, without Christ, and without hope in the world? No, if we are fellow citizens with the saints and belong to the household of God, it becomes us to have our conversation in heaven; from whence we look for the great God, our Savior.

We should imitate His instructive example who, for the joy set before Him, endured the cross, despising the shame. With unreluctant cheerfulness, we should trace the most thorny road which leads to the seats of bliss. With undaunted fortitude, we should disdain the frowns and flatteries of the world, when they divert us from the path of duty. With unfainting patience, we should pass through the trials and tribulations of the present state, knowing that our light afflictions, which are but for a moment, work for us a far more exceeding and eternal weight of glory (2 Corinthians 4:17). If by the sovereign appointment of heaven we are called to suffer the loss of all things in the cause of our adorable Master, we may cheerfully make the sacrifice. What is the wrath of man in comparison with the wrath of an omnipotent God? Man may persecute us to death, but the grave places us beyond the reach of their cruelty and malice. They may dismiss us from an uneasy world, but they cannot exclude us the delights of paradise. They may remove us from this valley of tears, but this will introduce us into the joy of our Lord. "Blessed are the dead which die in the Lord, from henceforth, yea, saith the Spirit, that they may rest from their labors, and their works do follow them" (Revelation 14:13).

This naturally leads me to speak of my deceased friend and dear brother, the Rev. Mr. George Whitefield, whose sudden and lamented death occasioned the present discourse. I am not fond of funeral panegyrics, which are adapted to flatter the dead more often than instruct the living. But where persons have been distinguishingly honored by heaven, and employed to do uncommon service for His church upon earth, it would be criminal ingratitude to suffer them to drop into the dust without the most respectful notice. The memory of the just is blessed. Posterity will view Mr. Whitefield in many respects as one of the most extraordinary characters of the present age. His zealous, incessant, and successful labors in Europe and America are without a parallel.

Early devoted to God, he took orders as soon as the constitution of the established church in England allowed. His first appearance in the work of the ministry was attended with surprising success. The largest churches in London were not able to contain the numbers that perpetually flocked to hear his awakening discourses; the crowds daily increased. He was soon forced into the fields, followed by multitudes who hung with silent attention upon his lips, and with avidity received the Word of Life. The Spirit of God in uncommon measures descended upon the hearers. The secure were awakened to a salutary fear of divine wrath, and inquiring minds were directed to Jesus, the only Savior in a revolted world. The vicious were visibly reclaimed, and those who had hitherto rested in a form of godliness were made acquainted with the power of a divine life. The people of God were refreshed with the consolations of the blessed Spirit, and rejoiced to see their exalted Master going on from conquering to conquer, and sinners of all orders and characters bowing to the scepter of a crucified Savior.

His zeal could not be confined within the British Islands; his ardent desire for the welfare of immortal souls conveyed him to the distant shores of America. We beheld a new star arise in the hemisphere of these western churches, and its salutary influences were diffused through a great part of the British settlements in these remote regions. We heard with pleasure from a divine of the Episcopal communion those great doctrines of the gospel that our venerable ancestors brought with them from their native country. With a soul elevated above a fond attachment to uninstituted forms and ceremonies, he inculcated that pure and unadulterated religion for the preservation of which our fathers banished themselves into an uncultivated desert. In his repeated progresses through the colonies, he was favored with the same success that attended him on the other side of the Atlantic. He preached from day to day in thronged assembles, yet his hearers never discovered the least weariness, but always followed him with increasing ardor. When he was in the pulpit, every eye was fixed on his expressive countenance; every ear was charmed with his melodious voice; all sorts of persons were captivated with the propriety and beauty of his address.

But it is not for the fine speaker, the accomplished orator, that we are to celebrate from the sacred desk. These engaging qualities, if not sanctified by divine grace and consecrated to the service of heaven, are as the sounding brass and the tinkling cymbal. When misimproved, instead of conveying happiness to mankind, they render us more illustriously miserable.

The gifts of nature, the acquisitions of art that adorned the character of Mr. Whitefield, were devoted to the honor of God and the enlargement of the kingdom of our divine Redeemer. While he preached the gospel, the Holy Ghost was sent down to apply it to the consciences of the hearers. The eyes of the blind were opened to behold the glories of a compassionate Savior; the ears of the deaf were unstopped to attend to the invitations of incarnate love; the dead were animated with a divine principle of life. Many in all parts of the land were turned from darkness to light, and from the power of Satan unto God. Those doctrines which we had been instructed in from our infancy by our faithful pastors seemed to acquire new force and were attended with uncommon success when delivered by him; his discourses were not trifling speculations, but contained the most interesting truths; they were not an empty play of wit, but solemn addresses to the hearts of men.

To convince sinners that they were by nature children of wrath, by practice transgressors of the divine law, and in consequence of this exposed to the vengeance of offended heaven; to display the transcendent excellency of a Savior, and persuade awakened minds to confide in His merits and righteousness as the only hope of a guilty world; to impress upon the professors of the gospel the necessity not only of an outward reformation, but an internal change by the powerful influences of the Spirit; to lead the faithful to a zealous practice of the various duties of the Christian life, that they may evidence the sincerity of their faith and adorn the doctrine of God their Savior— these were the reigning subjects of his pulpit discourses. If sinners were converted, if saints were built up in faith, holiness and comfort, he attained his utmost aim.

He was no contracted bigot, but embraced Christians of every denomination in the arms of his charity, and acknowledged them to be the children of the same Father, servants of the same Master, and heirs of the same undefiled inheritance.

That I am not complimenting the dead, but merely speaking the words of truth and soberness, I am persuaded that I have many witnesses in this assembly.

He was always received by multitudes with pleasure

when he favored these parts with his labors. But he never had a more obliging reception than in his last visit. Men of the first distinction in the province not only attended his ministry, but gave him the highest marks of their respect. With what faithfulness did he declare unto us the whole counsel of God! With what solemnity did he reprove us for our increasing degeneracy! With what zeal did he exhort us to remember from whence we were fallen, and repent and do our first works, lest God should come and remove our candlestick out of its place!

Upon every occasion, he expressed an uncommon concern for our civil as well as religious privileges, the dear-bought purchase of our heroic ancestors. With what fervency did he pray that they might be transmitted, entire, to the most distant posterity. He embraced every opportunity in public and private to persuade us to lay aside our party prejudices and passions so that, with undivided hearts, we might unite in every proper method to secure our future prosperity.

Animated with a godlike design of promoting the temporal and spiritual happiness of mankind, after the example of his divine Master, he went about doing good. In this he persevered with unremitting ardor and assiduity till death removed him to that rest which remains for the people of God. Perhaps no man, since the apostolic age, preached oftener, and with greater success.

If we view his private character, he will appear in a most amiable point of light. The polite gentleman, the faithful friend, the engaging companion, above all the sincere Christian, were visible in the whole of his deportment.

With large opportunities of accumulating wealth, he never discovered the least tincture of avarice. What he received from the kindness of friends he generously employed in offices of piety and charity. His benevolent mind was perpetually forming plans of extensive usefulness. The Orphan House which many years ago he erected in Georgia, and the college he was founding in that province at the time of his death, will be lasting monuments of his care, that religion and learning might be propagated to future generations.

In the midst of these generous projections of public utility, this commissioned angel was dispatched to dissolve the vital tie that detained him upon earth, and permit him to ascend its native skies. His death was sudden, but not by him undesired. He often uttered an ardent wish to be absent from the body that he might be present with the Lord. He has finished his work, and we do not doubt that he has received the approbation of his Master and Judge: "Well done, thou good and faithful servant; enter thou into the joy of thy Lord."

He had a quick transition from the labors of the church upon earth to the more sublime services of the heavenly sanctuary. He is separated from the society of his friends below, but united to the nobler society of angels, archangels, and the spirits of just men made perfect. View him then not as perishing in the dust of death, but entered into a world of glory. Behold him worshipping before the throne of God, not with a company of frail and imperfect mortals, but with the general assembly and church of the firstborn, shining in the unspotted robes of holiness, uniting in their "hosannas" and partaking in their triumphs.

If you ask, what is this illustrious company and from whence do they come? I answer in the words of the angel, in the vision of St. John, "These are they which come out of great tribulation, and have washed their robes and made them white in the blood of the Lamb."

I have not, my brethren, drawn an imaginary portrait, but described a character exhibited in real life. I have not mentioned his natural abilities, which were vastly above the common standard. I have not spoken of the improvements he made in human learning in one of the most celebrated universities in the world. I consider him principally in the light of a Christian, and a minister of Jesus Christ, in which he shone with a superior luster, as a star of the first magnitude.

After all, I am not representing a perfect man; there are spots in the most shining characters upon earth. But this may be said of Mr. Whitefield with justice, that after the most public appearances for above thirty years, and the most critical examination of his conduct, no other blemish could be fixed upon him than what arose from the common frailties of human nature and the peculiar circumstances that attended his first entrance into public life. The imprudence of inexperienced youth he frequently acknowledged from the pulpit with a frankness that will forever do honor to his memory. He took care to prevent any bad consequences that might flow from his unguarded censures in the early days of his ministry; the longer he lived, the more he evidently increased in purity of doctrine, in humility, meekness, prudence, patience, and the other amiable virtues of the Christian life.

We are now called to remember not only his pathetic discourses, but his excellent example. We are to follow him as far as he followed Christ, the only unspotted pattern of perfection.

His sudden death calls aloud upon all to prepare for that great event which must decide our destiny forever; from the silent grave he seems to address us in the awakening language of our Lord to His own disciples: "Watch ye therefore, for ye know not when the Master of the house cometh; at even, or at midnight, or at the cock crowing, or in the morning; lest coming suddenly, he find you sleeping. And what I say unto you, I say unto all, Watch" (Mark 13:35-37).

The solemn calls, the faithful reproof, the compassionate invitations you have heard from this deceased servant of Christ will aggravate your condemnation if you die in impenitence or infidelity.

Be persuaded then to trifle no longer with your immortal welfare. Be awakened by the Word and providence of God, without delay to prostrate yourselves at the feet of our Almighty Savior and accept the offers of reconciling grace. Then, when delivered from the burden of the flesh, you will be united with all who are departed in the faith of God's elect, and with them you will inherit a kingdom, prepared for you from the foundation of the world, Amen.